THE ROMAN CATACOMBS
AND THEIR MARTYRS

THE ROMAN CATACOMBS

1. Valentine
2. Pamphilus
3. Bassilla — Hermes
4. Maximus — *ad Sanctam Felicitatem*
5. Thraso — *ad Sanctum Saturninum*
6. Jordani — *ad Sanctum Alexandrum*
7. Priscilla
8. Nicomedes
9. Agnes
10. *Maius — Ostrinum*
11. Novatianus — Viale Regina
12. Hippolytus
13. Cyriaca — Laurence
14. Castulus

15. *Ad Duas Lauros* — Peter and Marcellinus — *ad Sanctam Helenam — sub Augusta*
16. Gordianus and Epimachus
17. Apronianus — Eugenia
18. Campana
19. Balbina
20. Lucina
21. Callistus
22. Sebastian — ad Catacumbas
23. Praetextatus
24. Marcus and Marcellianus
25. Domitilla

26. Nunziatella
27. Commodilla — *ad Sanctos Felicem et Adauctum*
28. Timotheus
29. Thecla
30. Pontianus — *ad Ursum Pileatum*
31. Generosa — *ad Sextum Philippi*
32. Pancratius — Octavilla
33. Processus and Martianus — *Sancta Agatha ad Girulum*
34. *Duo Felices*
35. Calepodius
36. Small catacomb discovered in 1956

THE
ROMAN CATACOMBS
AND THEIR MARTYRS

Ludwig Hertling, S.J. and
Engelbert Kirschbaum, S.J.

Translated by M. Joseph Costelloe, S.J.

DARTON, LONGMAN & TODD
LONDON

DARTON, LONGMAN & TODD LTD
85 Gloucester Road, London SW7 4SU

ISBN 0 232 48042 7

Translated from the German work *Die Römischen Katakomben und ihre Martyrer* (1950) by arrangement with Verlag Herder, Vienna.

PRINTED IN GREAT BRITAIN BY LOWE AND BRYDONE (PRINTERS) LIMITED, THETFORD, NORFOLK. DE LICENTIA SUPERIORUM ORDINIS NIHIL OBSTAT M. T. BARTON, S.T.D., L.S.S. CENSOR DEPUTATUS. IMPRIMATUR E. MORROGH BERNARD, VIC. GEN. WESTMONASTERII, DIE 16A FEBRUARII, 1960. THE NIHIL OBSTAT AND IMPRIMATUR ARE A DECLARATION THAT A BOOK OR PAMPHLET IS CONSIDERED TO BE FREE FROM DOCTRINAL OR MORAL ERROR. IT IS NOT IMPLIED THAT THOSE WHO HAVE GRANTED THE NIHIL OBSTAT AND IMPRIMATUR AGREE WITH THE CONTENTS, OPINIONS OR STATEMENTS EXPRESSED.

INTRODUCTION

WHEN one leads a stranger through the Colosseum, he is sometimes asked where the tribune stood from which the emperor Nero viewed the executions of the Christians. Actually, Nero died some years before the Colosseum was built. Ignorance or forgetfulness of such a fact implies no moral defect. No one will blame another for not knowing which pillars in the Roman forum still rest on their original foundations, and which in later times have been re-erected from the ruins, nor for failing to distinguish between the actual remains of an ancient monument and later restorations and reconstructions. There is no essential connection between archaeology and character, or even culture.

But such lack of knowledge and ability is in a sense to be regretted: it precludes a full appreciation and enjoyment of the ruins of antiquity. Complete satisfaction comes only with an experimental knowledge of reality. I can receive a purely aesthetic pleasure from a statue in a museum without knowing whether it is a work of Lysippus or Canova. But a group of ruins or, in particular, a bare historical site speaks to me only if I can in spirit span the centuries or millennia and place myself in the midst of the vanished realities. Then that indescribable experience of actuality comes over me as I realize that my feet touch the same Via Sacra on which Horace once walked, or that I stand on the spot where Paul disembarked, or that my oar touches the same sea on which Christ rowed with His Apostles.

In the Roman catacombs this experience is particularly keen, so keen in fact that even the most uneducated can sense it. But it will be imparted in fullest measure only to one who through earnest study has obtained the necessary knowledge and discernment. Apart from this, a knowledge of the catacombs remains all too easily a half-picturesque, half-mythical curiosity, not unlike the tomb of Vergil at Naples on the steeps of Posillipo, or the house of Romeo and Juliet at Verona, or the tomb of Barbarossa at Kyffhäuser.

In the course of a tour through the catacombs, an educated man once asked me as we came before an open grave in which, as not infrequently happens, fragments of skeletons could be seen: "Are these martyrs' bones? and are they really genuine?" These questions are indicative of what many bring with them into the catacombs: a whole cloud of pious but vague notions about the martyrs, and at the same time an indefinite feeling that all may be a hoax. The two go together. One who lacks real knowledge and is enveloped instead in a mist of romanticism loses all security. The world of the martyrs presents itself to him as an epic saga, no truer than the Homeric poems or the history of Romulus and Remus.

This is not to say that the Christian legends do not also have their own value and *raison d'être*. One who wishes only to be edified and to steep himself in the spirit of the early martyrs may confidently take up Wiseman's *Fabiola*. There he will find the spirit of early Christianity vividly portrayed, just as the spirit of ancient Rome is portrayed in Vergil or in the first books of Livy. But surely there are individuals of a more reflective mind who wish to know what actually took place, and to these the following pages are directed.

We have endeavored to set before the reader something more than a mere series of propositions. We have tried to give a certain insight into the problems connected with the scientific investigation of Christian antiquity and an exposition of the techniques employed in solving them. On the other hand, we have striven to limit the scholarly apparatus to essentials. It would not have been difficult to give to the whole a scientific cast, with many notes, Greek and Latin citations, and lengthy discussions of critical controversies. The average reader, however, we are sure, will find it more pleasant and profitable to listen to a professor speaking in a familiar fashion from the abundance of his knowledge than to be overwhelmed by his professional lore, which after all he can hardly check for himself.

If these pages assist the reader who has at one time sojourned in the Eternal City, or who will some day direct his steps thither, to achieve that experience of reality, that nearness to life, which nowhere so unites us with the early Church as in Rome, they will have achieved their goal.

THE AUTHORS

The Gregorian University, Rome
Easter, 1949

FOREWORD TO THE SECOND EDITION

THE cordial reception which was given to our little book has encouraged us to publish a new edition. With it the desire of many readers can now be fulfilled for an exact account of the Apostle Peter's tomb. When the first edition went to press, the excavations under St. Peter's had not been completed. As a consequence, the tomb and the area surrounding it could not be described. This difficulty has since been removed, and we have thus been able to revise completely the chapter on "The Tombs of the Apostles" and bring it up to date. New illustrations referring to these excavations have also been added.

THE AUTHORS

Rome
Christmas, 1954

TRANSLATOR'S NOTE

THE translation of this book is due in large part to the generosity of the U. S. Department of State in granting me a Fulbright scholarship for study in Rome during the years 1950–1951. At the Gregorian University I had the privilege of assisting at the lectures in Christian archaeology of Father Kirschbaum, one of the four members of the pontifical commission for the exploration of St. Peter's tomb. I also had the constant assistance and encouragement of Father Hertling, professor of Church history, in the special problem which I was investigating.

As a token of gratitude for the many kindnesses which were shown to me by the faculty of the Gregorian University during my stay in Rome, and in particular the help which I received from Fathers Hertling and Kirschbaum, I am presenting this admirable little book to the wide circle of English readers for whom, unfortunately, Christian archaeology is practically an unknown field.

With the authors' permission a few slight changes have been made in the text, a number of new photographs and plans have been added, and the notes have been considerably expanded.

M. JOSEPH COSTELLOE, S.J.

St. Stanislaus Seminary
Florissant, Missouri
Pentecost, 1956

DURING the past three years a number of new discoveries have been made and new hypotheses for old problems have been proposed. An attempt has been made to incorporate the more important of these in this new printing of *The Roman Catacombs and their Martyrs*. It is the hope of the authors and translator that this work will find as favorable an audience in England and Eire as it has in the United States.

M. JOSEPH COSTELLOE, S.J.

CONTENTS

ILLUSTRATIONS

Plates are reproduced by permission of the following: 19 and 42—Alinari; 20 to 23 and 25—Rev. Fabbrica di S. Pietro; all the remainder—Papal Archeological Institute.

CHAPTER 1

THE EXPLORATION OF THE CATACOMBS

THE Roman catacombs, scientifically considered, are simply sites of excavation, exactly like Pompeii, Herculaneum, Ostia, the tombs of the Egyptian kings, and the *tells,* or accumulated mounds of debris in Palestine and Mesopotamia.

Our whole knowledge of human activity in the past is based upon two kinds of testimony — that which is written, for example, primitive texts, letters, and authentic historical narratives, and that which is monumental, which consists of the material remains of former times. The farther back we go in the history of mankind, the fewer written documents we have. The history of the high cultures of the ancient East, the Egyptian and the Sumerian-Babylonian-Assyrian, is known to us chiefly through the evidence of excavations, while our knowledge of the so-called prehistoric times is derived entirely from the things which men made and from their graves.

For the period of classical antiquity, that is, from around 500 B.C. to A.D. 500, we have both types of testimony — written sources in rich abundance and at times of "classical" perfection, and monumental remains in such quantities that not only can we trace almost without interruption the development of the more important events of the time, but we can also form a well-rounded picture of the general culture of the people, and get numerous insights into private family affairs, and even into the personal experiences of many individuals who have made no name for themselves in the larger course of history.

For the Christian era, which began almost contemporaneously with the Roman empire at the middle of these thousand years, we likewise have both types of testimony — the writings of the Fathers of the Church, many more of which are extant than of the classical authors, and the excavations and discoveries of Christian antiquity. Among these latter the Roman catacombs hold the highest place. Although in artistic yields they are much less rich than Pompeii, they far surpass this city of the dead near Mount Vesuvius in the richness of their inscriptions and in their direct relationship with historical persons and events. Pompeii represents only a minor section in the sphere of influence exercised by the Roman empire; the Roman catacombs lie at the very center of early Christian history.

A long time was, of course, required for these treasures, which are unique in their kind, to be discovered, examined, and understood.

Throughout the entire Middle Ages the catacombs were scarcely known. Men visited the famous sepulchral churches outside the walls of Rome and knew that under some of them, especially under St. Sebastian, St. Pancratius, and St. Agnes, there were subterranean galleries filled with sepulchers, but no one was interested in them. At times tillers of the Campagna would descend into lightshafts opening up to the fields or brush in order to bring up from them beautifully polished slabs of marble, which had an endless variety of uses. Many of these slabs have made remarkable journeys. Between the years 1912 and 1939, for example, ten pieces of a sepulchral inscription were found which Pope Damasus had set up for the martyr Hippolytus in the latter's cemetery on the Via Tiburtina. Medieval masons had used the inscription for the *opus sectile* of the ornate marble floor of the Lateran basilica.[1]

From the fifteenth century we have traces of pious pilgrims

Pl. 1. *Graffiti* of the "Roman Academy" in Callistus. At the top is the date, 1475, and directly beneath it is the name *"Pantagathus"* followed by other ancient names assumed by members of the society. Toward the bottom may be seen the name of the leader, *Pom(ponius Laetus) Ponti(fex) Max(imus)*.

who descended into the still wholly unexplored crypts and there immortalized themselves with scratchings on the walls, which are technically known as *graffiti*. The earliest of these are found in the catacomb of Callistus. They go back to the year 1432 when members of the Roman Academy with Pomponio Leto at their head went down into the catacomb to look for artistic relics of antiquity. They were, however, disappointed in their expectations. Since these half-pagan humanists had no interest in Christian antiquities, they made no mention of these fruitless excursions in their learned writings, though they left their names scratched upon the walls (pl. 1). Traces of such visits in the sixteenth century are to be found in the catacombs of Callistus, Praetextatus, Priscilla, and of Peter and Marcellinus.

An active interest in the catacombs began only with the sixteenth century at the time of the Reformation. Philip Neri, "the Apostle of Rome," loved the catacombs, though he knew only the galleries under St. Sebastian. He often passed hours there alone in contemplation, and he also brought his disciples there to visit them. Philip was himself no scholar, but he knew intuitively the significance and importance of the study of Christian antiquity. Under his influence his greatest follower, Caesar Baronius, began his *Annales ecclesiastici*, in which for the first time Roman manuscript collections were used to any great extent. Baronius thus became the father of scientific Church history. At this same time the famous Augustinian, Onofrio Panvinio, undertook a series of profound studies in Christian archaeology and Roman topography. In 1568 he published an original work on the early Christian cemeteries in which he listed forty-three names mentioned in the martyrologies and in other literary sources, but he could identify the sites of only three of them — St. Sebastian, St. Laurence, and St. Valentine.[2]

The age was thus intellectually prepared for the first really great discovery in the field of the catacombs in June, 1578. By pure chance some workmen, while digging outside the Porta Salaria for pozzuolana, a volcanic deposit used in making cement, came upon a well-preserved cemetery with many galleries at different levels, and numerous frescoes and inscriptions. All Rome was immediately seized with enthusiasm. Cardinals and scholars hastened to descend into the galleries to examine the marvels of this newly discovered wonderland. Among the first of these was Baronius, who recognized at once their scientific value. Pope Gregory XIII also took a lively interest in the matter. Everywhere the hitherto scarcely noticed subterranean corridors about the city became objects of exploration and study.

One of the most industrious investigators of this period was Antonio Bosio.[3] Encouraged by Pompeo Ugonio, a professor in the University of Rome, with astounding diligence he sketched and took notes on everything he saw in his wanderings through the ancient cemeteries. We still run across his name in great letters on different walls, vaults, and corners of the catacombs. This marking up the catacombs was a bad habit to which other famous explorers tenaciously clung. The fruit of Bosio's long years of investigation, which won for him the honor of being called "the Columbus of the Catacombs," was gathered together in his famous work *Roma Sotterranea,* published posthumously in 1629.

If there was no lack of enthusiasm and diligence at this time, much was to be desired in the methodical elaboration of the new discoveries. There were no known scientific principles at hand for the task. Moreover, solutions for problems were sought in the catacombs which they simply could not give. Foremost among these were questions of apologetics. From the objects found in the catacombs scholars tried to show that the Reformers were wrong in appealing to the writers of the early Church, since there was a perfect continuity between the teaching of the earliest times and the present. Now it is certain that this proof can be made, but it is much more difficult than, and by no means so obvious as, was at first imagined. The catacombs are nothing but cemeteries, and out of any number of sepulchral decorations and inscriptions it is impossible to reconstruct a catechism or system of dogmatic theology. This lack of explicit instruction was felt, and refuge was taken in the theory of a *disciplina arcani*, or "hidden teaching," which had prevented the early Christians from giving expression to many elements of their doctrine in pictures or in writing.

All this was joined to another error, which postulated that all the catacombs with their contents came from the time of the persecutions. Actually, by far the greater number of tombs, and a vast majority of the inscriptions and other remains date from the times of peace in the fourth and fifth centuries. The enthusiasm for the "martyrs" dominated not only the common masses, but also scholars to such an extent that they believed that everywhere, even in the most trivial objects, a connection could be established with the persecutions and the martyrs. Thus, the palm branches which were so frequently carved on the marble slabs closing the tombs were taken without further ado to be signs of martyrdom. The monogram of Christ ☧, which is found nearly everywhere, and which is an almost certain indication of a time after 313, was interpreted as *passus pro Christo* ("suffered for Christ"). The numerous glass objects which were found, either as flasks in the tombs or as broken bits pushed into the still fresh mortar, were taken to be bottles in which was preserved the blood of those who had died for the faith. These containers which were as a consequence once regarded as signs of martyrdom are now held to have been perfume bottles and fragments of drinking glasses which had been used at funeral banquets, and which were plastered to the graves as a means of identification.

This romantic attitude toward martyrdom was an impediment to sober scientific research. At the same time it caused an entirely false picture of the history of the first Christian centuries to be drawn. As soon as everything was put in relation with the persecutions, the catacombs came to be looked upon as places of refuge for the Christians in times of persecution. Consequently, all the liturgy of the community would have been carried on underground, and not a few Christians would have lived there. Such fantasies were augmented by the old legends of the martyrs which came to be more and more esteemed after the discovery of the catacombs. In the *Legend of Susanna* it is recorded of Pope Caius that fleeing from persecution he remained concealed in the crypts for years.[4] As a matter of fact, however, at the time of the historical Pope Caius (283–296) there was no persecution at all.

There was, moreover, a complete lack of historical perspective. On the one hand, the Christian community was held to be so small that it could be gathered into rooms, the most spacious of which was hardly the size of a living room; on the other, it was thought that there must have been hundreds of thousands of martyrs from the selfsame community. Actually, the faithful in the Christian community at Rome could hardly have numbered more than 70,000 or 80,000 at the time of Diocletian's persecution, and by far the greater number of these survived the persecution.[5]

Despite all this, the work of the investigators of the catacombs in the seventeenth and eighteenth centuries was not entirely fruitless. Not only are mistakes in a sense natural in every science until the right method is found and correct conclusions are reached, but in their works these early scholars preserved much precious material which would otherwise have been lost. They were primarily collectors. They copied pictures and inscriptions just as their contemporaries did in the field of secular archaeology. They thus saved, at least in reproductions, much that has since perished or disappeared. Unfortunately, they did not content themselves with transcribing and copying. They removed objects to museums and private collections. Not only were many of these destroyed in the process, as for example, the interesting portrait of the *fossor* ("digger") Diogenes in the cemetery of Domitilla, which was broken to bits in the attempt to remove it from the wall; but many others have lost their scientific import because their provenance is now unknown.

This unfortunate practice of removing ancient objects was not peculiar to the explorers of the catacombs. From Pompeii and Herculaneum, from Hadrian's Villa, from the Baths of Caracalla, and from nearly every other famous site, the finest objects have been carried off. For works of art, however, the loss is not so great as for inscriptions, which frequently have their particular value in the fact that they are located in a certain spot, or in that the place of their derivation is at least known. It may be said in general that the investigations of the first students and explorers of the catacombs have done hardly less damage to them than the ravages of time and the plundering hands of the barbarians. Only in the middle of the nineteenth century was there a turn for the better.

The new movement, which led to the truly scientific discovery of the catacombs, is connected above all with the names of two men: Giuseppe Marchi, S.J., and Giovanni Battista de Rossi. Marchi was the pioneer, De Rossi the follower and finisher of the work.

In the year 1849, the then twenty-seven-year-old De Rossi, while poking about some rubbish, found a piece of a marble slab with the letters of an ancient inscription upon it: . . . NELIUS MARTYR. This discovery was made in a long abandoned chapel which had formerly been dedicated to the memory of the martyr Pope Zephyrinus, but which was then being used as a tool shed. The chapel itself was located in a vineyard lying within the sharp angle formed by the Via Appia and the Strada delle Sette Chiese, an hour's walk from Rome. Endowed as he was with great talent and unusual insight, De Rossi completed the letters of his slab so that they read: [Cor]NELIUS MARTYR. But he did not rest with this happy addition. He rightly presumed that this piece of marble, like so many others that are found on the Roman campagna, would not have been carried far from its original site. He therefore concluded that the tomb of the martyr would be in the vicinity.

De Rossi knew that he had found his slab on the ground overlying a hitherto unexplored cemetery, since there was near

9

Pl. 2. The marble slab used to close the tomb of Pope Cornelius (251–253) in Callistus. The upper portion of this slab was the starting point for the great discoveries of De Rossi.

to the old chapel of Zephyrinus a lightshaft descending into a series of ramifying corridors. He also knew from ancient topographical data that Pope Cornelius had been buried in the neighborhood, in the as yet unidentified cemetery of Callistus. He now believed that he had discovered this cemetery, and that he would succeed in bringing to light the tombs of the popes of the third century, which according to the old sources must be there.

For such a project it was first necessary to buy the property under which the galleries lay. De Rossi went to Pius IX, who had recently returned to Rome, told him of his discovery and his hopes, and asked him to buy the vineyard. *Pio Nono,* being a real Italian with a flair for a joke and a little harmless teasing, showed little interest in the project. But after the audience he told Monsignor Merode: "I've chased De Rossi like a cat, but I'll buy the vineyard."

And so he did. De Rossi could now excavate without disturbance, and his predictions were fulfilled. He not only found on a subterranean tomb the missing part of his inscription, which now read: CORNELIUS MARTYR EP(*iscopus*), but also the papal crypt for which he was looking (pl. 2).

The pope now wanted to see the discoveries himself. Before the visit he took breakfast at the villa of the Knights of Malta on the Aventine, and remarked during the meal to those about him in such a way that De Rossi, who was present, had to hear him: "Archaeologists are dreamers and poets. They weave together so many fantastic ideas that ordinary mortals can't even understand them."

During his visit to the subterranean galleries and crypts, the pope was deeply moved. With De Rossi he put together the pieces of the third century papal inscriptions which had been found there, and he asked with tears in his eyes: "Are these really the tombstones of my predecessors who were buried here?" De Rossi could not refrain from paying the pope back for the teasing of a short time before. "It's all an hallucination, Your

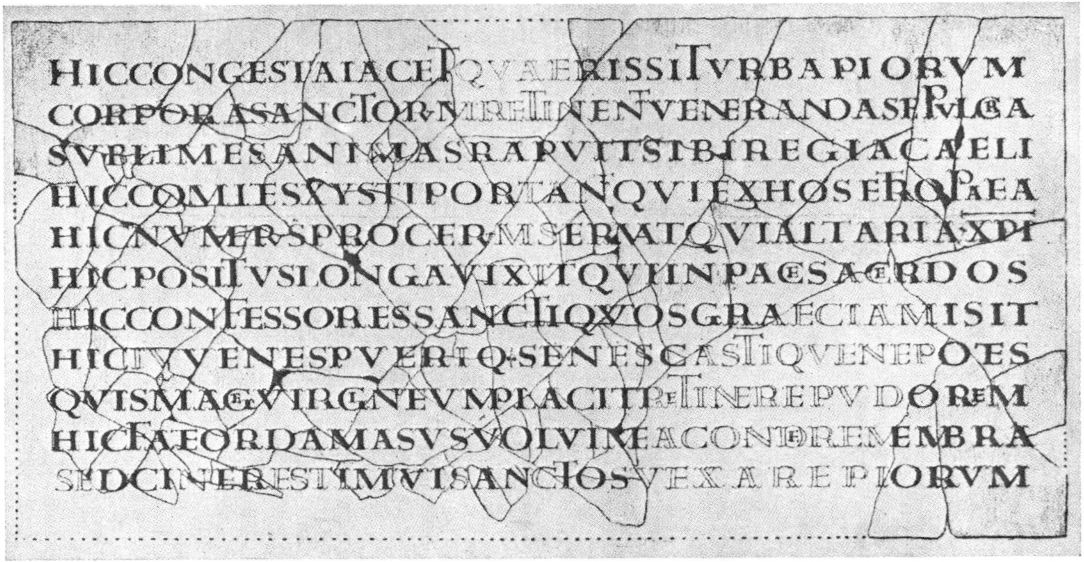

Pl. 3. Inscription composed by Pope St. Damasus to commemorate the martyrdom of Pope Xystus II and his "companions." The beautiful lettering is the work of the calligrapher Furius Dionysius Philocalus. The inscription was found in fragments by De Rossi in the papal crypt in Callistus.

Holiness," he said. "De Rossi," Pius replied, "you're a great rascal!"[6]

The papal crypt in the cemetery of Callistus was only one of the many discoveries which De Rossi made during his long life as a scholar, but it was certainly the most important. It was due not only to a lucky find, but also to the fact that he had hit upon the correct method for the study of the catacombs.

De Rossi began with the principle that for a systematic study of the catacombs it was necessary first of all to examine carefully the old written accounts of them. A whole series of these had long been known, but no one had ever correctly evaluated them. Several descriptions of the catacombs were extant which had been jotted down by ancient pilgrims as a kind of primitive guide for those who would come after them. Much that is contained in these so-called "itineraries" is confused and fabulous. The Latin is barbaric, but the topographical indications are in general precise and fairly complete. This is due to the fact that they were compiled at a time when the graves were for the most part still untouched, and when the inscriptions were still in place and legible.[7] Hardly less precious information is given by the old church calendars, the earliest of which was compiled in 354, a time when many people were still living who had experienced the persecution of Diocletian.[8] There are besides the metrical inscriptions with which Pope Damasus (366–384) adorned many of the martyrs' graves. Many of these epitaphs, beautifully lettered on marble slabs in a distinct and easily recognized style, are still extant, even if no longer on their original sites (pl. 3). The carving is the work of the calligrapher Furius Dionysius Filocalus, who described himself as *Damasi Papae cultor adque amator* ("friend and admirer of Pope Damasus").[9] The majority of these inscriptions were copied in antiquity and preserved in manuscripts of the Middle Ages. Valuable data with regard to persons and places have also been derived from them.

A unique document from the time of Gregory the Great (590–

604) is the *Papyrus of Monza*. Theodolinda, queen of the Lombards, sent a priest named John to Rome to get as many relics of the Roman martyrs as possible. He could not obtain any first-class relics since the pope was opposed to opening the tombs and dividing up the bodies of the saints.[10] He had to be content with remembrances which the faithful were accustomed to keep in place of relics, that is, with oil from the lamps which burned before their tombs. Even today such lamps are to be seen in St. Peter's and St. Paul's. The original list of the oils taken from the lamps before the martyrs' tombs is preserved in the treasury of the cathedral of Monza. Some of the oil flasks are also still extant with their respective labels.[11] This document also furnishes topographical data for the tombs of the Roman martyrs.

A final source of information are the legends of the martyrs. However fabulous a narrative it may be, its author who probably wrote in the fifth or sixth century, still had before his eyes the sites which he describes.[12]

From all of this humble material the state of the cemeteries in ancient times may be reconstructed with some measure of completeness. The tombs which were then pointed out and venerated as belonging to martyrs can thus also be known. On the basis of such information De Rossi concluded that the inscription of Cornelius would lead him to the cemetery of Callistus and the papal crypt. In this same manner we know today with certainty all of the old cemeteries. Not a single one of those visited by the ancient pilgrims has entirely disappeared. Only the cemetery *ad Clivum Cucumeris* has yet to be found, although its approximate location on the Via Salaria is at least known.

Another advance in method was in dating. The only sure criteria for this are inscriptions with consular dates. Since these are not very numerous, their removal is particularly to be regretted. If the place from which they have been taken is known, the age of that particular part of a cemetery can be deduced. The vast majority of dated inscriptions are from the fourth and fifth centuries. The oldest consular-dated Christian inscription belongs to the year 217. It is chiseled on one of the narrow sides of the great sarcophagus of Marcus Aurelius Prosenes, which is now preserved in the park of the Villa Borghese in Rome.[13] The sarcophagus does not come from the catacombs, but from the neighborhood of the Torre Nuova on the Via Labicana, where it was found in 1830. The inscription chronologically closest to that of 217 is perhaps the one on the tomb of Pope Pontianus, which, although it is not dated, is nonetheless to be assigned to the time of his death in 235, as is known from definite historical sources.

This does not mean that none of the cemeteries go back to earlier times. The oldest of these had their origins before the middle of the second century.[14] This has been determined by a study of the paintings and brickwork of the catacombs. The shape of carved or written letters, the abbreviations used for names, and in certain instances, the symbolism employed in the frescoes have also been of assistance in this matter. For the relative chronology, that is, for the mere determination of which parts of a catacomb are earlier and which are later, the disposition of the galleries and *cubiculi,* or burial chambers, is often decisive. Thus, for example, it is clear that in corridors which are higher than usual the ceiling was not raised, but the floor was dug deeper, so that the lower rows of tombs are the latest.[15] Many principles of this kind seem self-evident today, but here as in other sciences the work of generations was needed to establish them.

Today there are various branches of specialization in Christian archaeology which give an ever more profound knowledge of the field. The Pontifical Institute of Christian Archaeology erected by Pius XI in 1925 now guarantees such progress.

Pius IX, at the instance of De Rossi, founded the Pontifical Commission of Sacred Archaeology to have charge of Christian antiquities and to conduct new excavations. The juridical rights of the Holy See in this matter are officially recognized in the Concordat of 1929: "The supervision of the catacombs existing within the environs of Rome and in the remaining territory of the realm are reserved to the Holy See with the consequent burden of their care, maintenance, and conservation. It can, therefore, in accordance with the laws of the state and with the preservation of the possible rights of third parties, undertake needed excavations and transfer the bodies of the saints."[16]

A superintendent is appointed by the commission for the scientific direction of this work. The present superintendent is the noted Roman archaeologist Professor Enrico Josi. Individual cemeteries open to the public are entrusted to various religious communities. These communities place multi-lingual guides at the disposal of visitors, and they are responsible to the commission for the maintenance of the catacombs. They may not, however, undertake new excavations on their own initiative. As for the visits of the public, it is sufficient to note that before the war there were from 70,000 to 100,000 visitors a year to the cemetery of Callistus, which is entrusted to the Salesians of St. Don Bosco. Under special circumstances, such as the Jubilee Years of 1933 and 1950, this number has been surpassed many times over.

Even in recent decades some important new discoveries have been made in connection with the catacombs. In 1915 excavations were begun under St. Sebastian's which were destined to become famous within a very short time. In 1919 the *hypogeum*, or underground chamber, of a certain Aurelius Felicissimus was discovered by accident. It was soon recognized that he had been a member of a Gnostic sect. The year 1920 brought the discovery of the great cemetery of St. Pamphilus on the Salaria Vetus; and the following year, also on the Salaria, was found, or better, refound, the cemetery of the Jordani, the famous catacomb whose discovery in 1578, had so excited all the learned men of the time. Its entrance was blocked by a landslide shortly after its finding, so that not even Bosio could corroborate what had been seen by the first explorers. In 1926, near St. Laurence a small catacomb was discovered which does not appear in the old itineraries. It contains the grave of the highly controverted martyr Novatian. Finally, in 1956, on the Via Latina about half a mile from the Porta Latina, was discovered a small catacomb of the late third and early fourth centuries, which is not mentioned in the old itineraries but which contains the finest early Christian frescoes yet discovered.[17]

These discoveries, especially Pamphilus and Jordani, have yielded a wealth of inscriptions and well-preserved frescoes. Still it can be said that the era of great discoveries in the catacombs is now passed. Individual finds will always be made, but we can hardly expect any great surprises.

This is not to say that Roman archaeologists have nothing more to do. The material which the catacombs have furnished is so immense that no ancient excavated city of the world can compare with it in extent and importance. In its critical sifting there will be work for generations.

From the scientific point of view, the catacombs are like truly buried cities, sites for investigation of the first rank. But for the faithful, for the thousands of pilgrims who year in and year out descend into their crypts, they are something more: they are above all cities of devotion. And justly so. One who is not deaf to the highest sentiments pauses before the tomb of a great man, and visits with respect the house in which he lived, and scans with thoughtful eye a battlefield upon which the fate of the world has been decided. In the catacombs we have more than this. The individuals and events with which we here, despite the centuries, put ourselves in immediate contact, mean more to the believing Christian than the great men of world history and the battles which they fought.

But one who descends into the catacombs to strengthen his faith and to pray ought not to forget that he can only do so because men of science with conscientious labor and many a sacrifice have prepared the soil for him. Science gives him the security that he does not here treat of pious dreams and artistic fancies, but of reality.

18

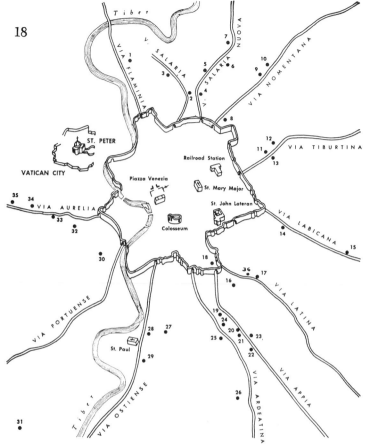

Fig. 1. THE ROMAN CATACOMBS

1. Valentine
2. Pamphilus
3. Bassilla — Hermes
4. Maximus — *ad Sanctam Felicitatem*
5. Thraso — *ad Sanctum Saturninum*
6. Jordani — *ad Sanctum Alexandrum*
7. Priscilla
8. Nicomedes
9. Agnes
10. *Maius — Ostrianum*
11. Novatianus — Viale Regina
12. Hippolytus
13. Cyriaca — Laurence
14. **Castulus**

15. *Ad Duas Lauros* — Peter and Marcellinus — *ad Sanctam Helenam — sub Augusta*
16. Gordianus and Epimachus
17. Apronianus — Eugenia
18. Campana
19. Balbina
20. Lucina
21. Callistus
22. Sebastian — ad Catacumbas
23. Praetextatus
24. Marcus and Marcellianus
25. Domitilla

26. Nunziatella
27. Commodilla — *ad Sanctos Felicem et Adauctum*
28. Timotheus
29. Thecla
30. Pontianus — *ad Ursum Pileatum*
31. Generosa — *ad Sextum Philippi*
32. Pancratius — Octavilla
33. Processus and Martianus — *Sancta Agatha ad Girulum*
34. *Duo Felices*
35. Calepodius
36. Small catacomb discovered in 1956

CHAPTER II

THE CEMETERIES

A MAP of the Roman catacombs shows them surrounding the city at a certain distance like a crown (fig. 1). For the most part they are situated along the highways which spread out from Rome in every direction and connected it with the rest of the world. In this the catacombs followed the example set by other early burial sites. The ancient Romans preferred to build their sepulchral monuments outside the city along their famous roads since it was forbidden by law to bury a person within the city walls.[1]

In the earliest accounts of the catacombs, we find that they are described with reference to the roads along which they lay. Since this topographical disposition is one of the essential characteristics of the catacombs, even today no better arrangement can be found for them.

The catacombs, however, are not all equally distributed along the various highways. The largest lie to the northeast, to the east, and to the south of the city. Those to the west beyond the Tiber are smaller. Thus along the Via Portuensis, which runs along the right bank of the Tiber, we find the catacombs of Pontianus, St. Felix, and Generosa. On the Via Aurelia, which leaves the city by the Porta San Pancrazio on the Janiculum, lie St. Pancratius, Sts. Processus and Martianus, and Calepodius.

Toward the north on the Via Flaminia there is only the

surface cemetery of St. Valentine. To the northeast on the Via Salaria Vecchia is to be found first the still unidentified cemetery *ad Clivum Cucumeris,* then St. Hermes, or Bassilla, and finally Pamphilus. Passing from there to the Via Salaria Nuova, one comes upon the catacombs of St. Felicitas, Thrason, Jordani, and the largest of this group, Priscilla. Toward the northeast, leaving the city by the Porta Pia, runs the Via Nomentana. Along it may be found the small catacombs of St. Nicomedes and St. Agnes, the large *coemeterium Maius,* and much farther on, St. Alexander.

Next in order is the Via Tiburtina, the road which leads to Tivoli, with the two cemeteries of St. Laurence, or Cyriaca, and St. Hippolytus. To these must now be added the small cemetery discovered in 1926 which lies in their immediate vicinity, and which probably belonged to the Novatians.

The Via Labicana, or Casilina, has the cemeteries of Sts. Peter and Marcellinus, and the small cemetery of St. Castulus.

The most important road of ancient Rome was the Via Appia, which runs toward the southeast, and which originally left the city to the south of the Circus Maximus by the ancient Porta Capena. After the erection of the Aurelian Wall, it issued from the gate which later came to be known as the Porta San Sebastiano. The Via Latina, which branches off to the left, has only a few Christian sepulchers in the small cemeteries of Sts. Gordian and Epimachus, and St. Eugene. Along the main road, on the contrary, we find the very important catacombs of St. Callistus, St. Sebastian, and Praetextatus. The Via Ardeatina branches off to the right with the catacomb of Domitilla. These four interdependent cemeteries form a veritable subterranean city. Some six miles of galleries have been explored and measured in Callistus, and eight in Domitilla.

The Via Ostiensis, which follows the left bank of the Tiber, has only the small cemeteries of St. Timotheus and St. Thecla. Somewhat farther from the river lies the much larger cemetery of Commodilla.

Ancient Roman tombs show two different types of burial. There are cremations and inhumations. In the former, the ashes of the dead were placed in cinerary urns, which in turn were preserved in richly adorned columbaria, or "dovecots." In the latter, the bodies of the dead were placed in stone or terra-cotta sarcophagi within a mausoleum. Both types of burial are often found in the same burial vault. In such cases the upper part of the mausoleum has the usual niches for cinerary urns, and the lower section contains the flatly arched niches destined for the reception of the sarcophagi. Inhumation was the original form of burial at Rome, and there were ancient families such as the Scipios who retained it exclusively. Toward the end of the second century after Christ the practice of cremation disappeared. It was never employed by the Christians.

The most characteristic feature of the catacombs is their location underground. The name "catacomb," however, does not come from this peculiarity, as might be imagined. "Catacomb" is only the specific designation dating back to antiquity of one of the many old Roman cemeteries, the *coemeterium ad Catacumbas*, later renowned as St. Sebastian's. *"Ad Catacumbas,"* from the Greek κατὰ κύμβας, is simply the designation of a particular site, and may be translated by something like "Sunken Valley."[2] Other cemeteries have similar place names, for example, *ad Clivum Cucumeris* ("at Cucumber Hill"), *ad Duas Lauros* ("at the Two Laurels"), *ad Ursum Pileatum* ("at the Capped Bear"). But since St. Sebastian's was known and accessible during the Middle Ages, all the subterranean places of burial received in the end the popular designation of "catacomb."

Underground cemeteries are now no longer in vogue. The question, then, may reasonably be asked as to why they were constructed at Rome. The answer lies in a consideration of the subsoil of Rome and its immediate environs. This consists of deep and extensive layers of a dark, soft tufa, which is easily cut, and which at the same time is quite strong.

Cave-like chambers and subterranean galleries were made where-
ever there was this kind of tufa or even soft sandstone. There
was, moreover, where the ground permitted it, an easy transfer
from the widespread practice of cutting tombs into the sides
of cliffs to excavating them beneath the surface of the ground.
Both types of tombs were known to the Etruscans, the burial
chamber hollowed out in a cliff, and the subterranean crypt
cut into the underlying tufa. Catacombs are thus found not
only at Rome, but also all over Italy wherever such stone is
to be found beneath the soil, as at Naples and in many places
in Sicily.

We must not, however, imagine that the Roman Christians
drove their underground galleries beneath the fields near any
of the great highways that they pleased, as if these were an
indefinite "No Man's Land" which could be pierced in any
direction. To excavate a catacomb it was at least necessary to
procure title to a piece of property, which was then recorded
in the official register.

The question has often been raised as to how the Christians
could inherit and acquire such pieces of property during the
times of persecution. There was no difficulty when the cemeteries were privately owned by individual Christians. But in
the third century, they passed at least in part into the possession
of the Church.[3] It must be assumed that measures taken against
the Christians as individuals did not *per se* deprive the Church
of all right of ownership. We know, for example, of a suit
between the Church at Rome and a corporation of innkeepers
over a plot of ground within the city. The case was decided in
favor of the Christians by the emperor Alexander Severus (222–
235; Ael. Lampr. *Alex Sev.* 49). In 257 an edict of Valerian
deprived the Church of proprietorship over the cemeteries, but
this was expressly restored by Gallienus in 260 (Euseb. *E.H.*
7.13.1).

A cemetery could only be erected on a specifically determined piece of land, which as we have already observed,

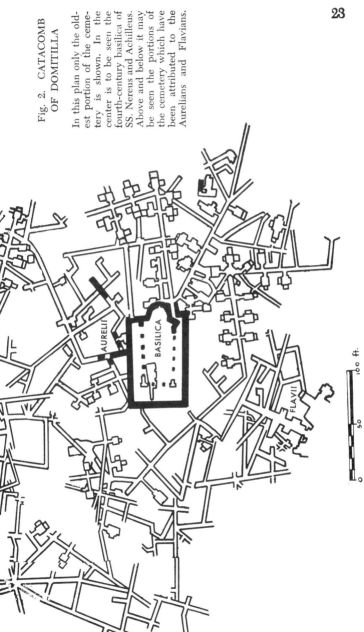

23

Fig. 2. CATACOMB OF DOMITILLA

In this plan only the oldest portion of the cemetery is shown. In the center is to be seen the fourth-century basilica of SS. Nereus and Achilleus. Above and below it may be seen the portions of the cemetery which have been attributed to the Aurelians and Flavians.

AURELII

BASILICA

FLAVII

0   50   100 ft.

had to be outside the walls of the city. It is still an unsolved problem whether the tombs were excavated underground at the very beginning, or whether the surface was first used and only later the area beneath because of a lack of further space for burials. Whichever may have been the case, the tombs had to remain within the boundaries of the determined piece of land, whether they were on the surface or beneath it.

The underground corridors had as a rule the following origin. A stairway was first dug into the ground, then a corridor slightly higher than a man was run off parallel to the surface at the foot of the stairs. Other corridors were then driven off at right angles to the original one, and these in turn could be connected with others which ran parallel to the first. There was thus formed a network which was at first fairly simple, but which gradually became more refined and complex (fig. 2).

The simplest way to use these galleries was to arrange the tombs along the wall, one over the other, and side by side (pls. 4, 5). But just as in modern cemeteries we find family burial vaults next to individual tombs, so also in the catacombs little rooms called *cubicula* with space enough for several graves were opened up at different places in the sides of the corridors.

The tombs themselves are of different types. The most distinguished is the marble sarcophagus, which itself could be quite varied in the richness of its artistry. Next to the sarcophagus in costliness is the so-called *arcosolium*. This consists of a kind of walled-up bin in which the corpse was placed beneath a semicircular niche carved into the wall. This type of tomb is found especially in the *cubicula,* but also in the corridors. Finally, there is the simplest and most common form of burial, the so-called *loculus.* This consists of a rectangular box-shaped niche, having its longest side running parallel to the surface of the wall and not pointed into it. If a tomb of this type was dug into the floor and not cut into a wall it is called a *forma.*

The corridors of a catacomb are as a rule completely occupied from top to bottom by such *loculi* placed one above the other.

Pl. 4. Typical corridor in a catacomb. Most of the tombs in the catacombs were opened by barbarians in search of plunder or by Christians who took the bodies from the cemeteries and buried them in the churches within the walls of the city to preserve them from desecration.

Pl. 5. A corridor in the catacomb of Pamphilus with the *loculi* still sealed.

Pl. 6. Coins of the time of the Emperor Aurelian (270–275) which were pressed into the fresh mortar at the sealing of a tomb in Pamphilus. These coins served as identification for the tomb which has no inscription.

Pl. 7. Terra-cotta lamp from Pamphilus with a portrait of the Good Shepherd. ◗

Pl. 8. Terra-cotta lamp with the stamp of the maker, once cemented on a tomb in Pamphilus. ⬇

Pl. 9. A gold glass with a representation of the multiplication of loaves still *in situ* in the catacomb of Pamphilus.

10. A glass bottle once d with perfumes ce- nted onto a grave in Pamphilus.

A visitor to the catacombs walking through these dark corridors and past this innumerable host of the dead is deeply impressed by the thought of the immense number of those who have here found their last resting place and of whom nothing remains but an empty tomb. The vast majority of *loculi* are today open and empty, though bones of the dead are occasionally to be seen.

Originally, of course, these tombs along the walls were carefully closed either with a slab of marble or several tiles laid next to each other. The edges of these were then sealed with mortar.

Only a small fraction of the slabs carry any inscriptions. Small objects such as coins (pl. 6), terra-cotta lamps (pls. 7, 8), ivory figurines, bits of colored porcelain, or pieces of glass decorated with figures in gold (pl. 9) were at times pushed into the fresh mortar sealing the tombs to serve as a means of identification. They also provided a modest decoration for the last resting places of the dead.

Occasionally, though not very frequently, small flasks are found fixed in the mortar (pl. 10). These held liquid perfumes with which visitors could sprinkle the slabs closing the tombs. This beautiful custom, which had been borrowed from the pagans, corresponds rather closely to our custom of placing fresh flowers upon the graves of those dear to us.

Comparing the Christian catacombs with our own cemeteries, we see at once a great similarity. Despite the different external surroundings, we find the same simple care and the same simple love for the dead giving expression in different ways to a common belief in everlasting life.

When there was no more room in a catacomb, various remedies were sought for the difficulty. Since the limits of the property would have been reached, further lateral extension was out of the question. Recourse was then had to deeper digging wherever the site permitted it. The simplest way to do this was to keep digging up the floor of the corridors.

Galleries were thus created of a remarkable height, and in which logically enough, the upper tombs are earlier than the lower. Often a lack of space even brought about the destruction of paintings which at an earlier date had served as pious decorations. Thus, for example, the center of a fresco representing the Good Shepherd in the catacomb of Callistus was destroyed by the cutting of a new *loculus,* nor was any attempt made afterward to restore the painting.

To increase the capacity of the underground cemeteries a second, a third, and at times even a fourth level were excavated beneath the first (fig. 3). Some of these later corridors thus reached a really remarkable depth.

With the passage of years several catacombs came to be excavated near each other. Attempts were then made to purchase the separating tracts of land so that the distinct and independent catacombs could be united. In this way, for example, the great cemetery of Callistus was gradually built up from separate catacombs.

Completely fantastic figures are sometimes given for the total number of Christians buried in the catacombs. A reasonable estimate of the number, however, can easily be made. The largest of the catacombs, Domitilla, has about eight miles of corridors, while the total length of the galleries of all the catacombs cannot be much more than sixty to ninety miles. The cemeteries which have been completely destroyed, or which have not yet been entirely excavated, are not so numerous as to change this estimate to any great extent. Four or five *loculi,* one above the other, are to be found on each side of a corridor. This means that for every six and one half feet there are about ten graves. If the total length of the catacombs is a little over sixty miles, the number of tombs would be about 500,000. If it is a little over ninety miles, it would be about 750,000 — the whole being, of course, only a rough estimate. This number may seem to be small when we consider the fact that the graves come from a period of nearly two and a half centuries, that is,

32

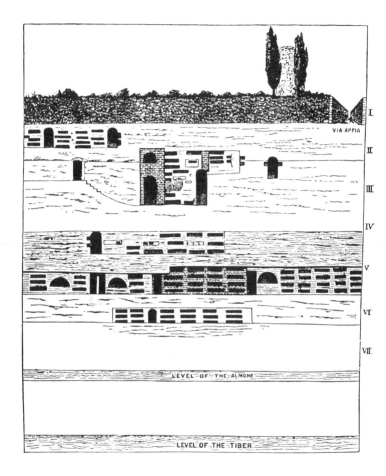

Fig. 3. COMPOSITE SECTION OF THE CATACOMB OF CALLISTUS

The Roman numerals on the right indicate various strata of tufa. The section
above the dark line dividing stratum V represents the "crypt of Lucina."
Strata V and VI represent another portion of the same cemetery.

from approximately 150 to 400. But it would be a mistake to imagine that the Christian community in Rome at this time was very large. About the year 200 there would have been only about 10,000 Christians at Rome, and toward 313, at the end of the persecutions, not more than 70,000 or 80,000. Even in the fourth century the Christians of Rome were for a long time a minority with respect to the pagans. Moreover, the number of the inhabitants of the city, which under Trajan and Hadrian had been perhaps a million, by the end of the second century had begun to decline rapidly.

The earliest Christian cemeteries at Rome had their origin in the private sepulchers of wealthy Christian families, just as the later Roman *tituli*, or parochial churches, had their origin as places of worship in private homes. This can be deduced from a study of the disposition of the primitive parts of the cemeteries, and also from the names of the original owners, as for example, Jordani, Praetextatus, Commodilla, Domitilla, Priscilla, and many others, which remained to indicate an entire complex, even after the original underground, or half-underground burial chamber had evolved into a system of subterranean galleries of different levels.

Of these primitive Christians the best known to us is Domitilla, from whom the great subterranean necropolis on the Via Ardeatina has taken its name. Domitilla was a granddaughter of the emperor Vespasian (69–79), and had married one of her grandfather's nephews, Titus Flavius Clemens. From early pagan and Christian sources we may conclude that both of them were Christians. Clemens was consul for the year 95. The emperor at the time was his cousin Domitian, son of Vespasian, and uncle of Domitilla.

We even know something about Domitilla's household. She had as her administrator the freedman Stephanus. In the year 96 he killed Domitian, most likely to avenge his patroness. Domitilla owned a piece of property on the Via Ardeatina within the region which is known today as the Tor Marancia, for an inscription which was found there states·that a sepulchral monument was erected on the site "with the kind permission of Flavia Domitilla."[4] She must also have owned a brick factory since there are still extant bricks bearing the stamp of a certain Felix, slave of Flavia Domitilla. We have, moreover, the epitaph of a certain Tatia, freedwoman of Flavia Domitilla, and the nurse of her mistress' seven children. We know that the two eldest of these children were destined to succeed to the throne, and that they had received the names of Domitian and Vespasian from their uncle the emperor. Their teacher was the famous rhetorician Quintilian, who obtained through their father, Flavius Clemens, the *ornamenta consularia,* that is, the insignia and honors of a consul without ever having actually held the magistracy.[5]

These various bits of information could point to a rich and noble, but hardly Christian family. The historians Suetonius and Dio Cassius, however, speak of the execution of Flavius Clemens in such terms that there can be little doubt that the reason for it was his profession of Christianity. Dio expressly states that he fell into disgrace with the emperor because of his impiety.[6] A further indication of his Christian faith lies in the fact that within the area of the Tor Marancia, where the inscriptions referring to Domitilla were found, there is a *hypogeum,* or underground chamber, whose walls belong to the first half of the second century, and which forms the nucleus of the immense Christian necropolis which was called in antiquity the cemetery of Domitilla.[7] Members of the Flavian family may have been buried in the oldest part of this cemetery, though there is no certain proof for such a belief. The Greek sepulchral inscription of Flavius Sabinus and his sister (Flavia) Titiana, which was found in the so-called "region of the Aurelians," one of the earliest sections of the cemetery, was probably thrown into the catacomb from a cemetery above ground after the area had ceased to be used as a place of burial (pl. 11).[8] We do not know if these Christian Flavians of the second century

Pl. 11. Remains of ancient tombs on the surface above the catacomb of Domitilla. The picture was taken during the course of excavations in 1926–1927.

were direct descendants of Clemens and Domitilla. They may possibly have been descendants of freedmen, but certainly they were connected in some way with this noble Roman family.[9]

While Flavius Clemens was completely forgotten in Christian legend, there remained at least a faint recollection of Domitilla within the Roman community. Though the evidence is not as clear as we might desire, her name seems to have been associated with the land under which the catacombs were excavated. When in the fifth or sixth century the legend of Nereus and Achilleus was composed, it was known that the name of the catacomb did not come from a martyr buried there, but from a Domitilla who had originally owned the property. In the legend the area is expressly described as the country home of Domitilla, but it confused and exaggerated everything. It made of the historical Domitilla, who had at least seven children, a virgin consecrated to God; and it linked her with the martyrs Nereus and Achilleus, who were buried in the cemetery of Domitilla, but who probably belong to a much later persecution (pl. 12).[10] In the fourth century visitors to the island of Ponza were shown the rooms in which a Domitilla had lived during her exile, but this early Christian seems to have been the niece rather than the wife of Flavius Clemens.[11]

It is a great misfortune that we do not know more about the domestic tragedy within the imperial household of the Flavians which reached its climax in the assassination of the emperor. It was certainly a domestic tragedy. Was it also a drama revolving about the right of succession? And did this in turn somehow involve the Christian faith? Since Clemens and Domitilla were Christians, their young sons would also have been Christians, even though their teacher was the pagan Quintilian. Or was Domitian unaware of their faith when he destined them to be his heirs to the throne, and did a later discovery of it bring about the ruin of their parents? How could Flavius Clemens in such circumstances have given his consent to the choice of his sons as the successors of Domitian,

Pl. 12. The execution of the martyr Achilleus carved on a column in the
basilica of SS. Nereus and Achilleus in Domitilla. The martyr's hands are
bound behind his back. The executioner has raised the sword to strike off
his victim's head. In the background is the cross with the victory crown.
Representations of such historical executions are very rare.

since he must have foreseen that such a course could only lead to catastrophe? Were the boys put to death with their father? Did the Christian community know anything of the struggle that was going on? And if it did, was it filled with hope or fear? A playwright could mold this material into a terrifying tragedy; an historian must be content with merely posing the questions.

The second of the very old cemeteries lies nearly opposite to Domitilla on the other side of the city. This cemetery, which bears the name of Priscilla, is also connected with a noble Roman family, but not so clearly as in the case of Domitilla.

In the oldest part of this cemetery is found the crypt of the Acilians. This family, whose eldest sons regularly carried the *cognomen*, or last name, of Glabrio, is much older than that of the Flavians, although it did not belong to the ancient patriciate. One of its ancestors was the consul Acilius Glabrio who in 191 B.C., at Thermopylae defeated Antiochus, king of Syria. Among his descendants was Acilius Glabrio, consul in A.D. 91, one of the many who, according to Dio Cassius, were put to death by the emperor Domitian. This historian, who is generally quite trustworthy, gives some significant details with regard to his downfall.

The emperor Domitian had a villa near Albano on the hill which is today crowned by the papal summer residence of Castel Gandolfo. He invited the consul to come there for the feast of the Juvenilia, and forced him to fight with a lion in the arena. There must have been some reason for such a command. Even the arrogant Domitian could hardly have permitted a consul in office to enter the arena as a gladiator. To the surprise of everybody Glabrio managed to slay the lion with his sword. According to Roman custom a man had to be set free for such an exploit. To avoid further traps that might be laid by the emperor, Glabrio seems to have gone into voluntary exile. But the emperor, who must have been humiliated by the stories told about the killing of the lion, continued his persecution and finally had Glabrio put to death. Later he so colored the affair as to make it appear that Glabrio had voluntarily played the part of a gladiator, and had thus acted in a way unbecoming a consul.[12]

These incidents which are recorded by Dio Cassius are not specific enough for us to maintain without further evidence that the consul Acilius Glabrio was a Christian, even though both Dio and Suetonius place his death in connection with that of Flavius Clemens. Here the discovery of a number of inscriptions in the so-called "*hypogeum,* or 'cellar,' of the Acilians" in the cemetery of Priscilla comes to our assistance.[13] The inscriptions are obviously connected with one another and bear the names of Acilius Rufinus, Claudius Acilius Valerius, Acilius Glabrio, Marcus Acilius, and Manius Acilius — Manius being the usual *praenomen* of the Acilii Glabriones. Of these, Acilius Rufinus was certainly a Christian, as is clearly indicated by the acclamation: ΖΗΣΗΣ ΕΝ ΘΕΩ ("May you live in God!"), but this epitaph belongs to either the third or fourth century. The inscriptions of the others give no indication of Christianity. In the second and third centuries the main branch of the Acilii Glabriones was certainly not Christian, as is known from a certain amount of historical information which we have with regard to a series of consuls of this name all descending from the lion-slayer.[14] Thus, at best, only a part of his descendants were Christian.

Moreover, the cemetery of Priscilla did not evolve simply from the "*hypogeum* of the Acilians." According to Styger we must distinguish three parts in the catacomb which were originally independent: the *arenarium,* or "sand pit," the *cryptoporticus,* or "hidden hall," and the so-called "*hypogeum* of the Acilians."[15] All three of these private burial grounds had their own entrances, and they were not connected with one another. After the middle of the third century they fell into disuse. Only in the fourth century, when the large public cemetery was created, were the three ancient nuclei incorporated into it.

If we look for a Priscilla among the Glabrios we come across

Arria Lucii filia Plaria Vera Priscilla, or more simply, "Arria Priscilla," wife of the consul of 152, Manius Acilius Glabrio Cornelius Severus.[16] A Manius Acilius and his sister Priscilla are named on one of the inscriptions in the hypogeum.[17] The consul of 152 also had a daughter Priscilla.

It cannot be denied that all of these conjectures are based on rather slim foundations. We have the lion-slaying consul of the year 91, who may have been a Christian. His descendants are buried above or near a crypt which later formed part of a Christian cemetery. Some of these descendants were themselves Christians. The cemetery was named after a Priscilla.[18] And, as we have seen, there were in the second century a number of Priscillas in the family of the Glabrios. These various details do not add up to a categorical proof, but it would be foolish to attribute them all to mere chance.

Traces of another noble family are quite probably to be found in yet another early cemetery, the large and important catacomb of Callistus. In his *Annales* for the year 56–57 Tacitus writes: "Pomponia Graecina, a noble woman, the wife of Aulus Plautius, who as I have recorded earlier received an ovation after his British campaign, was accused of practicing a foreign superstition and was left to the judgment of her husband. In accordance with ancient custom, he held the trial which was to determine the fate and good name of his wife before a family council and pronounced her innocent. Pomponia spent many years in constant sadness: for after the murder of Julia, the daughter of Drusus, through the machinations of Messalina (in A.D. 42), she lived for forty years dressed in mourning and lost in perpetual grief. During the reign of Claudius (41–54) she suffered no harm for her constancy, and afterwards (under Nero) it redounded to her credit" (*Ann.* 13.32).

This account seems to indicate that Pomponia was a Christian. The remarks of Tacitus about her *superstitio externa* and her puzzling manner of life, that is, her complete withdrawal from the social activities to which she was entitled as a woman of high rank, and the fact that no slanderous accusations could be proved against her, all point in this direction. The discovery of an inscription in the oldest part of the catacomb of Callistus referring to a certain Pomponius Graecinus makes this conjecture even more probable.[19] Among the Romans a similarity in the family name, that is, in the *nomen gentilicium,* such as Cornelius, Caecilius, or Pomponius, does not of itself indicate relationship since some of these names were very common. This was largely due to the fact that freedmen and their descendants took the family name of their former masters. But when in conjunction with the family name there is also found a characteristic last name, or *cognomen,* such as Cornelius *Scipio,* Caecilius *Metellus,* or Pomponius *Graecinus,* there is an indication of real blood relationship. The Christian Pomponius Graecinus could, then, have been a nephew, or more probably, the grandnephew of the Pomponia Graecina mentioned by Tacitus.

Tacitus dates the "sorrowful" life of Pomponia from the murder of the princess Julia, a distant relative of her husband. A causal connection can perhaps be here established in that Pomponia may have taken advantage of the period of mourning for her cousin-in-law to change her mode of life and withdraw from high society when less notice would be taken of it. That Pomponia should have already been a Christian in the year 43 is not impossible. In the second decade after the resurrection of our Lord there were a number of Christians in Rome even if none of the Apostles had as yet reached the city. If the enigmatic expression in the Acts of the Apostles: "And Peter going out, went into another place" (Acts 12:17), really refers to Rome, and if the liberation of the Apostle from the prison in Jerusalem is to be placed in the year 42, as many exegetes maintain, Pomponia could have been one of the first of those whom Peter personally converted to Christianity at Rome.[20]

To be sure, from what we know of Pomponia, we cannot positively maintain that the cemetery of Callistus was originally a crypt of the Pomponians. The reason for this is that everything in the cemetery has been so altered that the primitive nucleus can no longer be identified. Nevertheless, there must have been a definite connection between the cemetery of Callistus and the ancient Pomponians.

For the whole of the second century we hear nothing of the cemeteries, although at least three of them, namely, Priscilla, Domitilla, and Callistus, were already in existence. Only about the year 200 do we come across the important notice given by Hippolytus in the ninth book of his *Philosophumena* that Pope Zephyrinus (*ca.* 200–217) entrusted the administration of "the cemetery" to the deacon Callistus.[21]

In this same context we learn various details about the life of Callistus, whose name has remained fixed to the cemetery. At the same time we must remember that Hippolytus' account is an outspoken libel written after he had become the leader of a schism. According to him, Callistus had been a household slave. We may readily believe this since "Callistus" is a genuine slave name. His former master was a Christian, the freedman (Marcus Aurelius) Carpophorus. Following Roman custom, Callistus after his own enfranchisement would have been called Marcus Aurelius Callistus.

With capital furnished by his patron, Callistus set up a bank. His exchange was located near the *piscina publica* in what is now the district of San Saba. Hippolytus tells us that Callistus embezzled the money and had to flee. He reached a ship from Portus in the harbor, but was there apprehended by Carpophorus, who had set out in pursuit of him. In desperation Callistus dove into the sea, was fished out, and handed over to his patron, who took him to Rome and condemned him to forced labor. In the end Carpophorus yielded to the entreaties of the Christians. He freed Callistus so that he could pay off his debts, and even canceled what was owed to himself. Despite all this, Callistus was never in a position to pay back the loans which he had received. He therefore tried to extricate himself from his difficulties by a desperate stroke: he caused a riot among the Jews on a solemn Sabbath, was accused by them of being a Christian, was then scourged by the prefect of the city, Seius Fuscianus (consul in 188), and sent into exile in Sardinia, notwithstanding the fact that Carpophorus had testified in court that Callistus was not really a Christian, but only intent on being put to death.

All of this can scarcely have happened as it is told. Hippolytus obviously wanted to minimize Callistus' title of "confessor," which hurt his own position. Actually, a man with so scandalous a past could hardly have in later life been consecrated bishop. There may be some truth about the affairs of the bank. Callistus may have encountered occasional difficulties in meeting his financial obligations, but that he should have embezzled the funds is a calumny that can easily be laid against a businessman. He must have mastered his problems, for Pope Zephyrinus would never have entrusted the administration of the goods of the Church to one who had gone bankrupt. It is possible that the Jews denounced their troublesome competitor as a Christian, but it does not follow from this that there was anything irregular in Callistus' profession of faith as Hippolytus would like to have shown.

Callistus recovered his liberty through the pardon which Pope Victor obtained from the emperor Commodus for the exiles in Sardinia. Even here Hippolytus does not fail to give a tendentious interpretation to the events. In the list of confessors which Victor sent to the authorities in Sardinia, he is supposed to have purposely omitted the name of Callistus since he did not want to have this adventurer again at Rome. Callistus, however, with prayers and tears prevailed upon the officer in charge to let him off with the others. Victor was greatly upset, but since he could not alter what had been done, to get rid of Callistus and to keep him quiet, he sent him to Antium with a month's pay.

Again this is nothing but gossip. It would be more correct to say that after his release Callistus spent quite some time in the papal employ at Antium. The Church may have had possessions there which needed tending.. From the fact that Callistus received a stipend for his labors, we may conclude that he was already a member of the clergy. He may have been admitted into their ranks by Victor after his return from exile. This was an honor frequently conferred upon confessors at this time.

Victor's successor, Zephyrinus, recalled Callistus to Rome and made him his "archdeacon." Hippolytus does not fail to add that Callistus never departed from the side of the new pope, and that he completely won him over with his hypocrisy since Zephyrinus was of a very retiring nature. Without the irony, this simply means that Callistus did his duty as a deacon.

Of particular interest to us is the fact that Zephyrinus entrusted Callistus with the administration of "the cemetery." For the first time we hear of a cemetery belonging no longer to a private family, but to the Church of Rome as such. Without doubt the reference is to the cemetery which still bears the name of Callistus. The particular works which were executed there by Callistus are no longer identifiable, but they must certainly have been of no little consequence since his name has remained attached to the whole area despite the fact that he was neither the original founder of the cemetery, nor was he buried there. Callistus, who in the year 217 succeeded Zephyrinus in the papacy, suffered martyrdom in 222 and was buried in the cemetery of Calepodius on the Via Aurelia.

The papal crypt in Callistus seems to have been constructed only under Pope Fabian (235–250).

One of the very reliable notices in the *Liberian Catalog* is that Fabian also carried out numerous projects in the cemeteries.[22] We do not know exactly what they were. They could have been the excavation of new galleries, the decoration, restoration, and reinforcement of the old. Because of seepage and cave-ins the catacombs were in constant need of repair. Important in this account of Fabian's pontificate is that mention is made of a number of cemeteries which were subject to the direct administration of the Church, and which consequently no longer belonged to private individuals. The cemetery of Callistus, however, remained the principal cemetery, and in the third and fourth centuries it seems to have been the ordinary place of burial for the clergy. This is quite certain from the inscription which Pope Damasus placed in the crypt of the popes. The original inscription was discovered by De Rossi and pieced together from innumerable fragments. An inscription of the deacon Severus, who arranged for a family crypt "with the permission of Pope Marcellinus" (298–304), shows that clerics could also obtain burial for their relatives in this cemetery.[23]

In addition to the three oldest cemeteries there were at Rome toward the middle of the third century the catacombs of Commodilla, Praetextatus, Hermes, Jordani, and others.

From the present condition of the sites it is impossible to determine whether or not the persecutions of Valerian (257–258) and Diocletian (303–313) brought any ruin or desecration to the subterranean tombs. At least during the first of these persecutions the cemeteries were closed and confiscated.

When in the year 313 peace finally came to the Church, a new era gradually dawned for the catacombs.

The fourth century may be characterized as the period of transformation of the catacombs from cemeteries into places of pilgrimage, even though they continued to be used as places of burial to the end of the century. Contemporaneous with the development of the flourishing cult of the martyrs was the corresponding development of centers of forms of worship. The tombs of the martyrs were made into shrines. Over the tombs of some of these, for example, St. Agnes, St. Laurence, and Sts. Nereus and Achilleus, real basilicas were erected. Since the Christians of the fourth century wished to leave the graves of the martyrs untouched, these basilicas were built right into the catacombs. This meant, of course, that parts of the surrounding galleries with their sepulchers had to be sacrificed. Thus there evolved the rather peculiar type of half-buried basilica, which, though it was accessible to all through a flight of descending stairs, had a second floor at approximately ground level over the side naves, the so-called *matroneum*. At this same time basilicas were erected over the tombs of the Apostles Peter and Paul. All of these churches, which are known as cemeterial basilicas, are distinguished from the urban basilicas, such as St. John Lateran and St. Clement, in that the occasion for their construction was the veneration of a martyr's tomb. This determined the site of the building and the particular shape of the altar.

In the second half of the fourth century, Pope Damasus proved to be indefatigable in his labors for the catacombs. He redecorated most of the tombs of the martyrs and composed epigrams for them. These poems were inscribed in letters of classical perfection on great white slabs of marble and placed near the tombs, and thus added new luster to numerous sanctuaries. New entrances and stairways were also made to facilitate the approach to the various crypts.

With the fifth century began the decline of the catacombs. They not only suffered severe outrages during the continuous barbarian invasions, but the surrounding areas were laid waste as well. The Roman campagna, which had hitherto flourished with many villas and a thriving populace, became almost deserted. The inhabitants of the city were now surrounded by a wall that had become much too large for them. They had so declined in numbers that there was no further need for large cemeteries, and they now buried their dead within the churches of the city. No new Damasus arose to renovate the catacombs.

Nevertheless, they still remained places of prayer and devotion. Their fame in subsequent years extended particularly to northern Europe and drew to Rome many pious pilgrims. It was during this time that the *itineraria*, or "pilgrims' guides," made their appearance. These little works, despite their quaintness and frequent misconceptions, have rendered invaluable service to modern scholars.

Toward the middle of the eighth century Aistulf, King of the Lombards, sacked the Roman catacombs and carried off a good many relics.[24] With these thefts a new era began for the catacombs. The Roman pontiffs were no longer able to protect them from further damage or to restore the tombs now falling into ruin. Pope Paul I (757–767) decided to take a great number of the remains from their subterranean resting places and carry them to places of safety in the churches of the city. Later popes also, in particular Paschal I (817–829), sought to save the sacred relics in this way from irreverence and pillage.

Aistulf's plundering of the bones of the martyrs shows, on the other hand, the high regard in which they were held by this newly Christian nation. For a long time the veneration of the martyrs had been drawing pilgrims from the north to Rome. Was it not natural that they should have conceived the desire to have a share in these blessed treasures either by favor or by force?

There thus gradually arose a veritable war over the relics of the martyrs, which led unfortunately to some deplorable incidents. Most notorious are those connected with the Roman deacon Deusdona and his brothers Lunisus and Theodore.[25] While on a journey beyond the Alps, Deusdona made the acquaintance of Einhard, the learned friend of Charles the Great. Einhard was anxious to have some relics of the martyrs for his monastery of Mulinheim, later known as Seligenstadt, and Deusdona promised his assistance. He had under his care the catacombs of Sts. Peter and Marcellinus, so it was not too difficult for him to remove the bones one night. Thus Selingenstadt obtained the relics of Sts. Peter and Marcellinus. Not much later connections were made with another large German abbey, Fulda. Its abbot, Rhabanus Maurus, wished to increase the luster of his monastery in a similar way. He had one of his monks contact Deusdona. Fulda then received relics of the Roman martyrs Alexander, Sebastian, Fabian, Urban, Felicissimus, Felicitas, and Emerentiana. These, of course, were not always the complete remains of a martyr, but for the most part only small pieces of bone. Rhabanus Maurus was nonetheless highly pleased and richly rewarded Deusdona and his brothers. These achievements made the other French and German abbots all the more eager to obtain relics of the martyrs and their middlemen all the more audacious. In time relics of the most renowned martyrs of Rome found their way to many great cathedrals and monasteries beyond the Alps, where they were jealously guarded and became the objects of sincere reverence. It is not certain that the agents in dispatching the relics always acted with the most scrupulous honesty. Seligenstadt, at any rate, for a thousand years had believed that it enjoyed the possession of the holy relics of the martyr Hyacinth when in the year 1843 his bones were discovered in his still untouched tomb in the catacomb of St. Hermes. Nevertheless, many of the translated relics were certainly genuine. The overzealous bishops and abbots of France and Germany and their obliging agents at Rome thus only succeeded in greatly increasing and extending the honor and veneration shown to the Roman martyrs.

CHAPTER III

THE TOMBS OF THE POPES

WE KNOW where both of the Princes of the Apostles were buried, but no authentic tradition has survived with reference to the tombs of St. Peter's first successors. Still we have definite information about the order of succession of the early popes. The oldest papal catalog which we possess was drawn up by Irenaeus between 170 and 180 (*Adv. Haer.* 3.3.3). A hundred years after the death of the Apostle Peter there could still have been in Rome individuals who had personally known his disciples. The register of the popes at this time comprised only twelve names: Linus, Anencletus, Clement, Evaristus, Alexander, Xystus I, Telesphorus, Hyginus, Pius, Anicetus, Soter, and Eleutherius. Irenaeus, however, does not seem to have been the first to draw up such a list. Even before him, Hegesippus, who visited the churches founded by the Apostles to examine the unity of tradition in the faith, had compiled a catalog of the bishops of Rome (Euseb. *E.H.* 4.22.1–3).

In the course of time the list naturally grew longer, and it has come down to us in many different forms. Errors crept into it through mistakes in spelling and pronunciation, but these can easily be corrected by checking them with the earlier texts. The change of pronunciation in Latin and an ignorance of Greek brought about the corruption of many names. Some made

"Egenus," or even "Eugenius," out of Hyginus. Zephyrinus was written as "Geferinus" or "Severinus." The unusual name of Anencletus fared the worst. It appeared as "Anaclitus," "Anelitus," "Clitus," "Cletus," and in the end it was no longer known whether it was the name of one or of two popes. Many as a consequence inserted a superfluous Anacletus or Cletus before or after Clement. But since we have the very early list of Irenaeus, these later errors do not as a rule bother us.

The lists of Irenaeus and other early writers consist of a bare sequence of names without dates. These churchmen had no intention of writing a chronicle. They only wished to demonstrate the continuity of the Apostolic succession, and with it the certainty of the tradition of faith. Our knowledge of fixed dates for the popes begins only in the third century with the death of Pope Zephyrinus in 217. For the earlier period we must be content with relative chronology. We know, for example, that Anicetus ruled about the middle of the second century. This is deduced from the fact that during the reign of Antoninus Pius, quite probably in 155, Bishop Polycarp of Smyrna journeyed to Rome and there conferred with Pope Anicetus about the time for celebrating Easter (Euseb. *E.H.* 4.14.5; Jerome *De vir. ill.* 27).

As has already been observed, we know nothing about the tombs of the first popes. In the sixth century it was held that they were all located near the tomb of St. Peter, but this seems to have been only a conjecture of the times without any real foundation in actual discoveries or tradition.[1]

The first pope whose place of burial happens to be known is *Zephyrinus* († 217). He was buried in the open area above the cemetery of Callistus. The *Itinerary of Salzburg* gives the following description of the site: "On the same (Appian) Way near St. Cecilia there is an innumerable multitude of martyrs: Xystus, pope and martyr; Dionysius, pope and martyr; Julian, pope and martyr; Flavian, martyr; St. Caecilia, virgin and martyr. Eighty martyrs rest there underground. Geferinus, pope and confessor, rests above. Eusebius, pope and martyr, is far from there in a hollow. Cornelius, pope and martyr, is far from there in another hollow. Then you will come to the saintly virgin and martyr Soteris."[2] According to this account the tomb of Zephyrinus was thus above ground and so situated that the pilgrims visited it when they came up from the crypt of St. Caecilia and the neighboring crypt of Pope Xystus. They then descended again to the tombs of Eusebius and Cornelius and finally to that of Soteris. The burial place of Zephyrinus was, of course, not simply a grave in the open field but a mausoleum however unpretentious.

There can be no doubt about the location of the tomb of St. Caecilia, the papal crypt, and the sepulcher of Cornelius. The problem is to locate the mausoleum of Zephyrinus. The *cella trichora*, or small triapsidal chapel, almost immediately above, and near the present-day entrance to the crypt of the popes comes at once to mind. It was here that De Rossi found the fragment of the inscription of Cornelius. As a matter of fact, beneath the central apse of this *cella trichora* at a depth of six and a half feet is found a tomb surrounded by brickwork. Marucchi firmly believed that this specially protected tomb was the lost sepulcher of Zephyrinus.[3] The *cella* itself comes from the age of Constantine, but it stands in turn on more ancient foundations. These also could be part of the original mausoleum of Zephyrinus. But, as Wilpert has proved, the brickwork about the tomb beneath the central apse is more recent. He therefore looked for the tomb of Zephyrinus in another *cella* named after St. Soteris near the Via delle Sette Chiese.[4] This site, however, does not agree with the description given in the *Itinerary of Salzburg*. Marucchi's opinion may thus be the more probable.

During the seventh century the tomb of St. Tarsicius was also venerated in the mausoleum of Zephyrinus. But since we possess only a transcription of the beautiful epitaph which Damasus composed for this renowned martyr of the Eucharist, we no longer know the exact location of his tomb.

Callistus (217–222), the successor of Zephyrinus, was buried on the Via Aurelia in the cemetery of Calepodius. Nothing remains of his tomb, although there are traces of an oratory which Pope Julius erected there to his memory in the fourth century. That Callistus was not buried in "his" cemetery has been a source of surprise. The explanation for this rather singular fact is said to be found in the legendary account of Callistus' murder in Trastevere. Since there was no time to carry his body to the Via Appia, it was hastily laid to rest in the cemetery lying nearby on the Via Aurelia.[5] We know that Callistus died as a martyr and that at the time of his death there was no general persecution of the Christians. It is therefore not improbable that he fell a victim to the violence of a mob. From Trastevere to the papal crypt is a good hour's walk, but it is also a good forty-five minute walk to Calepodius. The need of haste therefore really explains nothing. Much simpler is the supposition that the papal crypt in Callistus was not yet in existence in 222.

We do not know where *Urban* (222–230), the successor of Callistus, was buried.

The series of popes laid to rest in the cemetery of Callistus begins with Pontianus (230–235). When De Rossi discovered the crypt of the popes, he found that everything in it had been wantonly destroyed (pls. 13, 14). The tombs were open, and the inscriptions lay smashed amid the debris. The inscriptions of only four popes were recovered: Anteros (235), Fabian (235–250), Lucius (253–254), and Eutychian (275–283). In 1909, when reinforcements made necessary by a slipping of the earth were being added to the neighboring crypt of St. Cecilia, a well was found filled with rubbish. Wilpert extracted from it the badly smashed inscription of Pope Pontianus (230–235).[6] There were also found in this same cemetery, but outside the papal crypt, the inscriptions of Cornelius (251–253), Caius (283–296), and Eusebius (310). According to the reliable index of A.D. 354, the so-called *Depositio episcoporum,* all of these popes were buried in Callistus. Besides these, Stephen (254–257), Diony-

Pl. 13. Crypt of the popes in Callistus as it appears today.

54

Pl. 14. De Rossi's restoration of the papal crypt as it was in the late
fourth century.

sius (260–268), Felix (269–274), and Melchiades, of whom no inscriptions have survived, were buried here, and also the martyr-pope Xystus (257–258).

Xystus was buried in the large tomb in the floor of the crypt where the altar now stands. The crypt contained sixteen *loculi*. Since Caius was buried outside the crypt, the last place in it must have been taken by his predecessor Eutychian († 283). But since from Pontianus to Eutychian only eight popes were buried in the crypt (with Xystus, nine), others who were not popes must also have been buried there. For anyone who has some measure of historical insight and who listens to the message of the stones, the papal crypt with its environs is one of the most impressive monuments in the whole compass of ancient Rome. Here one stands in the main current of ancient Church history.

Pontianus (230–235) held a synod in which he confirmed the deposition of Origen which had been pronounced by the bishop of Alexandria. His greatest achievement, however, was the settlement of the schism of Hippolytus.

Hippolytus, who was at odds with the bishop of Rome from 217 to 235, is one of the most remarkable personalities of the old Roman church.[7] Surpassed in his own age only by Origen in learning, of high moral seriousness, passionate, and an indefatigable worker to his old age, he was as a priest during the long pontificate of Zephyrinus (200–217), the great theologian of the Roman clergy. But even then he seems to have been embittered at not being able to carry out all of his own ideas. When, after the death of Zephyrinus, the deacon Callistus, to whom he was personally antagonistic, was chosen pope, and his own hopes for the honor were shattered, Hippolytus went into schism. He had himself consecrated by some unknown bishop, organized a separate community, and bitterly attacked Callistus. This state of affairs persisted under the pontificates of Urban (222–230) and Pontianus (230–235). In later years the followers of Hippolytus do not seem to have been very

numerous. At least he complains about the apostasy of many
of them. He had contacts with the imperial court and dedicated
his *World Chronicle* to the emperor Alexander Severus.

Alexander's successor, Maximinus Thrax, took up again the
persecution of the Christians. He directed his attack against
the bishops in particular. Since there were two Christian bishops
at Rome, Pontianus and Hippolytus, he banished them both
to Sardinia.[8]

We can only guess what happened there. It is certain, however, that in Sardinia Pontianus resigned his episcopal office.[9]
This was the first action of the kind in the history of the
popes. Moreover, it is also certain that before his death Hippolytus abandoned his schism and was reconciled to the church.
In his epigram on Hippolytus, Damasus states as much.[10] Even
if Damasus reached this conclusion only from the fact that
Hippolytus was honored as a martyr, he made no mistake in
so doing. In the Catholic Church a cult was never given to
schismatics or heretics, even if they died as martyrs. On the
other hand, since the popes did not lay down their office when
they went into exile — neither Cornelius nor Lucius nor Eusebius
had done so — we may suppose that Pontianus resigned the
dignity to make the same step easier for his rival. There may
here be lost one of the most beautiful episodes in the history
of the early Church. The two old men both doomed to death
strove with each other, and the magnanimity of one helped the
other to gain a great victory over himself so that he acknowledged
the great error of his life.

Pontianus and Hippolytus died in Sardinia. Their bodies
were brought to Rome. Pontianus was buried in the papal crypt
(pl. 15); Hippolytus found his last resting place in the cemetery
on the Via Tiburtina which was later named after him. There
the statue which now adorns the Lateran museum was erected
in his honor. The statue itself has little to tell us. The upper
part of the body and the head are modern restorations, and
the lower part is quite probably the statue of a Roman senator

15. The marble slab from the tomb of Pope Pontianus (230–235) in Callistus.

l. 16. Fragments of bones may still be seen in many of the *loculi*, but rarely complete skeletons as in this tomb in Pamphilus.

which was later reworked into a representation of Hippolytus. The saint is portrayed as seated upon a throne. Of great importance for us is the fact that a list of his writings as well as his computation of the paschal cycle are engraved on the sides of the chair. The latter was regarded at the time as a particularly learned achievement.

The second of the extant papal inscriptions is that of *Anteros* (235). He was elected pope after the resignation, but still during the lifetime of Pontianus. He died, however, within a few weeks. Anteros, like Callistus, was most probably a freedman since his name is one that was commonly found among the slaves. It must not be imagined, however, that Roman freedmen had the status of pensioned servants. Although they were looked down upon by the Roman aristocracy, the freedmen were industrious and often very wealthy individuals. Neither would it be correct to imagine, as sometimes happens, that the Christians of the first centuries were drawn almost exclusively from the lowest stratum of society. Both in its architecture and in its inscriptions the papal crypt plainly manifests a certain wealth and elegance which does not suffer in comparison with the best classical work of the kind.

The third inscription is that of *Fabian* (235–250). Cyprian speaks of this pope in terms of high praise.[11] His memory was also held in honor in the East, where in later times he was numbered among the wonder-working saints. Origen addressed a treatise to him in which he defended himself against a charge of heresy (Euseb. *E.H.* 6.36.4). The chief significance of Fabian's pontificate seems to lie in his administrative reforms. The organization of the lower clergy, noted by his successor Cornelius in his letter to Bishop Fabius of Antioch, was due to this pope. There were now seven deacons at Rome, each assisted by a subdeacon and six acolytes. Besides these fifty-six clerics there were forty-six priests and fifty-two who were either lectors, exorcists, or porters (Euseb. *E.H.* 6.43.11). At this same time the city was divided up into seven regions for the succor of the poor. From the school of Fabian came the following eminent pontiffs: Cornelius, Lucius, Stephen, and probably Xystus II and Dionysius as well. Fabian suffered martyrdom at the very beginning of the Decian persecution.

After a long vacancy, Fabian was succeeded in the papal see by *Cornelius* (251–253). We have more information with regard to the life of Cornelius than we have for most of the early popes, and even more than we have for his contemporary, the emperor Gallus. Many letters which Cyprian, the famous bishop of Carthage, wrote to him are still extant, as well as two letters which he wrote to Cyprian and one to Fabius, the bishop of Antioch. In a synod held at Rome in which sixty bishops took part, Cornelius excommunicated Novatian and his followers. He succeeded in bringing back to the Church five Roman priests who had gone over to Novatian. Among these was the priest Maximus. In the Vatican collection of inscriptions there was one of a priest, named Maximus. This inscription, which may be from the third century, is now to be found in the cemetery of Callistus near the tomb of Cornelius. It may be the epitaph of the Maximus who did public penance before Cornelius, but the name is so common that there is no certainty about the matter.

In the year 253, Cornelius was banished by the emperor Gallus to Centumcellae (Civitavecchia) and died soon afterward. His body was not brought to Rome until thirty years later. It was placed in a private crypt in the cemetery of Callistus. In later years his feast was celebrated on the fourteenth of September together with that of his friend Cyprian. Over his tomb Damasus placed one of his inscriptions. It was discovered there by De Rossi in 1852, but so badly damaged that only a few words were legible. Beneath it are small fragments of another inscription, which may be from Pope Siricius (384–399), the successor of Damasus. The crypt was later decorated with paintings which are relatively well preserved: on the left are Pope Xystus II and an unknown bishop Optatus, and on the right Cornelius and Cyprian. Marucchi attributed these pictures to the second half of the sixth century, Wilpert to the eighth.[12]

Cornelius' successor, *Lucius* (253–254), was laid to rest in the papal crypt. Immediately after his election Lucius also had been sent into exile, but he was able to return to Rome after the death of the emperor Gallus. We have a letter from Cyprian to him in which he congratulates him upon his exile and return (*Ep.* 61). It is rather odd that his name Lukios is given in its popularly abbreviated form of "Lukis" in the inscription on his tomb.

No inscription has been preserved of Pope *Stephen* (254–257), who was also buried in the papal crypt, nor is there one for his successor, the famous *Xystus II* (257–258). The tomb of this latter pope is, however, known. It is in a sense the focal point of the whole papal crypt.

In the *Ecclesiastical History* of Eusebius may be found a letter which Dionysius of Alexandria wrote to Xystus, but which perhaps did not find the pope alive (*E.H.* 7.9.1–5). The brevity of his pontificate during the course of Valerian's persecution furnished him with no opportunity for great works. He did, however, manage to effect a reconciliation with Cyprian, who had completely fallen out with his predecessor Stephen. Xystus achieved his greatest fame through his martyrdom.

Cyprian wrote to a friend: "Xystus was put to death in the cemetery on the eighth day before the Ides of August (August 6, 258), and with him four deacons" (*Ep.* 80.1). It is the next to last letter written by Cyprian. Five weeks later, on September 14, he himself suffered martyrdom. The circumstances of Xystus' death may be surmised in some detail from Cyprian's letter and from Damasus' epigram on the saint, the transcript of which has all the appearance of a reliable account.[13]

The scene is laid in "the cemetery," which can only mean the catacomb of Callistus. Damasus states that Xystus was preaching when the soldiers suddenly forced their way into the assembly. This implies that it was at a time when a solemn function was being held in a fairly large room near the base of the steps leading down into the catacomb. The papal crypt itself comes at once to mind. Damasus continues: "The congregation bared their necks to the soldiers. When the old man saw that they wished to deprive him of the palm (of martyrdom), he did not suffer it, but surrendering himself at once he offered his head (for the sword), lest the executioners should injure any of the others."

The gathering must have been held at night or in the early morning, since it is probable that the Eucharist would have been celebrated after the sermon. The congregation saw the soldiers rush in and naturally knew at once what would happen. They drew themselves up in a body before the bishop and faced the soldiers. No attempt was made to resist them, but all cried out with a loud voice that they were ready to die, and they accompanied their protestations with expressive gestures quite familiar in antiquity: they bared their breasts for the thrusts of the swords, or they cast themselves on their knees before the soldiers with their heads bowed waiting for them to be struck off. The soldiers were willing to strike, but then from the rear could be heard the "*Stop!*" of the aged bishop. It was like the "Halt! whom seek you?" of our Lord in the Garden of Olives which prevented a massacre of the Apostles. The clamor died down, the throng made way for the soldiers who pushed on toward the rear where the bishop was still seated upon his throne, just as when he had been preaching. Two deacons stood to his left and two to his right. The bishop was seized, led up the stairs to the open air and immediately beheaded with his four deacons. This summary execution corresponds exactly with the wording of Valerian's second edict with regard to the Christians, which provided that "bishops, priests, and deacons, should be executed 'on the spot,'" and thus apparently without any formal trial.[14]

Xystus was buried in the papal crypt. The slab with the

epigram describing the martyrdom of Xystus has disappeared, but Damasus also set up there a second inscription, fragments of which were discovered and replaced by De Rossi. In it Damasus refers to "the companions of Xystus," by whom the four deacons who also were buried in Callistus are obviously meant.[15] From later notices it may be concluded that at this time, even if not on the same day, the three remaining deacons were put to death. These may well have been Felicissimus and Agapitus, who were buried in Praetextatus, and Laurence, who was buried in a crypt in the Agro Verano later known as the *coemeterium Laurentii* or *Cyriacae*. Felicissimus and Agapitus are mentioned with Xystus in the *Depositio martyrum* of 354 for August 6, while Laurence is mentioned for August 10. There can be no doubt that these three are historical martyrs, but it is not certain that their martyrdom took place during the Valerian persecution of 258. The distinctive features of the legend of St. Laurence, the confiscation of the goods collected for the poor and death by fire on the gridiron, are more characteristic of the persecution of Diocletian; and hence it is possible that he at least belongs to this later period.[16]

We know nothing in detail about the next two popes, *Eutychian* (275–283) and *Caius* (283–296), whose inscriptions are still extant. Their pontificates fell within the period of peace which preceded the persecution of Diocletian.

Marcellinus (296–304), who died during Diocletian's persecution, but not as a martyr, was buried in Priscilla. Nothing remains of his tomb. There is, however, a reference to him in the inscription of the deacon Severus in the cemetery of Callistus. In Latin hexameters Severus tells us that he had built the *cubiculum* with its *arcisolia* for himself and his family "at the bidding of his Pope Marcellinus."[17] According to the *Liber pontificalis* the tomb of *Marcellus* (308–309), the successor of Marcellinus, was also in Priscilla, but the much more trustworthy *Depositio* of A.D. 354 makes no mention of it. Damasus' epigram for Marcellus has only survived in a transcript, and thus it furnishes us with no clue as to the place of his burial.[18]

Toward the end of the persecution of Diocletian, perhaps in 310, *Eusebius* was elected pope. He was at once banished by Maxentius to Sicily, where he soon died. His body was brought to Rome and placed in Callistus, very near the tomb of Pope Caius. The inscription which Damasus placed there seems to have been smashed by the Goths in the sixth century, for Pope Vigilius (537–555) had a copy of it made on a new slab, which is still to be seen in the crypt. Some fragments of the original have been discovered. In this epitaph Eusebius is described as a martyr. This was an honor which was also given to Popes Pontianus and Cornelius. It is strange, however, that the *Depositio* of A.D. 354 does not give him the title of martyr.

Pope *Silvester* (314–335) was buried in the basilica which he built above ground over the cemetery of Priscilla. This basilica, which was explored by De Rossi in 1890 and definitively excavated by Marucchi in 1907, lies directly over the crypt of the Acilians. Later popes, *Liberius* (352–366), *Siricius* (384–399), *Celestine I* (422–432), and *Vigilius* (537–555) were also buried in this basilica.

Apart from this, from the fourth century on there was no special place of burial for the popes. *Julius I* (337–352) built a tomb for himself in Calepodius on the Via Aurelia, where Callistus was laid to rest. *Damasus* (366–384), the great friend of the catacombs, chose for himself a remote spot in the cemetery of Callistus, because, as he himself said, he wished to be buried near the martyrs but dared not have a place in their midst.[19] The tomb of Pope *Marcus* (336) was not far from the crypt of Damasus.

Anastasius I (399–402) and *Innocent I* (402–417) were buried in the *coemeterium ad Ursum Pileatum* (the catacomb of Pontianus in Trastevere), and *Boniface I* (418–422) in St. Felicitas on the Via Salaria. Three popes — *Zosimus* (417–418), *Xystus III* (432–440), and *Hilary* (461–468), repose in the crypt of St. Laurence on the Via Tiburtina. *Felix III* (483–492) was buried in St. Paul's, and beginning with his successor, *Gelasius* (492–496), the popes for centuries were almost all buried in St. Peter's, where *Leo the Great* (440–461) had been the first to erect his sepulcher.

The bones of the popes buried in the catacombs, including those venerated from antiquity in the papal crypt in Callistus, were later translated to the churches of the city. With that their original tombs gradually fell into ruin and oblivion.

CHAPTER IV

THE TOMBS OF THE MARTYRS

THE special attraction which the catacombs have had for the faithful in both ancient and modern times lies in the tombs of the martyrs. A visitor to the catacombs today, however, may feel disillusioned when after hours of wandering through these subterranean galleries he has seen many interesting things and yet has not come upon the tomb of a single martyr, at least one in which the bones of a real martyr still rest (pl. 16). Every one is empty. Even the inscriptions are missing. The questions rise: Who were the martyrs? How many were there? What historical certainty do we have that the martyrs were ever buried here?

The simplest answer to the final query is to be found in the case of those martyrs in whose honor even in antiquity basilicas were erected over their still untouched tombs. These basilicas were indeed above ground, but they were as a rule so situated that the high altar stood directly over the tomb. In the front part of the altar was to be found an opening, the *fenestella*, which was connected with the *cataracta*, a hollow shaft inside the altar, and through which the faithful could lower small objects, for the most part *brandea*, that is, small pieces of cloth, to the tomb below. They then carried these away with them as relics. A somewhat simpler arrangement may still be seen in the altar of the basilica of Sts. Alexander, Eventius, and Theodulus on the Via Nomentana (pl. 17). The area around the sepulcher of Sts. Alexander and Eventius was cleared away so that the altar could be built around, and not simply over it. Pilgrims could thus reach through the *fenestella* and place objects directly upon the slab covering the tomb. This interest in relics may be the reason why in the cemeterial basilicas, and in these alone, the altar was so placed that the celebrant regularly stood behind it facing the people. An approach to the *fenestella* even during divine services was thus open to all. It may even be said that in the cemeterial basilicas the celebration of Mass was not the chief object of concern, but the visit to the tomb of the martyr.

The laying **out** of such a basilica entailed, of course, a great deal of destruction in the area immediately surrounding the martyr's tomb, and this destruction was further increased by the various transformations which most of the basilicas underwent during the course of the centuries. Still it is possible through excavations such as those which were carried out at St. Agnes to determine the original disposition of the tomb (pl. 18).[1]

Thus, wherever there are cemeterial basilicas with a known history reaching back to antiquity, we may be sure that there is to be found, or at least that there was once present on this precise spot a martyr's tomb, even though his bones may long since have fallen into dust. But such basilicas were built only over the tombs of the most famous and most highly respected martyrs, and their number is not large. The most important of these cemeterial basilicas are the two churches of St. Peter and St. Paul. In addition to these we have St. Agnes, St. Laurence, St. Sebastian, Sts. Nerius and Achilleus (on the Via Ardeatina), and St. Pancratius. It is archaeologically certain that all of these were historical martyrs. But for the vast majority of martyrs we have no such basilicas which can guarantee us the existence of their tombs. We must therefore have recourse to other criteria.

The simplest of these would be an inscription found on its

67

Pl. 17. Altar over the tomb of St. Alexander in the cemeterial basilica of St. Alexander, Eventius, and Theodulus on the Via Nomentana. In the center of the altar is to be seen the *fenestella*, or window, through which objects could be passed to the tomb. The inscription states that the altar was consecrated by the bishop of Nomentum in the fifth century.

68

Pl. 18. Excavation under the high altar of the cemeterial basilica of St. Agnes. The tomb lies at a rather shallow depth directly beneath the altar. It was an ordinary tomb in a

original site. But it must be an inscription which was set in place when the tomb was sealed, and not at some later date when the particular area was decorated. These original inscriptions have almost entirely disappeared. If we prescind from those of the martyr popes, we have only one of this type. It was found in 1845 by Marchi in St. Hermes and is now in the College of Propaganda.

There are some interesting details connected with the discovery of this inscription. Father Marchi himself gives us an account of them in his work on the catacombs:

"The evening of Good Friday, March 21, 1845, Giovanni Zinobili, a man quite unlettered, superintendent of a small group of workmen assigned to the care of the relics of the Apostolic Palace, which had been entrusted to the Most Illustrious and Very Reverend Monsignor Giuseppe Maria Castellani, Bishop of Porfirio and Sacristan of the reigning pontiff, Gregory XVI, came to me in the Roman College having in his hands a piece of paper on which could be read an epitaph which he had clumsily copied:

DP • III • IDUS SEPTEBR

YACINTHUS

MARTYR

"A few days before I had been in the cemetery of St. Hermes where Zinobili was working. I consequently asked him where he had found this precious inscription. He answered that he had found it in a room very close to the *arcosolium* decorated with mosaics, and that the stone was still sealed to the opening of the sepulcher. In my capacity as superintendent of the cemetery I forbade him to return to the room until I could accompany him there on Easter Monday. At daybreak on Monday I was at the cemetery with Zinobili, the architect Fontana, and the painter Bossi. . . . That morning I had Bossi sketch the mosaic while I measured the floor and the height of the crypt with the assistance of Fontana. Considering the importance of the discovery and the advisability of guaranteeing its authenticity in every detail, I gave orders that everything should be left in its original state and that the workmen should continue their excavations in other parts of the cemetery. I then returned to Rome and announced the important discovery to the sovereign pontiff and to his sacristan, Monsignor Castellani. They listened with lively interest, and then with the sketches and the inscriptions in my hand I went to my study and began a minute comparison between that which was still extant in the crypt and the written and nonwritten evidence which is to be found elsewhere with respect to the tomb and relics of Sts. Protus and Hyacinth."[2]

Father Marchi then gives a very detailed account of the opening of the sepulcher and the careful recognition of the sacred relics. Angelo Monti, a public notary who was among those who were present, made an exact record of everything that was done. A second examination of the relics was made April 29 on the Quirinal, again in the presence of the notary and the competent ecclesiastical authorities. To these was further added the professor of anatomy, Andrea Belli. The opinion of one of Rome's best chemists, P. G. B. Pianciani, was also sought. Only then was Marchi satisfied.

A similar case occurred some years ago in the discovery of a tomb with the inscription:

> NOVATIANO BEATISSIMO MARTYRI
> GAUDENTIUS DIACONUS FECIT
> (The deacon Gaudentius has erected this
> for the blessed martyr Novatian)[3]

This tomb is empty, but the inscription is on its original site in a small otherwise entirely unknown catacomb on the Via Tiburtina near San Lorenzo. The martyr Novatian, who does not appear in the itineraries or in the martyrologies, is probably the famous heresiarch of the third century whom Pope Cornelius excommunicated in the year 251 (Euseb. *E.H.* 6.43.2).

We thus have the extraordinary case that at Rome the only inscription of a martyr which is found today in its original place — *in situ,* as the archaeologists say — is that of a schismatic.

Notwithstanding the fact that the original inscriptions are so few, it is still possible to demonstrate the existence of other historical martyr tombs. These cannot indeed be determined by the shape of the grave or the kind of burial as was formerly maintained, when every large *arcosolium* was thought to be the tomb of a martyr. Nor can they be identified by the so-called "flasks of blood" (pl. 10) or other similar objects. But they can be recognized by the following rule, which today is universally accepted as valid: Wherever there are proved to be traces of an old, that is, of a primitive cult, the existence of a tomb and at the same time the historicity of a particular martyrdom are firmly fixed, even if the sepulcher itself is no longer recognizable.

As an example of this we may take the martyr Crescentio in Priscilla. The precise location of his tomb is not known. The itineraries attest only its existence while giving different names to the martyr. The *Itinerary of Salzburg* has "Crescencius," the sources for William of Malmesbury and the *Mirabilia Urbis Romae,* "Crescentianus." The *Liber pontificalis* refers to the tomb of Pope Marcellinus in Priscilla as follows: "In a crypt near the body of St. Crescentio." An inscription found in Priscilla states:

> FILICISSIMUS ET LEOPAR [*da emerunt locum*]
> BISOMUM AT CRISCENT [*ionem martyrem*]
> INTROITU
> (Felicissimus and Leoparda have bought a double tomb close to the martyr Crescentio near the entrance.)

Moreover there is found in this cemetery a *graffito:*

> SALBA ME DOMNE CRESCENTIONE MEAM LUCE. . .
>
> (Lord Crescentio, heal my eyes for me!)

Although we cannot fix precisely the date either of the inscription or of the *graffito,* and though we do not know the
exact location of the martyr's tomb within the general area,
these indications prove conclusively that Crescentio was an
historical martyr.[4] In order, however, to evaluate the force
of this argument we must have some knowledge of the origin,
and in particular, of the nature of the cult of the martyrs.

The cult of the martyrs had its origin in the cult of the dead
and at first had no other liturgical form than that employed
for the dead. Even in Cyprian's time no adequate distinction
was made between prayers for the dead and the invocation
of their intercession with God. The sacrifice of the Mass was
offered *for* the dead even if they happened to be martyrs.[5]
From the very beginning, however, the funeral cult of a martyr
was distinguished not only by the greater part which the
community had in it, but also by its more permanent character.
Since it was a matter of concern to both the bishop and the
community, it did not cease with the death of the martyr's
immediate relatives. The cult of the martyrs betrays its connection with the cult of the dead in that it was exclusively
associated with the grave. Antiquity hardly knew what might
be called an abstract worship of the saints. Later on, in the
Middle Ages, it occasionally happened that a legend was taken
on its face value, and honors were given to saints who existed
only on paper. But demonstrable instances of this sort are not
too frequent. In early Christian times this was hardly possible,
for a tomb could not be so readily discovered or falsified, at
least not in the midst of a community.

Some mistakes were of course made. The oldest Roman
calendar of saints, that of the year 354, has for August 8, on
the Via Ostiensis, the feast *Julianetis,* and thus of a martyr
Juliana. The *Martyrologium Hieronymianum* and the later martyrologies have *Juliani.* Such a change proves that this feminine
martyr was in later times believed to have been a man. The
inscription may have been abbreviated or difficult to read.

But this does not change the fact that there was a reliable tradition with respect to this martyr's tomb.

These considerations give us the right to conclude that there is a real martyr's tomb wherever we find actual traces of an early local cult of a martyr.

Definite indications of a primitive cult are given not only by basilicas, inscriptions, pictures, and *graffiti,* but even more than by anything else by references in the earliest liturgical calendars. We have for Rome two liturgical lists of martyrs, the *Depositio martyrum* of the year 354, and the *Martyrologium Hieronymianum,* whose primitive redaction as reconstructed by Kirsch is to be placed about the year 400.[6] Surprising, however, is the fact that the latter list contains the names of many more martyrs — about three times as many as the *Depositio.* This has led many critics to believe that after the middle of the fourth century, when an actual remembrance of the persecutions no longer existed, a whole series of cults was added.

This conclusion, however, will not stand up under careful examination. In the first place, there can be no doubt that the names of the *Depositio* of 354 refer to real martyrs. In the year 354 a half century had not yet passed since the end of the last persecution. Moreover, these cults were not introduced for the first time in this year. The *Depositio* is only a written form of the feast day calendar then in use. It obviously does not represent the whole of the existing calendar, but only memorial days of a definite liturgical type, namely, those on which the bishop and all the higher clerics repaired to the cemeterial basilicas.

The so-called *Martyrologium Hieronymianum* appears to be a calendar of another kind — a complete list of all the feasts celebrated about the year 400, without regard to their rank in the liturgy, whether they were solemnized by the presence of the bishop or not. There is consequently no reason for maintaining that feasts found in the *Hieronymianum* and not in the *Depositio* are later additions. We may thus consider the additional names in the *Hieronymianum* as also being the names of real martyrs.

This is not to say that in the year 400 there was still extant an actual remembrance or complete record of the great persecution of 303–305, or *a fortiori,* of the earlier persecutions. By the time of Pope Damasus (366–384) such knowledge had already been largely dissipated. Damasus, so far as we can determine from his poems — even granting that many of them have been lost — knew few concrete particulars about the persecutions, and even this little had not been obtained from immediate eyewitnesses. The case to which he refers in his epigram on Peter and Marcellinus, namely, that in his youth he had personally spoken with the man who had executed the martyrs is an exception.[7] About the year 400, a generation after Damasus, the Christians were certainly in a still less favorable position to reconstruct the martyrdoms from reminiscences alone.

Nevertheless, at the close of the fourth century and even later, there were to be seen the actual tombs of the martyrs, and for these there was no need of any tradition or conjecture. The cult of the martyrs was concentrated about them, and about them alone. Nor is there any need to doubt that the tombs in general were authentic and were known and undisturbed.

There were indeed cases in which the tombs of martyrs hitherto unknown were discovered, or were believed to have been discovered. The most famous example of this is the discovery of the relics of Gervasius and Protasius in Milan by St. Ambrose in the year 386. Many critics are skeptical about such discoveries, especially if they are placed in connection with visions and revelations. Such an occurrence also took place at Rome. In his epigram on the martyr Eutychius, Damasus tells us that the place of his tomb was shown to him during the course of a sleepless night. Such a statement is regarded by many historians as "a pious fraud," though one should be extremely cautious in prejudging men of the caliber of Ambrose and Damasus. But even if Damasus were deceived, and erroneously believed that the skeleton which he uncovered because of his supposed supernatural illumination was that of the martyr Eutychius, it does not follow that the list of martyrs received in this way any extraordinary increase of names.

We know that Damasus was actively engaged in excavating, enlarging, and restoring the cemeteries. In the course of this work he repaired tombs which had fallen to ruin and opened up an approach to others which had been shut off from visitors. Of Protus and Hyacinth he states: "The tomb lay deeply hidden under the fallen earth. Damasus brought it to light, for it contained blessed bones." Another inscription, set up by the priest Theodore near the stairway which he constructed as an entrance to the crypt, also refers to the great depth to which the tomb had been covered.[8] A literal interpretation of Damasus' words could indicate that there hitherto had been no knowledge whatsoever of this tomb. This would be an error, for the *Depositio* of 354 has the feast of Protus and Hyacinthus in Bassilla (St. Hermes) on September 11. Their feast was thus celebrated on this spot long before Damasus began his excavation. It was generally known that a martyrs' tomb lay here at a considerable depth, but there was no way of getting to it.

Damasus tells of another "discovery" in his epigram on Peter and Marcellinus. The bodies lay "hidden under the earth. Warned through your (that is, the martyrs') grace, Lucilla was pleased to translate your sacred bones to this more suitable place" (*coemeterium ad Duas Lauros* — Torpignattara).[9] This account has also been declared "suspect."[10] But the whole epigram needs only to be read to dissipate the doubt. The "rabid executioner," that is, the official who pronounced the sentence, had given orders that Peter and Marcellinus should be interred at the site of their execution so that no one might know where they were buried. The man who carried out this order told it himself to the youthful Damasus, and he still recalled the fact that both Christians had dug their own graves before they were put to death. The man, who apparently in the meantime had become a Christian, naturally knew the place in the thickets and must have revealed it to Damasus. Thus, when Damasus says "hidden," this does not mean that the place could not be found, but only that there were no external marks of identification over the martyrs' grave. Since the principal witness was still alive, it could be found without difficulty. The executioner may have made the spot famous long before this by telling others what had taken place there. Damasus does not say that the pious Lucilla obtained her knowledge of the site through a revelation, but only that she was urged by the saints to provide a more worthy sepulcher for them. We do not have the least reason for doubting the historicity of their martyrdom or the identity of the later renowned relics simply because in the course of events there is recorded a vision or supernatural illumination.

The critics of such narratives easily fall into the error of regarding the supernatural illumination as the key to these discoveries, but this does not seem to be the case for those for which we have sufficient information. An exception, however, should perhaps here be made for the discovery by St. Ambrose of the relics of Sts. Gervasius and Protasius. His contemporaries, St. Augustine, the deacon Paulinus, St. Gaudentius of Brescia, and St. Paulinus of Nola attribute the invention to a special revelation.[11] But even here the martyrs were not entirely unknown, for as St. Ambrose wrote to his sister in Rome immediately after the translation of the relics: "Now old men keep saying that long ago they heard the names of these martyrs and read their epitaph" (*Ep.* 22.12). The vision which Ambrose had, and the miracles which occurred after the discovery of the relics prove that they had not been deceived.

Finally, one may hold any opinion that he cares to about such discoveries. They will always be the exceptions. By far the greater number of martyrs' tombs were known from the very beginning, and did not have to be rediscovered later.

We may then restate our general principle: Wherever we

find positive indications of a primitive cult, there was a tomb; and wherever there was a tomb, there was an historical martyr.

We may thus confidently maintain that it is precisely the most renowned Roman martyrs who are most definitely historical personages. Laurence, Sebastian, Pancratius, Nereus and Achilleus, Processus and Martinian, Peter and Marcellinus, Agnes, Emerentiana, Tarsicius, Largus and Smaragdus, Tiburtius, Soteris, Parthenius and Calocerus, Abdon and Sennen, Protus and Hyacinth, Saturninus, Gorgonius, and many others really lived and died for their faith.

A further question that may be asked is whether the names known to us represent the totality of Roman martyrs, or whether there were still others whom we do not know. If the existence of a cult is to be our criterion in the matter, we must confess that we cannot name many more than a hundred historical martyrs at Rome.

But first of all we must be careful to note that the liturgical cult of the martyrs was introduced into Rome at a rather late date. While in Africa the practice seems to have been firmly established even before the Decian persecution, and thus before 250, and in Asia Minor it goes back even into the second century, we find it observed in Rome only after the Valerian persecution of 258. The martyrs of the first two centuries were in a certain sense forgotten, that is, they received no cult. We know of such martyrs only through other sources. Tacitus, a pagan historian, is our primary source for the *multitudo ingens* ("huge number") of Christians executed under Nero (*Ann.* 15.44). Irenaeus records the martyrdom of Pope Telesphorus. In his *Second Apology* Justin tells of the martyrdoms of Ptolemaeus, Lucius, and a third unnamed Christian. We have the official acts of the trial of Justin and his six companions, and also those of Apollonius. Obviously there were during this early period many more martyrs at Rome, but of whom no trace whatsoever has remained.

Of the martyrs of the third century only the bishops received the honor of a cult. These were Callistus († 222), Pontianus († 235), Fabian († 250), Cornelius († 253), and the schismatic Hippolytus († 235). This dignity, however, seems not to have been given until the second half of the third century. At least the title of martyr was only later engraved upon the extant tombstones of Pontianus, Fabian, and Cornelius. The priest Moses, or Musaeus († 251), did not at this time become the object of a cult. From this we can probably conclude that the other Roman martyrs of Decian's persecution also failed to receive this honor. It seems that even after the Valerian persecution only clerics obtained a cult. Among these we must reckon besides Pope Xystus II the deacons Felicissimus, Agapitus, and Laurence, unless indeed the latter's martyrdom occurred during the persecution of Diocletian.

It thus appears that almost all the Roman martyrs who were later honored there come from the period of Diocletian's persecution. From this fact alone it is clear that the sum total of martyrs must have been much greater than that of the demonstrable cults.

Moreover, even for the period after the introduction of the cult of the martyrs, we cannot immediately maintain that every martyr necessarily received a cult. His tomb had at least to be known. Christians who were murdered in flight or died in exile, and who had in this way become separated from the community could be martyrs in the fullest sense of the word, but they remained without a cult even after the persecution of Diocletian.

The question has often been asked whether or not there was in antiquity something like an ecclesiastical approbation of a cult, so that such an observance could originate, or continue to exist, only if ecclesiastical superiors examined the authenticity of a particular martyrdom and approved it. Evidence of a kind for such a provision is given by a text of Optatus in which there is a reference to a woman who was guilty of an abuse in showing a most extraordinary honor to a "non-recognized" martyr.[12] Without doubt there were certain criteria which were followed. Heretical and schismatic martyrs received absolutely no cult in the Catholic church. On the other hand, Cyprian believed that those confessors who died in prison "were worthy to be numbered among the martyrs."[13] The titles of "martyr" which were later added to the papal inscriptions indicate a certain official control, since they would surely not have been placed there by private individuals. We must not conclude from this, however, that there was a kind of formal approbation like the later processes of canonization. The far greater number of cults were spontaneous, that is, they arose from the zeal of the people and the local clergy.

Nevertheless, we must not imagine that the introduction, and especially the continuation of a cult was automatic. A variety of factors determined the "popularity" of a saint. Even today no rule can be laid down as to why one place of pilgrimage flourishes more than another. Among the martyrs' tombs there were some without doubt more interesting than others, and there were some that were less attractive. A tomb such as that of Sts. Chrysanthus and Daria, where there was a view through a window into a vestibule in which the bones of the Christians who had been stoned before their grave lay unburied, was certainly more spectacular than any polished tombstone. The legends of later times did much to make certain sites particularly fascinating. Thus it came about that on the Via Ostiensis, Largus and Smaragdus were much more popular than Memmia and Juliana, although these latter were just as truly martyrs as the former.

If what we have observed so far is true, then we must admit that the origin and evolution of a cult involved a certain element of chance.

In the first place, a martyrdom had to be definitely known. A pastor in a village today who is personally acquainted with all the families in his little community will know exactly in time of war those from his village who have been wounded, imprisoned, or killed, and who are missing. A pastor in a large city or great industrial area with a very fluid population will not have such definite information. True, with the passing of time he will succeed in putting up some sort of a memorial in his church, a more or less complete list of all the parishioners who have fallen. But this can only be effected with the continued co-operation of the military authorities who notify the respective families of the death of one of their members. The presumption too is, of course, that there is no reason for keeping the death a secret. If we apply this comparison to a persecution of several years' duration, such as that of Diocletian, and with reference to a great city like Rome, we can see at once the difference. It would have been highly imprudent for the bishop, clerics, or relatives of the martyrs to expect any co-operation from the state authorities. The relatives of the martyred Christian, whether they were pagans or Christians, had every reason, even if they knew about the execution, to keep it as secret as possible.

There was thus lacking during the years of persecution any automatic system of registration for those who died for the faith. Accident as well as deliberate selection determined the names of the martyrs who were included in the later catalogs. It does not follow from this, however, that we cannot trust the evidence of the fourth century, even if from the very beginning some mistakes were probably made. It only follows that the lists of the cults, such as those contained in the *Martyrologium Hieronymianum* of about 400, are not necessarily complete registers of all the actual martyrs. They were catalogs of cults, and not church histories. If during the years when the cult of the martyrs was in full bloom individual martyrs apparently fell into oblivion, this could have happened even more readily at the beginning when everything was still in a state of flux. An example of such a disappearance is the case of Nicander. His feast is recorded in the earliest calendar for June 17 in the *coemeterium ad Septem Palumbas,* but his sepulcher is not mentioned in the itineraries. We have also seen that there was some remembrance of Peter and Marcellinus at Rome, and of Gervasius and Protasius at Milan, though their cults were introduced only later. On the basis of such evidence we must presume that others were not remembered as long, and that as a consequence they received no cult whatever.

Thus far we have only the bare possibility. The question which now arises is whether or not we have positive indications that originally there were more martyrs than there were later cults.

From the fourth century on, Christians were firmly convinced that the names of the martyrs known through their cults represented only a fraction of the actual martyrs. This is already apparent in the itineraries, which for almost every cemetery, in addition to the martyrs expressly named, give further notice of large numbers of unidentified Christians who died for their faith. These are referred to in such general terms as, "and many saints are buried there," or "a multitude of saints under the main altar," or "an innumerable host of martyrs lie buried in the crypts." Frequently definite figures are given, for example, "three hundred and sixty-five martyrs in one grave." But the numbers given in the manuscripts, apparently even with respect to the same groups, almost never agree with one another. Sometimes the numbers are extraordinarily high, such as "800" or "1222."[14] These calculations are obviously worthless. The hypothesis has even been advanced that these supposedly mass burials owe their origin to a crass misunderstanding of the early custom of placing some mark of identification on the graves of the common dead when these carried no inscription. Anyone who has visited the catacombs can recall seeing numerous shells or other small objects which were pushed into the mortar while it was still fresh. It seems that numbers were also used for such marks of identification. De Rossi, for example, found the remains of a single child in a *loculus* with the number "LIX."[15] The theory has thus been advanced that the later belief in mass burials was occasioned by these numbers.[16]

But this is hardly tenable. However lacking the Roman Christians may have been in critical insight, they still did not believe that several hundred bodies were laid to rest in a *loculus* the size of a modest cabinet. Also — and this is the decisive factor — the numbers in our tradition should be constant, for the same number on the same grave would always have given rise to the same misunderstanding. Further, an error of this type cannot be attributed to such an experienced person as Damasus, and yet he wrote an epigram not only for the sixty-two martyrs buried near Chrysanthus and Daria, but also for a second group buried in a single grave in the same cemetery of Thrason of whom he knew neither the names nor the number.[17]

There can be little doubt about the reality of tombs containing the bodies of numbers of unknown martyrs, however misunderstood and exaggerated these may have been in later times. On the other hand, we should not imagine that they were excessively large. In the Roman cemeteries there are no indications of formal mass burials in which hundreds of bodies were placed at a single time. In the barbaric centuries of the early Middle Ages such ossuaries came into existence when the cemeteries, which had become dangerous and were falling into ruin, were gradually emptied, and whole convoys of bones were carried into the churches of the city. But these translations do not furnish us with a point of reference, for they were executed without any kind of historical judgment. What we do know of mass executions from the actual period of the persecutions is that they did not exceed groups of forty or fifty in number, and most were smaller.[18] Even so it cannot immediately be concluded that martyrs executed at the same time were always buried in a common grave. Pope Xystus II and his deacons were placed in different sepulchers. And, if Felicissimus, Agapitus, and Laurence are to be numbered among these latter, even in different cemeteries. Hasty interment in a common grave occurred only when there was no time for any other form of burial, and when there were no relatives at hand. This may often have been the case during the terrible confusion of Diocletian's persecution.

All of these considerations lead us to conclude that the number of actual martyrs was significantly greater than the number of demonstrable cults, and this is perhaps particularly true for the great persecution of the early fourth century.[19] Still we should not permit ourselves to be deceived with fantastic numbers. There certainly were not tens of thousand, or hundreds of thousands of martyrs at Rome during the persecution of Diocletian since the Christian community at that time did not number a hundred thousand souls.

CHAPTER V

THE TOMBS OF THE APOSTLES

So MUCH has been written about the tombs of the Apostles Peter and Paul that a whole library could be filled with it. This could create the impression that here is something about which nothing definite can be had, for so much learning and so many controversies would not be brought to bear on a simple and easily established fact. To correct this impression at once: the problems and difficulties connected with the tombs do not arise from the fact that we do not have enough information about them, but from the fact that we know too much, that is, the historical and archaeological data are so abundant that it is difficult to bring them all together into a harmonious whole. The fundamental truth that Peter and Paul were buried at Rome is not at all affected by these difficulties.

At the very beginning it must be noted that the question whether and how Peter was buried at Rome is not the same as the question whether he was actually in Rome, founded the Roman Church, and became its first bishop. The evidence which we have for this latter is entirely independent of the question of the tomb, and it remains so even if we had no certainty about the place of his burial.

If we wish to discuss the question of the tomb scientifically, we must prescind from all accounts that are legendary or hypothetical, whether they come from ancient or from more recent times, and hold fast to what can be historically and archaeologically proved.

From antiquity we have two fundamental texts which describe the tombs of the Apostles at Rome. The first of these is preserved in Eusebius and comes from the pen of an otherwise unknown Church historian Caius, who wrote at Rome about the year 200. The text reads as follows: "I can show you the trophies of the Apostles, for if you will go to the Vatican or to the Ostian Way, you will find the trophies of those who founded this church" (Euseb. *E.H.* 2.25.7).

That there is here a reference to tombs is clear from the general context. The only question to be asked is why Caius used the expression τρόπαιον ("trophy"), that is, a victory monument. Is this only a rhetorical figure for the noble grave, or did Caius see an actual monument? Eusebius, who was not himself acquainted with Rome, may have understood the "trophy" of Caius to be a monumental inscription since he speaks of the Πρόσρησις upon (ἐπί) "the cemetery there." Πρόσρησις (the Latin *appellatio, salutatio*) ἐπί could mean "the name of" or "the inscription on" the cemetery, while "trophy" can indicate any kind of monument.

The second text comes from the Roman liturgical calendar of the year 354. For *III Kal. Iul.*, that is, June 29, there is the notice: *Petri in Catacumbas et Pauli Ostense, Tusco et Basso conss.*[1] This may be interpreted: "The liturgical feast of Peter is held *in Catacumbas* (the site of the present church of St. Sebastian); that of Paul on the road to Ostia, in the consulship of Tuscus and Bassus (A.D. 258)." There is here no direct reference to the tombs, but only to the cult; still there is an obvious connection between cult and place of burial. The text presents two riddles: Why was the feast of St. Peter celebrated in 354 at St. Sebastian's and not in his basilica on the Vatican? What is the meaning of the date 258, that is, the year of the great Valerian persecution?

For the archaeological part of our investigation we may begin with the fact that Constantine built both basilicas in the early fourth century, the smaller on the Ostian Way for Paul, and the larger, on the Vatican Hill for Peter. The Petrine basilica, which remained standing until the sixteenth century, was completed as we know from an inscription only under one of his sons, probably Constantius († 361).[2]

The Pauline basilica built by Constantine was very modest in size. It faced the road and had the confession and apse toward the Tiber, that is, toward the west, as the cemeterial basilicas of the fourth century were regularly orientated. This first basilica, however, was soon replaced by another which was much larger. Since neither the tomb of the Apostle nor the street could be moved, an opposite orientation was given to the church, with its apse now directed toward the east in order to obtain a larger area upon which to build the church. The construction began, as the mosaic inscription over the triumphal arch clearly indicates, under the emperor Theodosius (379–395), and was completed under Honorius (395–423). The decoration of the interior, however, was only brought to completion through the sister of Honorius, the empress Galla Placidia, and Pope Leo the Great (440–461). The basilica stood essentially unaltered until the year 1823, when a great fire destroyed the entire nave and gravely damaged the transept and apse. The magnificent new construction completed by Pius IX, however, still gives today the general impression of the old basilica.

A visitor today to St. Paul's can see much more clearly than at St. Peter's that there was no free choice of site for the erection of the building. The location is about as inconvenient as possible. The basilica lies far from the city, very near the Tiber, and so low, that even in recent times high water has not seldom flooded the church. That a basilica should have been built on this site, which is further restricted by precipitous hills of tufa and the important road to Ostia, can only be explained by the fact that there was here a definite immovable tomb over which a building was to be erected.

The whole area is filled with ancient tombs. In the banks of tufa very near the basilica may be seen the remains of *columbaria,* and on the level ground there is a whole series of tombs which are now protected by a roof. The Apostle Paul must have been buried in such a tomb in the midst of a pagan cemetery. Under the present altar of the basilica, which is hollow and has two little windows with iron gratings to the east and to the west, lies a great marble slab with the inscription: PAULO APOSTOLO MART(*yri*). It was carefully examined by Hartmann Grisar.[3] From the style of the inscription and the shape of its letters he dated it as coming from the time of Constantine. Today the common opinion is that it comes from the time of the second basilica, that is, from the end of the fourth century. The slab has been pierced in three places, and these three holes come together into a small shaft twenty-nine and one half inches deep, which passes through the underlying masonry. The purpose of the holes was to allow the passing of small objects as near as possible to the tomb below. The slab along with its supporting masonry has never been removed. The whole site is probably still in the same condition that it was when it was arranged by Theodosius. We do not know what the original tomb looked like before it was covered with the masonry and slab. It was probably a simple *forma,* an earthen grave without a sarcophagus. Some kind of monument may have been erected over it, a "trophy" such as we now know from the tomb of Peter.

The area about St. Peter's sepulcher has been much more extensively transformed than that about the grave of St. Paul on the Via Ostiensis. The interior of St. Peter's basilica, with the bronze baldachin of Bernini, the papal altar beneath it, and the confession in front of the latter, is so familiar to every pilgrim to Rome, and even to those who have not been to Rome through countless pictures, that it is quite difficult to get an exact idea of the different structures which have been placed about and over the tomb.

The papal altar is a great rectangular block raised so high that it can be seen from every part of the basilica, even when the church is filled with people. Before the altar, toward the east, in the direction of the nave, sunk deeply into the floor is the vestibule of the confession, an open rectangular space whose eastern end has the shape of a semicircle. Within the balustrade which surrounds this antichamber burn the famous hundred oil lamps (pl. 19). Down below may be seen the marble statue of the kneeling Pope Pius VI. Opposite to this statue there is a filigreed bronze door which leads to a small empty chamber directly beneath the papal altar, the so-called "niche of the pallia."[4]

The floor of the confession lies at the level of the "old grottoes," a series of vaulted corridors spreading out beneath the pavement of the nave. Since their recent renovation, the pavement of these crypts is now slightly lower than the level of the floor of the Constantine basilica, which formerly occupied the site. To the west, and at a slightly lower level, there is a subterranean corridor which gyrates in a semicircle about the spot over which has been erected the papal altar. From the vertex of this semicircle, which lies on the longitudinal axis of the nave, there is an entrance into a cruciform chapel located within the semicircle. The eastern wall of this chapel is all but directly under the high altar, and actually supports it. If one were to bore through this wall he would come to the area beneath the papal altar to the niche of the pallia and the statue of Pius VI.

The papal altar is thus situated upon a high pedestal, or support, which rises from the level of the old basilica and whose base can be approached at this level from two sides, that is, from the east and from the west (fig. 4). In, or rather under this pedestal, is to be sought the tomb of the Apostle.

The earliest notices with regard to explorations and archaeological excavations within this complex date from the year 1594, when Clement VIII erected the present papal altar. Before

Pl. 19. The confession of St. Peter's. The bronze doors beneath the altar open up on a small chamber, the "niche of the pallia." Behind the rear wall of this niche is a cruciform chapel with a small altar.

90

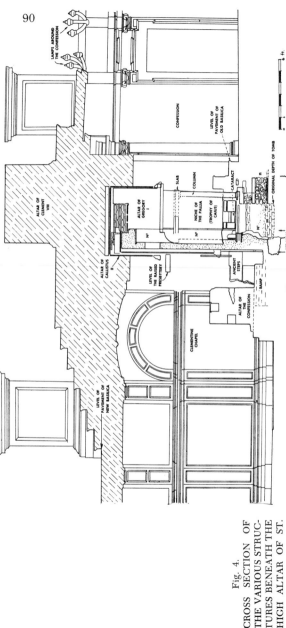

Fig. 4.
CROSS SECTION OF THE VARIOUS STRUCTURES BENEATH THE HIGH ALTAR OF ST. PETER'S

The confession is the open area directly east of the high altar (pl. 19). The altar of Clement VIII (1592–1605) conceals the altar of Callistus II (1110–1124), which was built around and over the earlier altar of Gregory I (590–604). In order to erect an altar over the shrine of St. Peter (pl. 23) which had been enclosed in marble and porphyry by Constantine (pl. 20), Pope Gregory raised the floor of the apse of Constantine's basilica about four and one half feet to form the "raised presbytery" (pl. 21). The niche of the pallia is con-

the niche, which is the central part of the "trophy of Gaius," is a portion of the red wall with its three superimposed indentations (N¹, N², and N³). Five tiles found in the drain beneath the ramp behind the red wall bear stamps indicating that they were made between A.D. 147 and 161. These give the approximate date for the whole complex, including the shrine over the tomb of St. Peter. The "cataract" is an open shaft through which objects could be passed to the tomb below. The Clementine chapel, unlike the con-

this, there had stood on this site the altar set up by Callistus II (1119–1124). Clement VIII had the new *mensa* built over the old and smaller altar of Callistus, without having this latter removed. During the course of this work, through cracks or fissures, a still earlier altar was seen beneath the altar of Callistus. This was taken to be the altar constructed by Pope Silvester (314–336). Clement VIII ordered these openings to be closed at once. Such is the account given by Grimaldi, a reliable witness.⁵ Later it was imagined that the pope himself, through one of the fissures, had seen the very tomb of Peter together with the golden cross, which according to tradition Constantine had placed there.

In 1615, under Paul V, the area in front of the confession was given its present form. During the course of this work a number of graves were found under the pavement, which were immediately taken to be the tombs of the first popes. Scholars of the time were convinced of the historical accuracy of the *Liber pontificalis;* and according to it, the first popes were buried in the vicinity of St. Peter's tomb. A confirmation for this was found in a broken inscription of which only the letters LINUS could be read. But LINUS, as De Rossi observed, can be the last part of several Roman names, such as, Catullinus, Anullinus, Marcellinus, and others.⁶ Moreover, the epitaph of the actual Linus would have been written in Greek. The other legible inscriptions which were found at the same time, MAESIAE TITIANAE C. F. (*Clarissimae Feminae* – "Noble Woman") and POMPONIAE FADIULAE C. F., have reference to members of the Roman aristocracy, but not to the popes.

In 1626, under Urban VIII, deep excavations were made to the right and left of the papal altar for the foundations of the bronze columns of Bernini's baldachin. We have very full accounts of these excavations. At varying depths of from eight and one half to fourteen and one half feet, and hence at some depth below the floor of the grottoes, solid ground was reached. Pagan tombs were again found, and coins dating back to the time of Faustina the Younger (145–176), the wife of the emperor Marcus Aurelius, Cornelia Salomina, the wife of the emperor Gallienus (260–268), and Maximian (286–305).[7] Sepulchers of the early Middle Ages were also unearthed.

From these discoveries and those of more recent times it is clear that the tomb of Peter lay in a pagan cemetery, which at the beginning of the fourth century, and thus shortly before Constantine built the basilica, was still in use.

During all these excavations, which were of a practical and nonarchaeological character, the original support or pedestal upon which the papal altar stands was not disturbed.

In 1940, in accordance with the express desires of Pope Pius XII, excavations were begun with the intention of investigating this pedestal. For ten years these excavations were directed by professors of the Pontifical Archaeological Institute: Bruno Apollonj-Ghetti, Architect and Lecturer in the Preservation of Roman Antiquities at the University of Rome; Antonio Ferrua, Secretary of the Papal Commission for Christian Antiquities; Enrico Josi, Superintendent of the Catacombs and Director of the Lateran Museum for Christian Antiquities; and Engelbert Kirschbaum, Professor of Archaeology and of the History of Art in the Gregorian University.[8] The archaeologists were assisted by two architects of St. Peter's, Enrico Pietro Galeazzi and Giuseppe Nicolosi. The direction of the whole undertaking lay in the hands of the late Monsignor Ludwig Kaas, Secretary of the Vatican Buildings.

The following is a summary of the results of these investigations:

1. What appears to be the high, or papal altar in the numerous pictures of the old basilica was originally something entirely different. During the erection of the basilica under Constantine there stood on this spot a block-like mass resembling a small house encased in marble and porphyry (pl. 20). This structure rose several yards in height, and hence it could not

Pl. 20. The shrine over the Apostle's tomb after it had been encased by
Constantine in marble and porphyry and surrounded by four ornate columns.

94

Pl. 21. Shrine and presbytery of St. Peter's at the time of Gregory the Great. The floor of the apse was raised so that the top of the monument could be used as an altar.

Pl. 22. Small column of the "trophy of Gaius," erected over the tomb of St. Peter about A.D. 160. The brickwork around part of the column is of a later date.

Pl. 23. A reconstruction of the "trophy of Gaius." Since nothing remains above the opening in the upper niche, the top part of the shrine has been conjecturally restored.

be used as an altar. Only later, probably toward the end of the sixth century, was the level of the surrounding area raised on three sides so that the top of the block was now no higher than a table (pl. 21).[9] It could now be used as the base for an altar. The original papal altar, which was then erected here, was covered over by the altar of Callistus II in the twelfth century. We do not know where the popes celebrated Mass in the basilica prior to the erection of the altar over the block, but it is quite possible that they offered the Holy Sacrifice on a portable altar set in front of it.

2. This marble-encased block of the age of Constantine contains within its interior the remains of a variety of early structures. There are, first of all, two small marble columns more than three feet high (pl. 22). One of these is entire; only a piece of the other is still extant. These columns supported a slab which projected from a wall lying behind them. The wall, because of its red color was christened by the excavators the *muro rosso,* that is, the "red wall." In the red wall between the two columns there is found a semi-circular niche. Directly above it, over the slab, there is a second and somewhat larger niche. From stamped tiles and other evidence, the date for the erection of the red wall with its niches and forecolumns may be fixed near the middle of the second century, about 160. The red wall was obviously built as a boundary to the sepulchral area and the passageway to this area, which are both located behind the wall to the west. The two niches with the slab between, and the columns in front of them, thus constituted a simple monument, and are quite obviously the "trophy" of which Caius wrote (pl. 23). Caius indeed meant the tomb, but the expression "trophy" indicates that there was more to be seen than a mere grave, namely, an easily distinguished monument near or over the grave. The date for the construction of the monument also agrees with what Caius has to say of it. When writing about the year 200, he refers to the trophy as

something long standing, and not a monument erected in his own day. When he wrote, it had been in existence for some forty years (figs. 5–7).

3. What is beneath the trophy? In front of the red wall there are several earthen graves. One of these lies directly beneath the lower niche in the red wall and extends eastward almost to the base of the columns in front of it. This grave, however, does not lie at right angles to the wall, but somewhat obliquely to it – a sign that it was not laid out after the erection of the red wall. A further proof of this is the fact that the wall passes over the grave, cutting off a part of it (fig. 8). All of these graves are *formae,* that is, rectangular excavations in the earth, and they were in part covered with flat tiles laid over them like a roof (pl. 24). A child's grave partially covered by the red wall and directly south of the trophy has a tile with a stamp that dates it between the years 116 and 123. Just east of the trophy is another grave with a stamped tile from the time of Vespasian (69-79).[9a]

At the foot of the red wall, exactly on the spot where the Apostle's grave must have been, were found a number of human bones. An anatomical examination of these skeletal remains has shown that they come from a single individual, a powerfully-built old man. This in connection with the place of their finding makes it highly probable that they are the bones of the Apostle. But the ground where they were found had been so disturbed that there is no complete certainty as to whether or not the bones actually lay in their original place.

In the grave and in its immediate surroundings were found hundreds of coins, which were obviously thrown there by the faithful. From the present floor of the niche of the pallia a "cataract," as it is called, examples of which are found in other martyr tombs, passes through all the various intervening layers to the tomb itself (pl. 25). The coins range in date from the early Roman empire to the end of the Middle Ages,

99

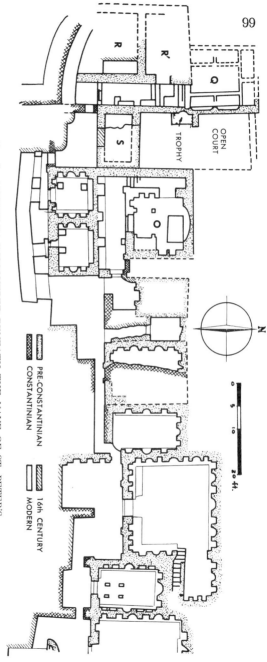

Fig. 5. MAUSOLEA DISCOVERED BENEATH THE NAVE OF ST. PETER'S

Only the mausolea nearest to St. Peter's tomb are here shown. More of the same general type were discovered to the east of these. During the second and third centuries these burial chambers were erected in two paralel rows separated by a narrow passageway. All of the mausolea had their entrances from the south. This was to prevent any water coming down the slope of the hill entering the vaults.

The mausolea most closely connected with the tomb of St. Peter are: O — a mausoleum built by the Matucci between A.D. 123 and 150, S — an unidentified mausoleum built shortly after that of the Matucci family, and R — the mausoleum of Flavius Agricola. R' is a porch attached to R, and Q is an enclosed area for inhumations which was probably never roofed over. Compare with Figure 6.

PRE-CONSTANTINIAN
CONSTANTINIAN
16th CENTURY
MODERN

0 5 10 20 ft.

N

100

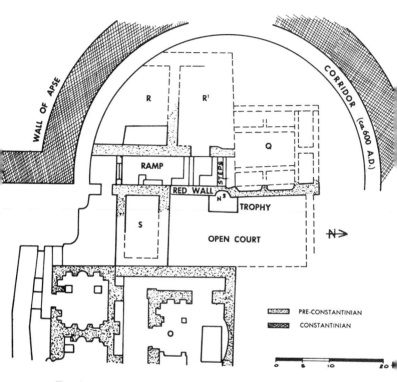

Fig. 6. PLAN OF THE AREA AROUND ST. PETER'S TOMB

The trophy of Gaius was set at the center of the apse of Constantine's basilica.
In front of the trophy was an open court and on three sides were mausolea erected
shortly before or after the middle of the second century A.D. O is a mausoleum
belonging to the Matuccii family. S is an unidentified mausoleum. R and R¹ are the
mausoleum and porch of Flavius Agricola. Q was an enclosed area used for inhumations. The only entrance to Q was by means of a ramp and steps to the west
of the red wall. N³ is the largest of three superimposed niches in the red wall
(see Fig. 4).

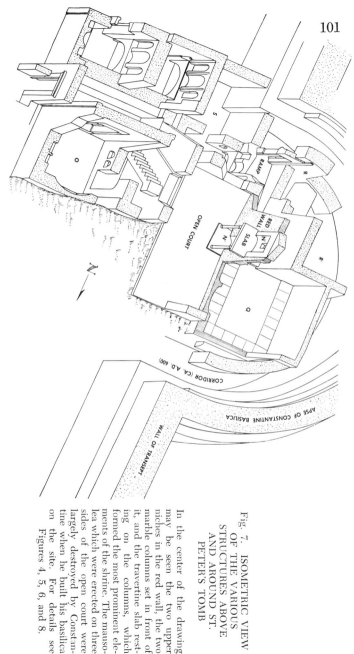

Fig. 7. ISOMETRIC VIEW OF THE VARIOUS STRUCTURES ABOVE AND AROUND ST. PETER'S TOMB

In the center of the drawing may be seen the two upper niches in the red wall, the two marble columns set in front of it, and the travertine slab resting on the columns, which formed the most prominent elements of the shrine. The mausolea which were erected on three sides of the open court were largely destroyed by Constantine when he built his basilica on the site. For details see Figures 4, 5, 6, and 8.

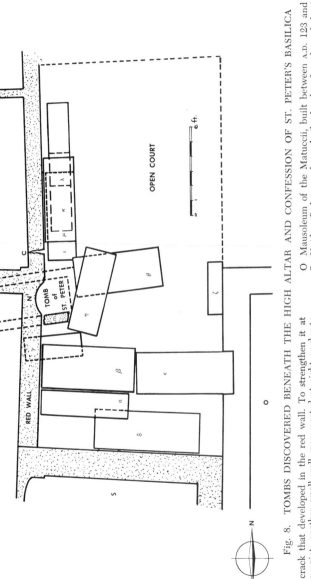

Fig. 8. TOMBS DISCOVERED BENEATH THE HIGH ALTAR AND CONFESSION OF ST. PETER'S BASILICA

C A crack that developed in the red wall. To strengthen it at this point, another small wall was erected at right angles to it. Into this buttress was built a small marble receptacle that later contained human bones.

Q Enclosed area for inhumations. Tiles used in the drain for this area, which passed beneath the ramp to the south of it, were made between A.D. 147 and 161.

O Mausoleum of the Matuccii, built between A.D. 123 and 150.

S Unidentified mausoleum built shortly after that of the Matuccii.

N¹ The lowest of three niches in the red wall.

γ Child's tomb with a tile made between A.D. 116 and 123.

θ Tomb with a tile from the time of Vespasian (A.D. 69–79). Tombs laid out after the erection of the red wall, were η,ι,μ,κ,λ.

ζ Small tomb which probably dates from the second century.

Pl. 24. Simple inhumations at Isola Sacra near Ostia. In a simple grave much like one of these St. Peter must have been buried.

Pl. 25. Subterranean shaft of the confession of St. Peter as seen from the north. A pagan tombstone was used as a cover for the grave in the late third or early fourth century. The hole cut in the slab formed part of the "cataract" which passed to the tomb below.

and come from almost every European country. The coins do not of themselves furnish an exact date since newly-minted pieces were not necessarily thrown there. They show, however, that the tomb began to be honored at a very early date.

It was no easy task to unravel all the clues afforded by the various structural remains which had been built in such a narrow and difficult place. But the issue is now clear. When Constantine built his basilica, the cemetery in which Peter had been buried was not only known, but there even stood in it a monument, or "memorial." Instead of removing this monument, Constantine enclosed it with masonry and so built the basilica about it that the enclosed memorial became the focal point of the building, occupying the site usually reserved for the high altar. The memorial itself comes from the middle of the second century, and the grave lying beneath it from the first. From Caius' text of about 200, it is evident that this grave was ever held to be that of the Apostle. We thus have today an uninterrupted archaeological proof, and we may say, an unusually happy one for the place of Peter's burial. In other excavations of this type we must as a rule be content with much less.

Many indeed have been surprised that no inscription referring to Peter was found. Monumental inscriptions, it is true, were hardly to have been expected. The pagan burial chambers of the second and third centuries which lie in the vicinity contain inscriptions with the names of the dead, but these are richly adorned mausolea with urn burials and sacophagi. The grave beneath the trophy is a simple excavation in the earth once covered over with flat tiles, and such graves did not as a rule bear any inscriptions. Still one might have expected that the faithful would have covered the parts about the grave with *graffiti* and invocations as was done in St. Sebastian's. On the outer side of a retaining wall, which was set at right angles to the red wall after this had developed an ominous crack, are a number of scratched invocations, but

the name of Peter is not found among them. This contrast with
St. Sebastian's is unfortunate, but it does not at all follow
that the faithful invoked another saint here on the Vatican
hill, but rather that at this site it was self-evident who was
the object of their prayers. Peter's name is found scratched
only once on the red wall, and once in the mausoleum of the
Valerii some seventy feet away.[10]

In the light of these critical investigations we can now say:
the discoveries connected with Peter's tomb are exactly what
they should have been. Formerly, the erroneous information
furnished by the *Liber pontificalis* caused an entirely different
disposition of the tomb to be imagined: the grave lay at some
fabulous depth enclosed in bronze plates and adorned with
a golden cross, and the remains of the saint were very probably
in an artistically wrought sarcophagus.[11]

When the Christians under Nero buried the body of the
Apostle, they did not construct the tomb of an Egyptian Pharaoh,
but they simply buried it as the dead were usually buried at
that time in Rome. It may be well to recall how famous
Christians were buried in later times when the cult of the martyrs
was flourishing. Cornelius, pope and martyr, received at the
end of the persecution a simple burial in a wall like thousands
of other Christians before him. For Peter, also, a special monument was erected only after the growth of the cemetery made
it necessary to build the red wall, and it was this addition to
the cemetery which occasioned the construction of a memorial
which would serve at the same time as a mark of identification.

We can now say that the site of St. Peter's tomb has at
last not only been definitely determined but that its original
appearance and its fate are also known. On the other hand,
these recent discoveries have not clarified the riddle of the
cult of the Apostle at St. Sebastian's on the Via Appia.

In the seventeenth century Cardinal Borghese completely transformed the old basilica of St. Sebastian. The original church
had three naves, but it was distinguished from other Roman

basilicas not only in that pilasters were used instead of columns, but also in the fact that the side aisles or naves were led about the apse. The altar stood in the middle of the central nave, but there was no confession. The size of the church was noteworthy, the interior measuring 174 by 92 feet and the whole edifice including narthex and atrium being over 270 feet long. It was thus, after St. Peter's, the largest of the cemeterial basilicas until the erection of the second basilica of St. Paul by Theodosius at the end of the fourth century (pl. 26).

The exact dates for the building of the basilica are not known. From an inscription it may be deduced that it was in use in the year 356/7.[12] But construction must have begun at least under Constantine († 337). It may even be that the basilica comes from pre-Constantinian times. Its style of masonry would in no way contradict this earlier date. The fact also that the plan of the old St. Sebastian's differs so much from that of the other Roman churches of the fourth century may be another indication of an earlier age. But it cannot have been built before Maxentius (306–312), or more precisely, before the restoration of ecclesiastical property by this emperor in 310.

Although the church contained the tomb of the martyr Sebastian from the very beginning, it was always called in antiquity "the basilica of the Apostles." Only in the early Middle Ages was it known as "the basilica of St. Sebastian."

During the excavations undertaken in 1915 by Anthony de Waal and Paul Styger, an area of very great interest was uncovered under the front, or eastern part, of the nave (pl. 27). Here was found a rather large space shaped like a trapezoid which at one time had been partially covered by a roof resting on pilasters bordering on an open court which resembled a Pompeian peristyle. The whole eastern wall of this area is covered with *graffiti* in which the names of the Apostles Peter and Paul repeatedly appear with invocations of every possible sort (pl. 28). The inscriptions are in both Latin and Greek, and some even in Latin written in Greek characters:

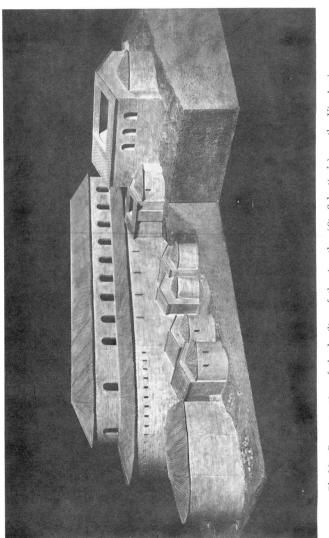

Pl. 26. Reconstruction of the basilica of the Apostles (St. Sebastian's) on the Via Appia as seen from the south. The tomb of St. Sebastian is found in the building to the right. To the left is the "Platonia," which was probably a mausoleum erected in the fourth century for the martyr Quirinus.

Pl. 27. The excavations in the nave of St. Sebastian's shortly after their inception in 1915. In the left center may be seen a portion of the east wall of the *triclia*. Directly beneath the zigzag lines is a flat red surface upon which many *graffiti* were scratched.

Pl. 28.   *Graffiti* in the *triclia* with petitions to Peter and Paul.

"Paul and Peter, pray for Victor!"

"Paul, Peter, pray for Eratus!"

"Peter and Paul, protect your servants! Holy souls, protect the reader!"

Several of the inscriptions refer to the strange custom of the *refrigerium*, a kind of funeral banquet that was here celebrated in honor of the Apostles.

"I, Tomius Coelius, have held a *refrigerium* for Peter and Paul."

"On the fourteenth day before the Kalends of April (March 19), I Parthenius, have held a *refrigerium*. In God. All of us in God."

"Dalmatius has celebrated a *refrigerium*."

"I have held a *refrigerium* for Peter and Paul."[13]

We know that the Christians held funeral banquets near the tombs of their relatives just as the pagans did, but that such a meal represented a cult act is only known from these inscriptions. This area, from which a stairway led down to a deep spring, has been called by archaeologists the *triclia*, or "dining room." After the erection of the basilica, the *triclia* could no longer be used since it had been filled in and covered over by the pavement of the basilica. A long controversy has been waged with regard to the dates of the *triclia*. The most recent discussion of the matter has attributed the *graffiti* to a consular date corresponding to the year 260. They could hardly have been written much earlier.[14]

In conclusion, among the important data for St. Sebastian's belongs the inscription of Pope Damasus: *Hic habitasse prius* ("Here formerly dwelt").[15] Unfortunately, we do not know where it was originally placed. Its entire text survives only in a transcript, but an incomplete copy of the thirteenth century was found near the crypt of St. Sebastian. The poem may be translated: "Whoever you are who asks about the names of Peter and Paul, you should know this: here the saints formerly dwelt.

The East sent its disciples, a fact which we frankly admit. Having followed Christ through the stars they have reached heaven and the kingdom of the blessed. By reason of their bloody martyrdom, Rome has received a greater right to call them her citizens. May these verses of Damasus be referred to your praise, you new stars."

The sentence of particular interest is: "Here the saints formerly dwelt." The "here" has lost some of its original value since the original location of the inscription is now unknown. For us, as a consequence, it merely signifies: "where the basilica now stands." But what is the meaning of "the saints formerly dwelt here"?

The task of the historian is to find a theory which will satisfactorily explain all these different data. About the year 200, and earlier, the bones of the Apostles were found on the Vatican and on the Ostian Way. When in the fourth century the emperor Constantine began to build on these two sites, the same state of affairs prevailed. There was, however, a cult of both the Apostles together *ad Catacumbas*, going back at least to 260. Peter's feast was still celebrated in 354 *ad Catacumbas*, while at this time Paul's was celebrated on the Via Ostiensis. In the whole matter the year 258 plays a deciding role. — These are the facts, all the rest is theory.

Already in late antiquity it was believed that the bodies of the Apostles were placed at one time *ad Catacumbas*. There were various opinions as to how this came about and how long the bodies remained there. In the sixth century the *Liber pontificalis* has this to say about Pope Cornelius (251–253): "At the request of a matron named Lucina, during the night he removed the bodies of the blessed apostles, Peter and Paul, from the catacombs. The blessed Lucina first took the body of the blessed Paul and placed it in a plot of ground which she owned along the road to Ostia where he had been beheaded. The blessed Cornelius took the body of the blessed Peter and laid it away near the place where he had been crucified, among the bodies of the blessed bishops near the temple of Apollo on the Golden

Hill on the Vatican, by the palace of Nero, the 29th of June."[16]

In a letter written in 594, Gregory the Great gives an account of the theft of the relics: "At the time of their martyrdom, faithful came from the East to take away their bodies because they had been their countrymen. They carried them as far as the second milestone from the city to the place called *Catacumbas,* and there set them down. But when the entire multitude of them came together and tried to carry them further, they were so greatly terrified by violent thunder and lightning that they fled in different directions and did not dare attempt anything of the kind again. Then the Romans, who had deserved it through the goodness of the Lord, coming out of the city, raised the bodies and placed them where they are now to be found" (*Ep.* 4.30).

The apocryphal *Passio Petri et Pauli* gives the story as follows: Men from the East came and stole the bodies. A mighty earthquake, however, alarmed the Romans. They set out in pursuit of the robbers and captured them "at a place called *Catacumbas,* near the third milestone on the Via Appia."[17] There the blessed bodies were buried for a while, but after a year and seven months they were brought back to their original tombs.

The consensus of opinion today is that the history of the theft rests simply upon a misunderstanding of a line in Damasus' inscription which reads: *discipulos Oriens misit* ("the East sent disciples"). The "disciples" were taken to be Eastern Christians who wanted to steal the bodies of the Apostles, whereas Damasus was actually referring to the Apostles themselves.

The *Itinerary of Salzburg,* which is later than Gregory, has no account of the robbery, but it does refer to a temporary burial *ad Catacumbas:* "There are the tombs of the apostles Peter and Paul in which they rested for forty years."[18]

In later times further attention seems to have been given to the account of the *Liber pontificalis,* for a privilege of the year 1520 for the church of St. Sebastian which was discovered by Hartmann Grisar states: "Behind the church are the catacombs in which there is a well in which the bodies of the apostles Peter and Paul were hidden for the space of 252 years, and from which they were taken by the supreme pontiff Cornelius at the request of the blessed Lucina."[19] The same document speaks of the tomb of St. Peter as being "where he had been placed by his disciples," and the same words are used for the tomb of St. Paul.

That all of these accounts have no foundation in an authoritative tradition, but are only tentative explanations, is quite obvious. They are, in fact, contradictory: no deposition at all *ad Catacumbas,* but only portents associated with the theft of the bodies; temporary deposition *ad Catacumbas,* and translation only under Pope Cornelius.

The explanations given today are just as contradictory. The following possibilities may be considered:

1. Peter was originally buried *ad Catacumbas,* and was later transferred to the Vatican.[20] This must have taken place before 200, and now, in the light of the recent excavations under St. Peter's, even before 100, that is, soon after his martyrdom. This gives no explanation why there was a cult in the late third century *ad Catacumbas,* and why in the fourth century a basilica was erected there, since the body had not been there for a long time. Moreover, there is no apparent reason for such a translation in the second, or even in the first century. That the Christians wished to have the bodies near the place of their martyrdom is no such proof. First of all we do not know where they were executed — this is only deduced from their place of burial. Secondly, in early antiquity tombs were honored, but not places of execution. In later times, it is true, this could happen. In Carthage, for example, a basilica in honor of Cyprian was erected on the site of his martyrdom, though his body was not brought there. Finally, this theory does not take into consideration the year 258, and in this year something significant must certainly have taken place.

2. Peter was originally buried on the Vatican.[21] In the year

258 his relics were transferred to the cemetery *ad Catacumbas,* but very soon they were brought back to their original resting place, even before the basilica was built on the Vatican. The reason for this translation was the Valerian persecution (257–258) during which the cemeteries were confiscated. At the end of the persecution, when Gallienus restored the cemeteries to the Christians, the relics were returned to the original tombs. This theory seems to be the most popular today. It has the advantage of explaining the cult *ad Catacumbas* in the second half of the third century. This cult indeed had to continue even after the removal of the relics, since the official feast of St. Peter in the year 354 was still celebrated *ad Catacumbas* despite the fact that the relics were no longer there.

According to Lietzmann, a positive proof of a real translation of the relics may be found in the notice of the calendar of 354. In three different places it gives in addition to the day of the month on which a feast was celebrated the date of a year. For the feast of Sts. Peter and Paul we have the consulship of Tuscus and Bassus, or the year 258. For the feast of Parthenius and Calocerus, on May 19, and also for the feast of Bassilla, on September 22, we have the ninth consulship of Diocletian and the eighth of Maximian, òr the year 304. The original feast of Parthenius and Calocerus was apparently celebrated on February 11, and Bassilla seems to have been a martyr of the third century. These notices then would not indicate the day of their deaths, nor the day of their first depositions, but the day of their second burial, or translation.[22] On the other hand, the only feast in this calendar which we know for certain is a translation, and not the day of death, is that of Pontianus and Hippolytus on August 13, but no indication is here given of the year. Moreover, if the year 258 indicates the translations of Peter and Paul, then the calendar would say that in this year Peter was carried to St. Sebastian's and Paul in the same year to the Via Ostiensis. But this was certainly not the case.

The difficulty which is frequently lodged against this position, namely, that the bodies of the dead could not be exhumed without the permission of the *pontifex maximus,* can easily be answered.[23] The burial laws were in actual practice not so rigorously observed. This can be proved by numerous examples. Moreover, there would here be a case of a secret translation. Still it may be objected: if the bones which were found under the trophy on the Vatican are actually those of the Apostle, as seems highly probable, then the manner in which they were found in the earth does not favor a translation and retranslation. In such a case, the relics, which would by this time have been greatly decomposed, would have been placed in some kind of a container at the time of their retranslation, and would not have been laid simply in the bare ground.

3. The bodies of the Apostles were never *ad Catacumbas.*[24] The cult was celebrated there, and precisely in the year 258, since at this time no liturgical celebration could be held in the pagan cemeteries on the Vatican and on the road to Ostia. Since it was at this time that the cult of the martyrs came into vogue at Rome, it is easy to see that the two Apostles, the principal martyrs of Rome, would not be overlooked. At a later date, after Constantine had built the two basilicas, the cult naturally returned to the two original tombs; but the site *ad Catacumbas,* where the feast had originally been celebrated, always remained an object of veneration. Consequently it was also marked by a basilica.

The chief difficulty with this hypothesis is the inscription of Damasus: *Hic habitasse prius,* since "to dwell" and "dwelling" in reference to the dead can mean nothing except the place where the bones rested. But the question is whether this is also valid for the cult of the saints.

A saint does not actually "dwell" in a sarcophagus or in a *loculus,* but in his sanctuary — though invisibly — where he is honored, where he is active, where he hears the prayers addressed to him. As a rule the sanctuary coincides with the place of burial, but it can also be elsewhere. When the Roman breviary for

February 11 speaks in the following manner of the pilgrim shrine of Lourdes: "Here the Immaculate Virgin is honored as in her own proper dwelling (*In hac sua veluti sede Immaculata Virgo jugiter colitur*)," no one of the faithful, not even the simplest, understands this to mean that Mary dwells there corporally like any ordinary mortal; and still less do they believe that she is buried there. In antiquity men did not think otherwise. When the archangel Michael appeared to the bishop of Siponto on Mount Gargano and told him that it was his intention "to dwell in this place here on earth and to protect it,"[25] no one, neither the bishop nor the faithful, thought that the archangel was buried there.

The *habitasse* of Damasus can thus be understood as a reference to a simple cult without the necessity of a burial. More difficult is the *prius*. When Damasus wrote his verses, the basilica *ad Catacumbas* in honor of the apostles was standing, and they were there honored. Consequently, he could not have meant it in the sense of "formerly," "once upon a time," the Apostles were honored there. Something must have happened before the time of Damasus so that it could be said: "at one time, but now no more."

Moreover, the site of the basilica seems to militate against the hypothesis of a simple "imaginary" cult. The basilica is built upon a very definite and determined spot, much in the same way as the great basilica on the Vatican. The land on which St. Sebastian's stands slopes sharply. The important retaining walls which were necessary on the side toward the valley can still be seen today, as well as the deep foundations which had to be sunk into the ground already pierced by catacombs. All of this could have been avoided if there had not been a specific place in mind which had to lie at the center of the basilica. Had it been a question of an imaginary cult, then the basilica would simply have been erected elsewhere.

4. This consideration leads us to a further theory which also has its advocates.[26] There is not here a question of a place of

burial, but of an actual dwelling, the house in which the apostles lived during their lifetime. In such a case, Damasus was, of course, able to say: *habitasse prius*. To support this theory the *graffito* DOMUS PETRI ("the house of Peter"), which was discovered in 1912 in one of the old side chapels of the basilica, is commonly brought forward. This chapel lies considerably lower than the basilica, and is built against the walls of its foundation on the side toward the valley. But since it cannot be older than the basilica, neither can the *graffito* be earlier than the fourth century. It may even be of a much more recent date. It may have been written by a pilgrim who read the inscription of Damasus and took the *habitasse* literally. Hence, it has no value as an independent tradition.

The chief objection to this theory is that in antiquity a mere place of remembrance without the relics of a martyr did not become a place of cult. This may be answered by noting that this same difficulty is found in each of the theories proposed, since all must at least admit a cult at an empty tomb. There is, moreover, a canon of an African council, of a later date it is true, which states: "A sanctuary to a martyr may only be erected where his bodies or relics are, or where an uninterrupted tradition guarantees his house, property, or place of execution."[27]

Again, the year 258 is not clarified by this theory. The only thing that can be said about it is that this would be the year in which the cult of the dwelling was introduced.

5. The *memoria* to the two Apostles and the *basilica Apostolorum* which was later erected over it were not cult centers for the Catholics but for the Novatianists.[28] After the election of Pope Cornelius in 251, the bitterly disappointed Novatian led his followers into schism. Since they could no longer make use of the actual tombs of Peter and Paul as places of worship, they established a rival cult of the two apostles *ad Catacumbas,* probably in the year 258. The shrine would have passed into the hands of the Catholics either before the pontificate of Pope Damasus, since this pope in his epigram *Hic habitasse prius*

showed a marked interest in the site, or perhaps only later in the fifth century when the sect was suppressed. In support of this theory Dom Mohlberg points to the rather strange character of the *triclia*, the fact that the original *basilica Apostolorum* received the new name of St. Sebastian, and that the omission of the name of Pope Cornelius from the *Depositio martyrum* which gives the year 258 may indicate that it was edited by Novatianist sympathizers. But the omission of Cornelius' name from the *Depositio martyrum* and the *Depositio episcoporum* may indicate only that he did not die as a martyr at Rome but as an exile at Centumcellae. Moreover in the *Depositio martyrum* there is a notice to the effect that the Novatianists stole the body of the martyr Silanus (*Silanum martirem Novati furati sunt*) which Mohlberg must maintain is an anti-Novatianist interpolation. The theory in reality adds little to those which have already been considered, for it postulates a tradition common to both Catholics and Novatianists that the Apostles had either lived on this spot or had been temporarily buried there.

6. Since according to Roman law a person could not be buried in more than one place, his tomb should be identified with the spot where his head was deposited.[29] During the persecution of Valerian it would have been difficult for the Christians to remove the bodies of the two Apostles from their respective sepulchers, but it was possible to remove what remained of their heads. This was done, and the relics were enshrined somewhere in the *triclia* on the Appian Way.[30] Sometime before the completion of the Vatican basilica the relics of St. Peter were again translated and deposited in a marble receptacle built into the small wall set at right angles to the red wall after this had started to crack.[31] Later they were again moved, first to the altar of the confession, and then in the ninth century to the Lateran basilica, where they are to be found today in one of the two reliquaries over the high altar.[32]

Of the various theories that have been proposed to account for the cult of the Apostles *ad Catacumbas*, this last seems to be the most satisfactory. Nothing need here be said of the opinion still held by some that Peter was never in Rome nor ever buried there since it has its origin neither in the literary evidence nor the archaeological data but elsewhere.

CHAPTER VI

THE PERSECUTIONS

EARLY Christian writers and historians consistently refer to Nero as the author of the persecutions, even though it was known that Christian blood had been shed by others before him, at least in the deaths of the deacon Stephen and the apostle James. Tertullian, for example, states that "Nero was the first to rage with Caesar's sword against this sect," and he refers to the invalidation of all of Nero's acts except what he describes as the *institutum Neronianum,* the measures which he took against the Christians.[1] The precise formality under which the Christians were condemned by Nero and his successors and their respective legates is a matter which has been widely discussed. Many have maintained that a special law was passed directly proscribing Christianity. Others have maintained that already existing criminal laws were extended to cover the adherence to the new faith. Still others, following the lead of Theodor Mommsen, have held that the Christians were not legally prosecuted but merely subjected to the general coercive or "police" powers of the magistrates. None of the numerous solutions to the problem that have thus far been proposed are completely satisfactory. This is due largely to the fact that the data for the persecutions is frequently interpreted in terms of the legal rights of individuals as these are conceived today. But such rights were not clearly indicated in Roman criminal law.[2]

According to Tacitus, a "huge multitude" of Christians were put to death by Nero (*Ann.* 15.44). The horrors of his reign are also mentioned in a letter of Pope Clement written about the year 95 (1 Cor. 5, 6). We should not, however, take this "huge multitude" too literally since the Christian community in Rome at this time numbered at most a few thousand. After the first mass executions, which probably took place in the year 64, further measures could have been taken against individuals. We need not imagine that the emperor was personally present for the trials. The apostles Peter and Paul could thus have been executed in 67 while Nero was in Greece (from September, 66, to March, 68). Though the Christians experienced difficulties outside of Rome, it is not definitely known whether any at this time were put to death in the provinces (1 Pet. 4:13–19).

Drawing on a certain Brettius, or Bruttius, an otherwise unknown historian, as his source of information, Eusebius makes mention of a great persecution under Domitian (81–96). The only Roman Christians known to have suffered for their faith at this time are Flavius Clemens, who was executed, and his wife and niece, both named Domitilla, who were banished, and Acilius Glabrio, if he actually was a Christian, who was put to death. Under Trajan a policy was adopted with regard to the Christians which practically achieved a juridical status. The perplexity which could envelop a judge in dealing with the Christians is clearly exemplified by the letter of Pliny the Younger, governor of Bithynia, to the emperor. This letter and Trajan's answer or rescript are so important for the history of the persecutions that they should be cited at least in part:

To the Emperor Trajan

I have recourse to you, my Lord, in all my doubts. . . . Never having been present at any trials of the Christians, I do not know what means and limits are to be observed in examining or punishing them. . . . This is the way I have dealt with those who have been denounced to me as Christians: I asked them if they were Christians. If they admitted that they were, I asked them again a second and a third time threatening them with capital punishment. If they still persevered, I ordered them to be executed. For I felt certain that whatever it was that they professed, their contumacy and inflexible obstinacy obviously demanded punishment. There were others of a like madness, but since they were Roman citizens, I had them sent to Rome . . . (Plin. *Ep.* 10.96).

Trajan to Pliny

You acted rightly, my dear Pliny, in handling the cases of those who were denounced to you as Christians. It is not possible to lay down any general principle which may be used as a fixed norm in such cases. No search should be made for them. If they are denounced and found to be guilty, they must be punished, but with this restriction: If anyone says that he is not a Christian, and shall actually prove it by adoring our gods, he shall be pardoned as being repentant, even though he may have been suspect in the past. Unsigned accusations must never be admitted, for they would set a dangerous precedent and are not in keeping with the spirit of our age (Pliny *Ep.* 10.97).

Three provisions are to be noted in Trajan's rescript:

1. "No search is to be made for the Christians." No public official was obliged to initiate a process against an individual even though he was known to be a Christian. However, he had to accept the case if an accusation was laid before his court. This is in keeping with the spirit of Roman criminal law. The greatest difference between Roman and modern penal procedures lies in the fact that the Romans did not make use of a public prosecuting attorney. A judge in a *cognitio extra ordinem* could initiate a process if he so desired, but he normally waited for an accusation to be lodged by a private individual.

2. Whenever anyone was accused of being a Christian, the judge had to take up the case and punish the offender.

3. An exception, however, was to be made in favor of those who expressed a willingness before the judge to abandon their Christian faith, and who gave proof of it by taking part in one of the usual acts of pagan worship. In such a case the process was to be terminated.

Though Trajan expressly stated in his rescript that no general principle could be laid down for handling the Christians, the directions which he gave to Pliny seem to have been consistently applied by other imperial magistrates. It effectively created what may be described as the martyr's dilemma. The critical element in the juridical action taken against the Christians did not consist in the actual determination of the crime. It was so easy to determine whether an individual was a Christian or not, and thus guilty or not, that there was scarcely any need for investigating this detail. Rarely, if ever, did one who was accused seek to save himself by denying his former adherence to Christianity. The whole process was directed much more at persuading the accused to perform some religious act which would make his release possible. As a consequence, nearly all of the instances for which there is adequate evidence have the appearance not so much of a criminal trial as of a contest between the judge and the defendant to determine which of the two was the stronger.

For the most part the magistrates were anxious to free the Christians. They were motivated more by forbearance than by a thirst for blood. Arguments, promises, threats, torture were not as a rule employed to obtain a confession of crimes committed, as in other cases, but to break the will of the accused.

Thus it is not entirely accurate to speak of a "denial of the faith," or of an "apostasy from the faith." What an individual thought or believed was a matter of indifference to the Roman magistrate. Dionysius, bishop of Alexandria, for example, during his trial in 257 before the deputy-prefect of Egypt Aemilianus, was asked: "And who prevents you from honoring this god also (Christ), if he is a god, along with those who are by their very nature gods (Euseb. *E.H.* 7.11.9)?" It was not, then, a question of creed but of *belonging to the Church*. The Christian should be compelled to perform some act which would prove that he had withdrawn from the Christian community.

It was up to the Christians not to lose constancy at the moment of crisis. In a very real sense greater heroism was demanded of them than of soldiers waiting for death on the field of battle. For it does not depend upon a soldier whether he gets hit or not. He cannot escape the danger, but the martyr could. There was only the need of a wave of his hand or a word from his lips and all danger was passed.

Even the best disposed pagans had great difficulty in comprehending the obstinacy of the martyrs. What was asked of the Christians, from their point of view, was little enough. Perennius, prefect of the city and an experienced and respected judge, asked Apollonius in astonishment: "Are you willing to die for such opinions (*Acta Apol.* 29)?" The emperor Marcus Aurelius, who sacrificed every personal inclination to duty, had only censure and a shake of the head for the obstinacy of the martyrs (*Meditations* 11.3).

Not a few of the magistrates were ashamed of the part which they played in the trials of the Christians for in the main they had more the character of a show of violence than of a judicial procedure. When Scapula, the prefect of Carthage, was persecuting the Christians, Tertullian addressed an open letter to him in which he protested: "How many magistrates more determined and ruthless than you are have refused to have anything to do with such cases!" He then cites a number of examples: At Thysdris, Cincius Severus suggested to the Christians the answers they should use to gain their acquittal, obviously without compelling them to offer sacrifice. Vespronius Candidus refused to condemn a Christian, declaring that the accusation of disturbing the peace had not been proved against him. Before undertaking such a case, Asper declared in the presence of the lawyers and assessors that it grieved him to do so. When the accused Christian after a brief torture declared that he was ready to offer sacrifice, he was set free without being compelled to go through the ceremony. Thus Asper plainly showed that he considered such a victory of no consequence. Less subtle was Arrius

Antonius, governor of Asia, who expostulated with the Christians drawn up before his tribunal: "Fools! If you want to die, you have cliffs and halters" (Tertul. *Ad Scap.* 5).

Trajan's rescript to Pliny was followed by other imperial constitutions. Hadrian (117–138), and possibly Antoninus Pius (138–161), stipulated that no riotous actions should be tolerated, and that no attention should be paid to popular outcries against the Christians.[3] Such cases were constantly coming to the fore. A typical example of this kind is the martyrdom of the venerable bishop of Smyrna, Polycarp, in the year 156, for which we have a description from eyewitnesses.[4] The rescript of Marcus Aurelius to the governor of Lyons in 177 is substantially the same as the one addressed by Trajan to Pliny (Euseb. *E.H.* 5.1.47).

Whatever may have been the number of martyrs before Decius, it was certainly much greater than what can be deduced from direct evidence. Tertullian wrote against the Gnostics: Shall all the thousands who were baptized before Marcion and Valentine came upon the scene (before the middle of the second century) have been baptized to no purpose, and shall "so many martyrs have been crowned in vain (*De praescrip.* 29)?" Of the various local persecutions cited by Tertullian in his letter to Scapula, we have no other information. The only reference to the Christians executed by Pliny in Bithynia is to be found in his letter to Trajan. The theological speculations of the Alexandrian school about the martyr as "the true Gnostic" prove that toward the end of the second century martyrdom was not uncommon. Only by chance do we hear of so many Roman Christians being in exile in Sardinia in the year 190. Tertullian exclaims: "How often does a hostile mob, by-passing the regular courts, assail us! In their Bacchanalian fury they do not even spare those Christians who are dead but snatch them from their graves" (*Apol.* 37). In Carthage, long before the reign of Decius, there were certain practices among the Christians which were observed during the persecutions. Cyprian writes: "Under my predecessors it was ever the custom for the deacons to visit the prison and there satisfy the desires of the martyrs with their counsels and with the precepts of Holy Writ" (*Ep.* 15.1). And Tertullian, after his apostasy to Montanism, ridiculed the sumptuous banquets which the Catholics were accustomed to furnish for the confessors (*De ieiunio* 12). Such established customs could not have been effectively created by the few known African martyrs prior to the time of Decius. If, then, for the second century we cannot as yet speak of many thousands of martyrs, nevertheless, since the Christian communities were rather small, we must not imagine that this was too tranquil and bloodless an age.[5]

The martyrdoms of the second century were rather sporadic, so that we can hardly distinguish definite periods of persecution followed by periods of peace. In the third century, on the contrary, the years 202, 235, 250, and 258 are known as years of actual persecution. The position of a Christian in the second century was such that he had to consider the possibility of being haled into court at any moment and being executed, especially if he had any personal enemies. But at the same time it is quite probable that there were many places where one could grow old without ever seeing a Christian put to death.

The martyrdom of Justin at Rome (ca. 163) illustrates this state of affairs. In the years before his trial, Justin had not concealed his faith. He had openly directed his two apologies to the emperors. His school was open to all. In the second of his apologies, addressed to Antoninus Pius, he wrote: "I expect to be waylaid and placed upon the rack, perhaps by Crescens, that lover of empty bombast (φιλόψοφος καὶ φιλόκομπος). He is not worthy to be called a lover of wisdom (φιλόσοφος) since he publicly condemns us for something of which he has no knowledge, namely, that we are impious and godless" (*II Apol.* 8). Justin's expectation was fulfilled.

In the third century the persecutions present an entirely different picture. The driving force behind them is no longer a public or private prosecutor, but the empire itself. No longer was a pursuit made of private individuals; the war now raged against the Church.

The first of these general persecutions was that of the emperor Decius (249–251). It was conducted throughout the whole empire according to a unified plan, and obviously aimed at smashing Christianity with a single blow. Enough records of this persecution have survived to enable us to reconstruct in some detail the technical aspects of the procedure.

The most valuable evidence which we have are the *libelli*, or certificates of sacrifice. Forty-one of these pieces of papyrus, original documents of the first rank, have been found in the sands of Egypt, thirty-four coming from the village of Theadelphia in the Fayum. It is worth examining one of these *libelli* more in particular:

> *First hand:* To those who have been appointed as witnesses of the sacrifices; from Aurelius Diogenes, son of Satabous, of the village of Alexandru Nesus, aged seventy-two years, with a scar over his right eye. I have always and without interruption sacrificed to the gods, and now in your presence according to the command which has been given, I have offered sacrifice, and poured a libation, and tasted the flesh of a sacrificial victim, which I ask you to testify. Farewell! I, Aurelius Diogenes, have presented this petition.
>
> *Second hand:* I, Aurelius Syrus, saw you and your son sacrificing.
>
> *Third hand:* (only four letters extant).
>
> *First hand:* In the first year of the emperor Caesar Caius Messius Quintus Traianus Decius Pius Felix Augustus, on the second day (of the month) of Epiph (June 26, 250).[6]

From this splendid document, from which only a photograph and fingerprints are missing, the following may be deduced: Sacrificial commissions were set up even in the smallest towns, before which one had to offer sacrifice in order to obtain one of the *libelli.* A special edict had been issued to this effect. What was commanded was the single performance of the required acts. It was not sufficient that one had taken part in a sacrificial ceremony in the past. The following rite had to be gone through: A few grains of incense had to be placed upon coals burning in a censer set before a statue; a libation, that is, the pouring out of a few drops of wine, had to be made; and the flesh of a sacrificial victim had to be tasted — all of which acts were freighted with significance. The writing of the *libellus* and its signing by the different individuals probably lasted longer than the sacrificial ceremony itself.

The plan was not ill conceived. The form, an ordinance directed to all, avoided the odium of a proscription against a particular group. The complaints of the Christians about the unfair execution of the law were thus removed. It was in fact no permanent regulation, but merely a command to perform a single act. We have no reason for suspecting that Decius introduced a compulsory sacrifice that had to be repeated at definite intervals. The rescript of Trajan which stated that the Christians should not be sought out remained unchanged. It was up to the individual to declare himself to be a Christian or not.

The government apparently succeeded in keeping the whole matter secret until its simultaneous revelation throughout the empire. At least the Christians were completely taken by surprise. The bishops would certainly have known that nothing very good was to be expected from the new ruler. They would have counted upon hardships and, likely as well, on individual executions such as had hitherto been common during a time of persecution. For such trials they had prepared their flocks. But not even the bishops had suspected the new techniques of this persecution. The execution of the imperial edict thus created immediately an enormous panic among the Christians.

We have several descriptions of this panic from eyewitnesses: from Cyprian, the bishop of Carthage, Dionysius, the bishop of Alexandria, and a fragmentary account from Rome.[7]

According to these accounts the same succession of events took place everywhere. First of all a rumor about an imminent persecution, which created an atmosphere of universal fear, was spread abroad. Then came the edict in a form which no one had anticipated. We do not know the order in which the people were summoned, since even in the taking of the census different methods were employed. In the larger cities the order of the streets was probably followed, the list of the owners of the individual houses or apartments being used as a starting point.[8] Fixed days were probably allotted for the individual wards or streets of a city, but even then it was no small task.

At Rome at least three simultaneous commissions were set up on the Capitol, and opposite the temple of Jupiter another statue was placed to speed up the work. Secretaries were seated ready to supervise the registering and to summon the individuals for the sacrifice, and after it was completed to affix the notice of this fact — we would say the seal — upon the sacrificial certificate. For those who had not brought with them from home the certificate already filled out, there was a bureau set up on the approach to the Capitol where the official formulae could be obtained. Both Christians and pagans appeared before the commissions all mingled together, the pagans, for whom the whole thing was a joke, laughing and jeering at the Christians, and the latter concealing the smart of their consciences with all kinds of protestations.

One cloud of sacrificial smoke after another went up to heaven, and the blood of one sacrificial victim after another flowed over the stone altars, so that below, where the Cloaca Maxima flowed into the Tiber, the waters could be seen flowing with blood. If we may judge from what happened at Carthage and Alexandria, many a prominent Christian was accompanied with cries of derision when he attempted to disappear into the crowd with his signed and sealed *libellus*. "The throng of bystanders heaped mockery upon them seeing them to be complete cowards, afraid to die and afraid to offer sacrifice," observes Dionysius. And Cyprian adds to this: When it was evening and the officials worn out by the monotonous labor were anxious to return to their homes, other Christians voluntarily presented themselves and asked them to continue their task, so that they might at least sleep in peace.[9]

On the following day the same routine began again, and so it went for days and weeks. At this time, Rome still had perhaps half a million inhabitants. Even if everyone did not have to put in a personal appearance, still it can be imagined what a throng there must have been. For each one had to have his *libellus* before a fixed date or otherwise be automatically treated as a Christian.[10]

There were also, of course, among the Christians individuals of a more realistic temperament. They did not permit themselves to be taken in by the universal panic, and from the first took a close look at the proceedings. They soon noticed that on the different sacrificial commissions there sat many an official who was not exactly an uncorruptible Cato. There were those who provided *libelli* for individuals who had not offered sacrifice, in return of course for a small consideration for their trouble. One did not have to go to the Capitol at all to get such a handy *libellus,* but could obtain it in a private dwelling after the close of the working hours. It was not even necessary to go in person, for there were trusted individuals who were gracious enough to procure a receipt of the sort — also of course for a small tip (Cyp. *Ep.* 55.14). Moreover, there were many officials so accommodating as to wink a bit at the proceedings and to fulfill them in a very perfunctory manner. They furnished the head of a family with a *libellus* for himself, his wife, and children, or even for several parties together.[11] We have examples of this type from Egypt. According to Cyprian, many besides including their wife and children and all their household servants included also their serfs and tenants (*Ep.* 55.13). This simplification of business was very convenient, not only for the officials but also for the Christians.

In this way the sacrificial commissions, when their term of office finally expired, would have reported an extraordinarily high number for those who had sacrificed. The victorious record of the complete extirpation of Christianity was filed away in the imperial chancery, while the Christians themselves reasonably intact stood before their indignant bishops with the accursed *libelli* in their hands, many hardly knowing how they had been obtained.

To speak of wholesale apostasies as is commonly done today by many historians is, therefore, only partially correct.[12] The spiritual misery was assuredly great. Thousands of Christians had sinned, but they had not on that account ceased to be Christians. If one regards this persecution as a crucial struggle between the Roman empire and the Church, then the victor was certainly not the empire. For instead of destroying the Church, it had only created a host of penitent sinners. The actual victor was the Church, only it was for her a victory over which she could not rejoice.

The reason why the Christians did not fare better than they did at this time need not be sought in a general decline in morals, but rather in the new technique employed in their persecution. The Christians were taken by surprise. The same thing happened to them as to the apostle Peter in the forecourt of the High Priest. Peter was really ready to suffer death for his Master, but he had pictured it to himself in an entirely different fashion. Only after his denial did he realize what he had done. Something similar happened at this time to the terrified Christians. The rigorous Cyprian himself summed up the results of the persecution with the words: "Although we deserved even worse for our sins, God in His goodness so directed the matter that all which has occurred seems rather to have been a trial than a persecution" (*De lapsis* 5).

This is not to say that in the persecution of Decius there was not also a whole series of steadfast Christians who did not permit themselves to be taken by surprise, but with single-minded constancy responded to the call of martyrdom. In the first rank of these belongs Pope Fabian, who was executed on January 29, 250, immediately after the outbreak of the persecution. The bishops of Antioch and Jerusalem also met death at this time as martyrs. Many saved themselves from death only through flight.

After the execution of the first victims, the persecution continued. Not only were those Christian confessors who were not immediately put to death detained for a long time in prison — for Rome we have a long list of names, chiefly of clerics, of such a group — but new imprisonments were also made. The authorities apparently realized that the Christians had not been exterminated, and they were now taking in the gleanings. There were thus further martyrdoms. Many who had proved to be weak in the first panic now expiated the false step they had taken.

With the death of the emperor Decius in the spring of 251, there followed immediately a period of calm; but in 253 the emperor Gallus had Pope Cornelius imprisoned and taken to Centumcellae (Civitavecchia), where he soon died. In 257 under the emperor Valerian a great persecution broke out again.

It was obvious that the means employed by Decius had not achieved their goal. A new plan was consequently brought to the fore. Most of all, no blood should flow. The aim was rather to break up the organization of the Christian communities. The bishops were therefore to be banished, the gathering places of the Christians, the homes used as churches, and their cemeteries were to be closed and confiscated. We still possess fragments of the judicial examinations of the bishops of Carthage and Alexandria who were sent into exile at this time.[13]

The confiscation of church property was something new. Prior to this, action had only been taken against the Christians themselves, but it was now recognized that the strength of their resistance lay in their liturgical assemblies. The present intention was to render these impossible.

A curious fact is that this first edict of 257 does not seem to have been executed at Rome. On August 2, 257, Pope Stephen died, and in the same month his successor, Xystus II, was duly elected, though in other parts of the empire bishops were already being sent into exile. Xystus seems to have remained unmolested even later in Rome. Moreover, nothing seems to have been done to the Roman cemeteries.

In the summer of 258 the second edict of persecution was issued, and with it blood began to flow. In accordance with the general principle of the persecution, the edict was directed primarily against the clerics. We possess several fragmentary acts of the martyrs of this time, especially those leading to the executions of Cyprian, the great bishop of Carthage, on September 14, 258, of Fructuosus, bishop of Tarragona, with two deacons, on January 21, 259, and of the African martyrs Marian and Jacob in April, 259. Pope Xystus II with at least four deacons was executed in Rome on August 6, 258. Noteworthy in this persecution is the fact that it reached its peak during Valerian's hopeless campaign against the Persians, which ended in the annihilation of the Roman army and the capture of the emperor. When Gallienus, son of the captured emperor, took over the government, the executions came to an end; and the new ruler even permitted the Christians to recover their confiscated churches and cemeteries (Euseb. *E.H.* 7.13.1).

Peace now reigned for several decades, but in 303 persecution broke out again, and this persecution, which is associated with the name of Diocletian, was the bloodiest of all. The whole bureaucracy and system of police, which reached a considerable degree of perfection under this emperor, was brought into play. A series of laws and ordinances was issued which embraced almost everything which up to that time had been ordained with respect to the Christians. Here and there compulsory sacrifice was reintroduced; churches were destroyed; cemeteries and other ecclesiastical possessions were confiscated. A new element in this persecution was the ferreting out of ecclesiastical libraries and archives, and an enormous number of documents were destroyed. Most of the executions took place in the eastern half of the empire, where the persecution continued almost without interruption until 311.[14]

The different provinces of the west half of the empire did not all experience the same intensity of persecution. Nothing much happened in Gaul and Britain where the well-disposed emperor Constantius Clorus, the father of the later renowned Constantine, did not as a rule put into execution the edicts against the Christians emanating from the central authority. On the other hand, the persecution was fierce in Africa and in Rome.

From Africa there is extant a whole series of acts from which we can derive a very distinct picture of how the persecution was handled in the beginning, when the goods and writings of the Christians were expropriated. Some years after these events, during the Donatist controversies, the official reports describing the search of the houses were copied out, and they have thus in part come down to us. An account from Cirta in Numidia (the modern Constantine) shows us how the judicial commission went from house to house, from the episcopal residence to that of the last lector, and took everything that was found in the nature of writings or alms for the poor.[15] Often enough the Christians succeeded in deceiving the commissioners by palming off old pieces of paper or other worthless objects and concealing what was valuable. Those who refused to hand over anything were imprisoned and in certain instances executed. We still possess the *acta* dealing with the martyrdom of the bishop of Tabyzica in Africa who was put to death because he refused to hand over the books, and also those of the deacon Euplius of Catania († August 12, 304).

At Rome a thorough searching of homes was also undertaken. During the course of it, the episcopal archives along with others fell into the hands of the persecutors. We know where the archives were kept later in the century. They were in a building which Pope Damasus enlarged, and next to which he erected the basilica known in later years as San Lorenzo in Damaso. The building which housed the archives thus practically stood on the site which has been occupied since the fifteenth century by the splendid Palazzo della Cancelleria. It was already there in 313, when the popes took possession of the Lateran palace. It is probable that the destruction of the archives took place on this spot in 303.

The surrender of the Christian writings was regarded by the Christians as a sin, since it was considered by both parties, by the persecutors as well as by the persecuted, as a kind of denial of the faith. An accused Christian could purchase his freedom through the surrender of the writings just as he could by making a sacrifice.[16]

But this does not mean that in every case the resistance was carried to the extreme, even when the police were already in the house. The Donatists were the only ones who later treated Christians from whom anything had been taken as apostates and traitors. They maintained that they possessed *acta* which showed that during this persecution Pope Melchiades had surrendered Christian documents. Still they had no proof for such an assertion.[17]

The Donatists are a typical example of that joyless tendency which arose immediately after the passing of a persecution. When the danger had passed, in the consciousness of their own blamelessness, some began to look down upon their weaker brethren and their failings. This had been the attitude of the Novatians after the persecution of Decius. Even today there are historians who are never satisfied with describing the many "defections from the faith" during the persecutions of the first centuries. Yet surely the much-abused *lapsi* suffered far more for their faith and gave proof of greater constancy than has ever been evinced by their severe *post factum* critics. In the Catholic Church such an attitude was never fostered. Those who had remained steadfast were respected and honored, but no stones were cast at the others.

From the later edicts of toleration we know that in 303 the fixed properties of the Christians were confiscated as well as the scriptures and liturgical goods, but we do not know how extensively this was done. From the mere wording of the decrees of restoration we cannot draw immediate conclusions with regard to the extent of the confiscations. In the *Liber pontificalis* there is a reference which may be very old to the property of a pious woman named Cyriaca which had been confiscated by the *fiscus,* or treasury, during a time of persecution.[18] Without doubt this estate is to be identified with the land containing the cemetery of Cyriaca under St. Laurence in the Agro Verano. Whether the same fate befell all the cemeteries is not certain. In Callistus an inscription has been found with a consular date of 307. But it does not necessarily follow from this that the cemetery escaped confiscation, since it is possible that the Christians during the tranquil period under Maxentius secretly repossessed parts of their ancient burial grounds, even before they were officially restored to them.

With his usual acumen, De Rossi attempted to prove that the papal crypt in Callistus and the surrounding part of this cemetery were for a long time hidden from sight by sand, and he maintained that this took place at the beginning of the persecution of Diocletian in order to protect these sites from destruction during the expected confiscation.[19] But even if this did happen, it would not follow that the expropriation later actually took place.

Without being able to form a clear picture of the details, we may nevertheless believe that in the year 303 there was a great deal of confiscation and destruction of Christian property at Rome. Moreover, we have clear indications that the years 303–305, and even later, were a time of terror for the Christian community.

One of these indications is the list of popes. With only a few exceptions we know not only the number of years which the popes of the third century reigned but also the dates of their consecration and death. It can thus be deduced that the consecration regularly took place on a Sunday, a custom which from the fourth century on became the standing rule, and that whenever possible, it was on the Sunday after the death of the preceding pope. Pope Anteros, for example, died on January 3, 236, and on January 10, his successor Fabian was consecrated. Lucius died March 5, 254; the consecration of his successor Stephen took place on March 12. Thus the see was as a rule vacant for only a few days. Only in three places in our list are long periods of vacancy indicated. Between the martyrdom of Pope Fabian (January 20, 250) and the consecration of his successor Cornelius (March, 251), there was an interval of over a year. After the martyrdom of Xystus II (August 6, 258) almost two years passed before the election of his successor Dionysius. Both of these vacancies took place during critical periods of persecution, that is, during the reigns of Decius and Valerian. The third long vacancy occurred after the death of Pope Marcellinus († January 15, 304), and thus during the persecution of Diocletian. It lasted for four years.

The reason for this phenomenon should not be sought so much in the fear of danger. Every newly elected bishop realized that he was entering into a dangerous post. As Cyprian well observed, the emperor Decius would much rather have heard of a new rival for his throne than of the election of a new bishop of Rome (*Ep.* 55.9). Pope Xystus II was hurriedly consecrated at the very moment when the Valerian persecution was breaking out. The long vacancy of the see after his martyrdom was not due to the lack of a candidate but to the fact that the community had not been assembled. The election of a bishop at this time required the harmonious co-operation of laity, clerics, and neighboring bishops. During an active persecution all such activity came to a halt. No one knew what had happened to the others — who were dead, who had been seized, who had fled, who had apostatized. The election of a new bishop is ordinarily a sign that matters had returned to normal.

The unusually long vacancy of the episcopal see during the persecution of Diocletian leads us to conclude, therefore, that this was a period of particular violence. Pope Marcellinus died in 304. The exact date of his death is not certain, though it may have been October 24 or 25. The last days of his life are veiled in obscurity. According to the *Liber pontificalis,* Marcellinus offered incense to the gods when commanded to do so, but a few days later he repented of his crime and was condemned to death by Diocletian with three other Christians. This account is based on a lost *Passio Marcellini,* which seems to have given undue credence to slanders circulated about the pope.[20] When the persecution of the Christians under the new emperor Maxentius had died down, a new election was held. Pope Marcellus was consecrated in May or June, 308, and died in exile the following year.[21] His successor Eusebius was promptly sent into exile and died in 310 after a few months in Sicily. Only after the universal edict of toleration issued by the emperor Galerius in April, 311, was Melchiades elected. This took place on July 2, 311, and from then on begins again the uninterrupted succession of popes.

There is ample evidence that at the outbreak of a great persecution very many Christians would take to flight. The testimony taken during the Donatist controversies clearly shows that both clergy and laity would "take to the mountains" as a matter of course. Flight from persecution was regarded by the Catholics as something permissible, and was not treated as cowardice. Only Tertullian, and that, after he had gone over to the Montanists, scoffed at the Catholics, who knew no passage in the Gospels so well as the one which advises: "When they shall persecute you in this city flee into another" (Mt. 10:23). And he adds that there were bishops who showed themselves to be "lions in peace, but deer in battle" (*De corona* 1). The Catholics did not think so. The bishops who fled before the persecution of Decius in 250, Cyprian of Carthage, Dionysius of Alexandria, Gregory the Wonder-worker of Neo-Caesaria, were held as ornaments of the Church.

We must not imagine that such a flight was something pleasant. Home and possessions had to be left behind. In his account of the Decian persecution, Eusebius cites a letter of Dionysius, bishop of Alexandria, picturing the distress of the times: "What need is there to speak of the multitude of those who wandered in the deserts and mountains, and there perished from hunger and thirst and frost and diseases and robbers and wild beasts (*E.H.* 6.42.2)?" Similar misfortunes befell the Christians of Pontus a few decades before the persecution of Diocletian. Gregory the Wonder-worker tells us that during a barbarian invasion many of them fled to safer territory, but there they were sold by their "hosts" into slavery. There were even Christians involved in this wretched business, a fact which greatly grieved Bishop Gregory.

We may therefore conclude that many of the Roman Christians who fled during the persecution of Diocletian returned to their homes only after long and devious journeys, and that many, perhaps the majority, never again saw them.

There can be no doubt that in the terrible years of 304 and 305 a great deal of Christian blood was shed at Rome. Most of the martyrs who were later honored in Rome may come from this period.

In 306 Maxentius, the son of Maximian Herculeus, the persecutor of the Christians, usurped the title of emperor. Although he was not recognized by the other emperors, he was able to maintain himself at Rome and in Italy until 312. At the outset Maxentius showed himself friendly to the Christians, at least if we can believe the historian Eusebius. As a matter of fact, the bloody martyrdoms at Rome seem to have come to an end during his rule (Euseb. *E.H.* 8.14.1). Still the Church and individual Christians had much to suffer. The Church property, moreover, still remained confiscated; and the Church itself remained practically without a bishop until 311. In this year the higher ranking emperor Galerius issued his edict of toleration in Nicomedia; and Maxentius, who always maintained the fiction of a regular association within the imperial college, hastened to execute the edict at Rome and began with the restoration of ecclesiastical property.[22] On October 28, 312, he lost his life in the battle at the Milvian bridge, and the new emperor Constantine granted the Roman Church a true and lasting peace.

Just as it would be an exaggeration to imagine that the victims

of the persecutions amounted to many millions of martyrs — at
the time of Diocletian there may have been in the whole empire
from six to ten million Christians — so it would be false to judge
the terror of the persecutions only by the number of those who
were executed. That a Christian escaped with his life did not
mean that he had suffered nothing at all from a persecution.
Exile, painful tortures, flight, confiscation of property, or at least
business losses, the separation of families — something or other
of this sort was experienced by very many, if not by the majority
of Christians. At the very least there lay upon all, as well in
the earlier period of single persecutions as later during the mass
persecutions, a continual anxiety, a feeling of insecurity and
outlawry, and persistent problems of conscience. One needs only
to read the *De idololatria* of Tertullian, where he speaks of the
various vocations and occupations with their concomitant con-
flicts and dangers, to obtain a notion of how difficult it was for
a Christian of the time to hew to the straight line of duty as a
citizen, as the head of a family, and as a member of the Church,
and to realize what great sacrifices the faithful had to make in
their private lives because of the threat which even in fairly
quiet times hung over them. In those centuries the mere fact of
being a Christian required of each one a real measure of constancy and a readiness for martyrdom, even if in his lifetime one
may never have been arraigned before a judge or stretched upon
a rack. Thus we can understand the overwhelming feeling of
relief and the enthusiasm with which the Christians greeted the
emperor Constantine when at last he secured for them a legal
status within the Roman world.

CHAPTER VII

ON THE WAY TO MARTYRDOM

THE tombs of the martyrs are the last stopping place at which all the martyrs have alike arrived. Even if we had all the tombs of those who suffered for the faith and knew all their names, we still could not write a history of the persecutions nor even imagine how they were carried out. For this we must employ the accounts left by eyewitnesses. Unfortunately, so far as Rome itself is concerned, not many documents of this sort are extant. There are no such beautiful narratives of the Roman martyrs as the acts of the martyrs of Lyons of 177, or of Perpetua and Felicitas and their companions at Carthage in 202. For Rome we have transcripts of only two judicial processes, or at least accounts which were drawn from these authentic sources: the *acta* of Justin and his companions († ca. 163) and of Apollonius († ca. 185). This lack of documentation was felt even in antiquity, and to remedy it all kinds of tales about the fate of individual martyrs were pieced together, but unfortunately this took place at a time when a living memory of the events had long since disappeared. During the barbarous times of the fifth and sixth centuries there thus came into existence those compositions known as "legends," which the faithful of later centuries took for authentic accounts, but which are actually no more historical than Wiseman's *Fabiola* or other modern novels about the martyrs.[1]

The prefecture of the city, or as we would say, the court of justice, lay at the extremity of the Oppian Hill somewhat below the spot where today stands the church of San Francesco da Paola. The stonework which is to be seen there comes from the Middle Ages, but the beautifully fluted marble columns in the neighboring church of San Pietro in Vincoli may well have been taken from the old prefecture of the city. We no longer know the actual appearance of the building, nor even if the "bloody scourges," of which Martial speaks, were hung outside as a kind of heraldic shield, or whether the poet only wished to say that within the building the dreadful torture chamber was to be found (Martial 2.17.2). Next to this building, immediately to the northeast, lay the raucous residential area of the Suburra.

Here then we must imagine the trials of the Christians were usually held, and here also must have been the prison in which most of them awaited their lot.

One of the Roman prisons mentioned by ancient authors was situated in the praetorian camp.[2] Here were to be found such prisoners as had been sent from the provinces to Rome to be judged by the prefect of the praetorium. Among these was the apostle Paul, who in the year 61 received permission from the prefect to take up his dwelling in a private house in the neighborhood of the barracks.[3] The prison on the Tiber from which the church San Nicolao in Carcere has taken its name may belong only to the Byzantine period.[4] On the other hand, the age-old public prison at the foot of the Capitol, the Tullianum, still stands. We do not know whether this prison, in which King Jugurtha was starved to death, and in which Vercingetorix was detained, was used in the later years of the empire. That the apostles Peter and Paul were kept there before their execution is not improbable, even if there is no ancient evidence to prove it. During the period of the great persecutions, when the Roman forum no longer served as a place of justice, the prisoners must have been detained at the prefecture of the city. Nevertheless from the Tullianum we can derive a picture of what a prison of this sort must have been.

Roman criminal law did not recognize the wasting away of one's life in prison as a penalty. The jails served as a place to keep the accused during the penal investigations, and at the same time they were used as a place of torture. Debtors also sat in prison, there to rot until they paid up. The Christians were not thrown into prison as a punishment, but in order that they might become docile and offer sacrifice.

The prisons were so constructed that they lacked almost everything for the most elementary needs of life. The *squalor carceris,* or "filth of a jail," is a commonplace in ancient writers, and by it we must understand not merely a lack of cleanliness, but of everything connected with the convenience and dignity of man.

The Tullianum consisted of, and still consists of, two vaulted rooms of moderate dimensions, one placed over the other. A descent can be made into the lower room only by means of a ladder through a hole in the separating vault. No thought was given to ventilation or even sewerage. When no light was burning, it was pitch dark. The prison at Carthage, where in 202 Perpetua and her companions waited for martyrdom, seems to have been of this type. In her memoirs Perpetua speaks very plainly of the darkness, which at first caused great alarm. She also speaks of the crowding and the intense heat and the blows of the guards (*Passio Ss. Perp. et Fel.* 3.3–4). When Felicitas, the companion of St. Perpetua, gave birth to a child it was in prison three days before the games were to take place. While she was in labor one of the guards asked in wonder: "If now you so grieve, what will you do when you are thrown to the beasts, which you despised when you refused to sacrifice?" To this she answered: "It is now I who suffer, but there another in me will suffer for me, because I shall suffer for him" (*Passio* 15.3). The Christians of Carthage succeeded in obtaining some relief for the prisoners, so that they could at least pass some hours each day in a court or garden; and Perpetua, who was herself a young mother, even received and nursed her child in prison.

Death in prison was of frequent occurrence. In 177 Bishop Pothinus of Lyons died from the rigors of his confinement. In 251 the priest Musaeus died in prison at Rome. Cyprian wrote that such individuals should be recognized as true martyrs even if they had not suffered torture and death at the hands of the executioners.[5]

The last joy which the priest Musaeus had on earth was a letter of consolation which the bishop of Carthage addressed to him and to the other Roman confessors (Cyp. Ep. 37). In a gallant manner Cyprian reminded them of the fact that they had already been in prison for over a year — longer than the period of office for the highest magistrates, and of which these latter were so proud. They had seen, or rather they had not seen, all the four seasons of the year. There is a saying in Rome today: "Where the sun does not enter, the doctor does." Only one who has lived in Rome can imagine what it would mean not to catch sight of a sunbeam there for a whole year together.

Cyprian had learned of the plight of the Roman confessors from a young African who for a considerable time had been imprisoned with them. This young man, whose name was Celerinus, could hardly have been twenty years old. He came from a family of martyrs. His grandmother Celerina died for the faith in an earlier persecution, and also two of his uncles who had been soldiers. The young Celerinus happened to be in Rome in the winter of 249–250 when the persecution broke out. We do not know what he was doing there. It was probably not the pursuit of higher studies, for his letter to the confessor Lucian, which Cyprian included in his collection, with its mediocre Latin does not exactly portray a college education (Cyp. Ep. 21). Celerinus was imprisoned along with the Roman Christians at the very beginning of the persecution, and he distinguished himself through his singular steadfastness. He was even brought before the emperor Decius himself. When he could in no way be induced to offer sacrifice, he was placed in the prison stocks. Such prisoners were chained with their legs stretched as far apart as possible and left to lie upon the ground. Celerinus passed nineteen days and nights in this position without being able to move (Cyp. *Ep.* 39.2). He was then released from prison for some unknown reason, perhaps merely because he was not a native of Rome. He made his way to Africa and sought out Cyprian in his hideout. Cyprian wrote that if there were any doubting Thomas suspicious about Celerinus, he had only to look at him to see what he had suffered. Apparently the young man after the course of several months could still hardly walk. Cyprian ordained him lector and wrote to his clerics in Carthage that if Celerinus had not been so young he would have immediately ordained him priest — his constancy had merited it (*Ep.* 38.2). He should in the meantime receive the emoluments of a priest (*Ep.* 39.5). His ordination would be held later when he should have reached the required age.

The fact that they could receive visitors was for the Christians a ray of light. In this matter the superintendents of the jails appear to us to have been truly humane. Since practically all the prisoners were chained either to a wall, to the floor, or to one of the wardens, strict segregation from the outer world was hardly necessary. The prisoners could receive food, light, and other little comforts as circumstances permitted. They could be encouraged, and any business which they might have on hand could be furthered. This care for the imprisoned confessors was in time of persecution one of the chief duties of the clerics. The Church coffers were always open for such work. "They must lack nothing," Cyprian wrote to his clerics (*Ep.* 5.1). The laity also devoted themselves to this labor of love, and in fact to such an extent, that Cyprian had to warn them of excessive zeal. They ought not to go *en masse* into the prison, for if the permission was abused, it would in the end be withdrawn (*Ep.* 5.2). The priest Novatian, subsequently the founder of the sect bearing his name, was regarded with great disfavor because for a long time he failed to visit his brethren in prison (Euseb. *E.H.* 6.43.16). Later he also made such visits. In the preceding century this solicitude of the Christians for the imprisoned confessors was noted and ridiculed by the pagan Lucian (*Peregrinus* 12–13).

Of particular importance, of course, was the spiritual welfare of those in prison. The priests sedulously offered Mass for the prisoners. Here also Cyprian advised the use of prudence. Many wished to celebrate the liturgy with great solemnity. Cyprian gave orders that never more than one priest assisted by one deacon should offer Mass in prison, and they should not always be the same individuals. Thus suspicion would be lessened (*Ep.* 5.2).

This all took place before the eyes of the guards, who naturally enough knew that the visitors were Christians, and Christian priests. That made no difference. So long as no formal accusation was laid against an individual, he was left in peace, even if it was positively known that he was a priest, and hence guilty of exactly the same crime as those in chains. The prison personnel was, of course, more inclined to wink at what was going on when an occasional tip was dropped. Nevertheless it was a dangerous task for the clerics.

In such circumstances it is no surprise that the prisoners received letters from the outside and, in their turn, wrote or dictated extensive tracts. Nonetheless the prisons always remained frightful, and true places of martyrdom.

What were the thoughts and feelings of the Christians as they waited in prison not knowing whether they were to be executed or not? Perpetua in her memoirs narrates a conversation which she had with her younger brother, who had been arrested with her. The youth thought that in the circumstances she might dare to ask God for a sign as to what would happen to them. During the following night Perpetua did in fact have a dream in which she seemed to mount a ladder to heaven, and there received a morsel of food from a venerable old man, which symbolized the reception of Viaticum. In the morning she told her brother what she had dreamed, "and we understood it to mean that we would suffer martyrdom, and we began to have no further hope in this world" (*Passio* 4.6). In the same acts a later discourse is recorded, when the prisoners already knew that they must "battle" with wild beasts. One of them, Saturninus, declared his desire to be thrown to all the beasts, so that he might win a more glorious crown. Another, Saturus, who dreaded a bear more than anything else, thought he would suffer martyrdom by the single bite of a leopard (*Passio* 19.1,3).

Their chief care, and the object of their prayers, was that all should persevere to the end. Perpetua had been baptized only a few days before her imprisonment, when she already knew what was in store for her. At the moment of her baptism she was inspired by the Holy Spirit to ask no other special grace from the sacrament "except patience to endure" (*Passio* 3.3). In the account which the surviving confessors of Lyons drew up about the martyrdom of their companions, it is stated that during the initial tortures ten of the Christians proved to be weak. This caused "great pain and boundless sadness" to the others (Euseb. *E.H.* 5.1.11). In this instance, apostasy was of little immediate avail since those who denied the faith were still detained in jail, not as Christians, but "as murderers and foul persons"; but at least one of these, a woman named Biblis, recovered her senses under renewed torture and declared herself to be a Christian (Euseb. *E.H.* 5.1.25–26). Among the confessors of Lyons was a slave girl, Blandina. The Christians, and in particular her mistress, who was herself one of the confessors, were afraid that "through the frailty of her body, she would not find courage enough to even profess her faith" (Euseb. *E.H.* 5.1.18). The fear proved to be groundless, for Blandina remained steadfast to the end, the most courageous of them all.

Perpetua lays bare the natural sentiments of the martyrs where she writes of the visits of her father. The old man was not a Christian and acted as if he were completely beside himself. In the prison he threw himself upon his knees before his daughter, kissed her hands, and with tears begged her not to inflict such a disgrace upon him. Perpetua does not conceal how difficult this was for her, and how it grieved her that of all her family the only one who could not rejoice over her martyrdom was her father. She sought to console and persuade him, but to no avail (*Passio* 5.1–3).

Rather seldom in our sources do we find an eager longing for martyrdom. For that, the matter was too serious and too frightful. There were to be sure instances of youthful enthusiasm, such as that of the sixteen-year-old Origen who was shut up by his mother at home, and whose clothes she finally had to hide to prevent him from running to the provincial court and proclaiming himself to be a Christian (Euseb. *E.H.* 6.2.5). The bishops had, in fact, expressly forbidden such voluntary surrender for martyrdom. One could go as far as did the later renowned Anthony, who in the year 311 hastened from his retreat in the wilderness to the capital Alexandria where the persecution had broken out. He did not go directly to the judge, but he was plainly to be seen among the spectators encouraging the martyrs as best he could and going with them to the place of execution. The judge finally gave orders that the man with the wild beard and shaggy pelt and his fellow monks should not be given access to the court. Anthony shaved himself, put on a clean cloak, and again appeared in the crowd. Eventually he returned to his retreat, troubled in heart that he had not received the grace of martyrdom (Athanasius *Vita Anton.* 46).

The venerable Ignatius, bishop of Antioch, who was brought to Rome during the reign of the emperor Trajan (98–117) "to fight" with wild beasts, sent a letter to the Christians at Rome earnestly beseeching them not to do anything which might prevent his martyrdom. He wished to forestall the intercession of those who possessed some influence at the imperial court: "Permit me to be the food of beasts, through whom one may reach God. I am the wheat of God, and I am to be ground by the teeth of wild animals, so that I may be found the pure bread of Christ" (*Rom.* 4.1). The priest Musaeus and the other Christians imprisoned at Rome in the winter 250–251 wrote to Cyprian: "No one should regard it as an act of mercy that our execution is being continually stayed. This delay is no boon since it is an obstacle to glory, makes us wait for heaven, and shuts off the marvelous vision of God (Cyp. *Ep.* 31.5). Toward the end of his life, Cyprian himself possessed a great longing for martyrdom. He had received word that Pope Xystus II had been executed in the cemetery at Rome. The fact that he had been apprehended while preaching to his flock appeared to the bishop of Carthage as the ideal martyrdom of a bishop. The deacon Pontius writes about Cyprian's last days: "He was filled with an eager desire to preach, for he hoped that his longed-for martyrdom would occur at a time when he was speaking of the things of God to his people."[6]

The inner calm and courage with which the martyrs met their death may be seen in the last words of Perpetua's diary: "This much has happened up to the day before the games. But of the games themselves, if anybody should care to write of them, he may do so" (*Passio* 10.7). It is almost as if she had said with a smile: "One cannot ask me to write about my own execution." But still there is nothing in her words of vanity or ostentation.

During the course of imprisonment the confessors were often led before the judge for questioning. "As often as you are questioned," Cyprian wrote to the Christians imprisoned at Rome, "so often do you make a profession of your faith" (*Ep.* 37.1). These interrogations, however, as we have already seen, were not employed to prove the guilt of the accused. From the very beginning it was perfectly well known that they were Christians. Rather, during these hearings they were urged to offer sacrifice, and if necessary, torture was employed to constrain them.

A number of accounts are still extant of such processes. Some were jotted down by witnesses who heard the discussions in the courts. Others were later copied by the Christians from the official minutes of the proceedings. In them are to be found some magnificent answers given by the martyrs. The proconsul ordered Polycarp, the aged bishop of Smyrna: "Swear by the genius of Caesar and I shall let you go free. Revile Christ!" Polycarp replied: "For eighty-six years have I served Him, and He has done me no wrong. How can I curse my King who saved me (*Martyrium* 9.3; *E.H.* 4.15.20)?" The proconsul Saturninus asked the martyrs of Scilli in Africa after he had vainly sought to persuade them to apostatize: "Do you want time to reflect?" The leader of the group, Speratus, answered: "In a matter such as this deliberation would be wrong" (*Passio Ss. Scilit.* 11).

The Valerian persecution was directed particularly against the spiritual leaders of the Christians. Paternus, the proconsul of Carthage, thus asked Cyprian to give him the names of the other bishops and priests in and about Carthage. Cyprian gave as his answer: "You have wisely provided in your laws that there should be no informers. Consequently, I cannot reveal them, or hand them over to you, but they will be found in their respective cities." "This is the very information I am asking from you," was the judge's retort, to which Cyprian replied: "Since our rule of life forbids a man to voluntarily present himself before a judge, and since your own would not approve it, they cannot surrender themselves; but if you look for them, you will find them." Paternus replied: "I shall find them all right" (*Acta Cyp.* 1.5–7).

As a rule the judges refused to become involved in religious controversies, and only exceptionally did they pose any questions about the Christian tenets. Junius Rusticus, prefect of the city, a former teacher of Marcus Aurelius, and himself a student of philosophy, asked the philosopher Justin: "Is it your opinion that you will go to heaven and there obtain some noble recompense?" To this Justin replied: "It is no opinion, I know it for the truth, and am convinced of it" (*Acta Just.* 5.3).

The ninety-year-old bishop of Lyons, Pothinus, was asked by

the judge: "Who is the God of the Christian?" He received as his answer: "If you are found worthy, you will know" (Euseb. *E.H.* 5.1.31).

When arguments bore no fruit, recourse was had to torture. For a whole day the young Blandina was tortured without cease, but she found strength and comfort in repeating: "I am a Christian woman, and nothing wicked is done by us" (Euseb. *E.H.* 5.1.19).

While the deacon Euplius was being racked at Catania, the judge kept plying him with questions. The painful dialog was taken down even in its least details by the court stenographer:

> When he was being tortured, Euplius said: "I thank You, Christ. Protect me while I suffer these pains for You."
>
> "Get rid of this madness, Euplius," pleaded the judge Calvisianus. "Adore the gods and you will be set free."
>
> "I adore Christ," replied Euplius. "I despise demons. Do what you will, I am a Christian. This has long been my desire. Do what you will. Yet more! I am a Christian."
>
> After he had been tortured for a long time, Calvisianus ordered the hangmen to stop and said: "Miserable wretch, adore the gods. Worship Mars, Apollo, and Aesculapius."
>
> "I worship the Father, Son, and Holy Spirit," answered Euplius. "I worship the Blessed Trinity, apart from which there is no God. May those gods perish who did not make heaven and earth and whatever is in them. I am a Christian."
>
> "Sacrifice, if you wish to be freed," said the prefect Calvisianus.
>
> "I am now sacrificing myself to Christ, who is God. There is no more than I can do. Your attempts are vain. I am a Christian."
>
> Calvisianus gave orders that he should be tortured again more cruelly. And while he was being tortured, Euplius said: "Thanks to You, Christ! Christ, come to my assistance! For You, Christ, I am suffering these torments." And when he had said this again and again, his strength finally failed him. And though he could no longer make any sound he kept repeating with his lips these and other words.[7]

After being subjected to torture, the martyrs were returned

to prison where they waited further questioning until finally the judge decided to pass sentence.

The sentence of execution was given with a certain formality. The accused were brought forth for a last time and asked if they persisted in their refusal. Then the judge with his assessors withdrew behind a curtain and there dictated the sentence, which was written in large letters upon a tablet by the court clerk. The judge then came out from behind the curtain, sat upon the judgment seat, and read the sentence from the tablet. Before doing this, he sometimes gave the reasons for his sentence. The proconsul Valerius Maximus, for example, before his condemnation of Cyprian observed: "For a long time you have lived in a sacrilegious frame of mind, and you have gathered very many men about yourself in an accursed conspiracy, and you have set yourself up as a foe to the Roman gods and the sacred rites of religion; nor have the devout and most sacred *principes,* Valerian and Gallienus Augusti, and Valerian, the most excellent Caesar, been able to call you back to the observance of their religious ceremonies. And therefore, since you, the sponsor and the standard-bearer of most impious crimes, have been apprehended, you shall be an example to those who have joined you in your wickedness. Right order shall be restored by your blood" (*Acta Cyp.* 4.1–2).

The actual written sentence was very short: "It is the will of the court that Cyprian be struck with the sword" (*Acta Cyp.* 4.3). Or it could be like the following: "Speratus, Nartzalus, Cittinus, Donatus, Vestia, Secunda, and the rest have confessed that they live according to the Christian rite; and since they have obstinately persevered when granted the opportunity of returning to the Roman manner of life, they are to be executed with the sword" (*Passio Ss. Scilit.* 14); or, "I order the Christian Euplius who despises the commands of the emperors, blasphemes the gods, and does not wish to change his mind to be executed by the sword" (*Acta Euplii* 3.1).

There is a widespread opinion that most of the martyrs were

put to death in combats with wild beasts. This is partly due to the fact that some of the best and clearest accounts which we have from antiquity, such as the acts of the martyrs of Lyons of the year 177 and those of Carthage of 202, describe such contests with wild animals. They were, it seems, not uncommon. During the reign of Trajan, Ignatius of Antioch was condemned to fight with beasts at Rome. The people of Smyrna wanted the proconsul to give Polycarp to the wild beasts, but their request was refused since the time for the games was already passed. The war cry raised against the Christians, "The Christians to the lion!" shows how natural such a course of action must have been. But one lion, as Tertullian noted in a bitter jest, would never have sufficed for all the Christians (Tertul. *Apol.* 40.2.). In his *Ecclesiastical History*, Eusebius narrates the exposure of a youth to wild beasts which he himself witnessed during the persecution of Diocletian (Euseb. *E.H.* 8.7.4).

Criminals, including Christians, could be sent to Rome for the games if they were strong and agile enough to provide entertainment for the people.[8] However, no great performance in the arena could have been expected from the old bishop Ignatius. From this it may be concluded that death for the Christians from beasts was more common at Rome than elsewhere.

In antiquity there were three kinds of buildings for public spectacles: the theater, the circus, and the amphitheater. The theaters, of which a magnificent example, the theater of Marcellus, still stands in Rome, were not used for the baiting of beasts. The circuses, on the other hand, were not only used for chariot races, but also for combats with wild animals. The arena of the Circus Maximus at Rome was originally separated from the seats of the spectators by a ditch to prevent the escape of the animals. This ditch was, however, later filled in, and it seems that such games were from this time on held in the amphitheaters specially erected for them. There were two of these at Rome, the Colosseum, and the smaller Amphitheatrum Castrense. Its outer rim was incorporated into the city wall by Aurelian. It may be seen today near the basilica of Santa Croce in Gerusalemme. The martyrdom of St. Perpetua and her companions took place in the Amphitheatrum Castrense of Carthage. At Rome the usual place for such spectacles was most probably the Colosseum.

This presumption, however, rests only on general considerations. We have not a single bit of evidence for it from antiquity. Not once in the legends is the Colosseum indicated as the place of execution for the martyrs. Nor do the Middle Ages furnish us with such a tradition. Only from the seventeenth century on did the arena of the Colosseum come to be regarded as soil consecrated by the blood of martyrs.

Whatever may have been the site for such contests, they were not the ordinary means of execution. By far the greater number of Roman martyrs must have been put to death with the sword. In the only cases for which we have the judicial processes, that is, the martyrdoms of Justin and his companions, and Apollonius, this manner of execution is expressly indicated.

With regard to Justin and his companions, it is stated that they were executed "at the usual place" (*Acta Just.* 6.1). It would be worth knowing where this place was. In ancient times criminals were executed as a rule on the Ager Esquilinus in front of the Porta Esquilina. This gate lay between Santa Maria Maggiore and the present Piazza Vittorio Emmanuele, where remains of the ancient Servian wall may still be seen. The area in front of the gate was notorious. It contained a great cemetery for the poor and numerous pits into which refuse, dead animals, and the bodies of slaves and executed criminals were hurled. In the environs of the present Via Napoleone III more than seventy of these dumps have been discovered.[9] They plagued the whole area with their foul odors, so that even to the present day the name of the Dea Mephis, who was honored there in a sacred grove, has remained as a proverb.

In this "flayer's yard" was the ancient place of execution.

On the advice of Maecenas, the emperor Augustus, who did so much to improve and adorn the city, completely renovated this region. He filled the site with earth, at times to a depth of twenty-six feet, and on the reclaimed land on both sides of the Via Praenestina, he laid out beautiful gardens. Horace discovered that one could not only go for a pleasant walk on the Esquiline but even safely live there, where only a short time before bleached bones could be seen lying about (*Sat.* 1.8.8–16).

Nevertheless, the place of execution seems to have remained in this neighborhood, since Suetonius states that during Claudius' reign those who falsely claimed Roman citizenship were struck with the sword on the Esquiline field (*Claud.* 25). From the prefecture of the city it was only a short distance to this spot. It is quite possible that many a Roman Christian made his *via crucis* along the present Via Giovanni Lanza, or perhaps more exactly, along the Via in Selci.

We do not know if this site continued to be used as the ordinary place of execution. A spot once chosen for such a purpose is not as a rule readily changed, but for the later period we have no definite information. It is certain, however, that other sites could have been used. From the history of Peter and Marcellinus, as recorded by Damasus, we know that at times this must have been the case.

Wherever it was that the Christians were put to death, their executions did not bear the semblance of a triumph. Exteriorly they did not differ in the least from the executions of common criminals. But the moral grandeur of a martyr is essentially the same, whether he preserved his constancy in the arena before thousands of raving spectators, or whether he perfected his martyrdom forsaken by all upon a pitiless flayer's field.

CHAPTER VIII

THE EUCHARIST

THE Eucharist during the centuries of persecution was, just as it is today, the focal point of the Church's liturgy and of personal piety. There is an abundance of evidence for this going back to the earliest times, not a little of which is to be found in the catacombs.

The primitive Christians of the Pentecostal community in Jerusalem "continued breaking bread from house to house" (Acts 2:46) in remembrance of the Lord's precept: "Do this for a commemoration of me" (Lk. 22:19). Paul also in the early morning "broke bread" (Acts 20:7) in the assembly of his converts, and he wrote to the Corinthians: "The chalice of benediction which we bless, is it not the communion of the blood of Christ? And the bread which we break, is it not the partaking of the body of the Lord?" (1 Cor. 10.16.) For Ignatius, disciple of the apostles and martyr, the Eucharist is in a special way the sign of Church unity.[1]

The earliest description which we have of the rite of the Holy Sacrifice of the Mass comes from the middle of the second century. According to Justin, philosopher and martyr, the celebration took place on Sundays. Selections were first read from the Old and New Testament, after which the "overseer" delivered a homily. When this was finished, all stood to pray, and when the prayer was ended, they gave each other the kiss of peace. Bread and a cup containing water and wine were then brought to the bishop. Over these he prayed and gave thanks (*eucharistia*) to the best of his ability, and when the prayer was offered, the entire congregation answered "Amen." The bread and the wine mixed with water over which the prayer of thanksgiving had been pronounced was then given to those who were present and carried by the deacons to those who were not. "This food is called by us the Eucharist, and no one may eat of it who does not believe in our teaching and is not baptized to the remission of sins and a new birth and does not live as Christ has commanded. For we do not partake of this as ordinary bread and ordinary drink, . . . since we have been taught that this food is the flesh and blood of Jesus, the Word of God made man." After the ceremony a collection was taken up for the poor (*I Apol.* 65–67).

Justin was writing for the pagans, and he thus gives a rather external description of the Eucharistic service. Some fifty years later the so-called *Egyptian Church Order* was composed. In this precious little work, which is now known to be a Coptic translation of the *Apostolic Tradition* of Hippolytus of Rome, the prayers used at Mass are given. After the presentation of the offertory gifts, the bishop begins his dialog with the people, which even today in every rite serves as an introduction to the canon: *Dominus cum omnibus vobis — Et cum spiritu tuo. Sursum corda vestra — Habemus ad Dominum. Gratias agamus Domino — Dignum et justum.* There then follows the true and proper Eucharistic prayer, the canon, in which are included the words of consecration. After saying "Do this in commemoration of Me," the bishop continues: *Recordantes igitur* . . . (today's *Unde et memores*). There is, however, as yet no fixed formula for the prayer. Its contents are determined, but the words are left to the improvisation of the celebrant. Only the introductions and conclusions, such as, the *Sursum corda* and the dismissal of the faithful at the end with *Abite in pace* (in later times, *Ite, missa est*), are fixed, and likewise the words immediately preceding the consecration.[2]

The *Didascalia Apostolorum,* or as it is sometimes known, *The Catholic Teaching of the Twelve Apostles and Holy Disciples of Our Saviour,* a church order which was probably composed in Syria in the early third century, gives us the ritual which was followed in the divine service. The eastern part of the room is reserved for the priests. They are seated on both sides of the episcopal throne. The men in the congregation are separated from the women, and the boys from the girls, unless they are children who are still with their parents. One of the deacons takes his place at the entrance to the room and, after all have entered, sees to it that everyone is in his proper place and that "no one whispers, or falls asleep, or laughs, or makes signs."[3]

Despite all this, there were relatively few regulations for the first centuries. The liturgical functions took place either in private dwellings or, where these had been erected, in buildings especially destined for religious services. Some years ago a Christian church which can be dated with certainty in the first half of the third century was excavated at Dura Europos in Syria. It is the earliest structure of this type that we possess. There are several rooms, including a baptistery, ordered about a little court. The largest room, the church proper, is about sixteen and a half feet wide and about thirty-nine feet long. In the year 303 the whole congregation, which was assisting at Mass, was surprised and arrested at Abitina, a little city near Carthage. The bishop had apostatized by handing over the Scriptures to the civil authorities and hence was not present at the time. Fifty Christians were taken into custody including Saturninus, the officiating priest, three lectors, eighteen women, and a number of children.[4]

Conditions at Rome were, of course, much different. From a letter of Pope Cornelius written in 251, we know that at Rome there were at this time besides the bishop "forty-six priests, seven deacons, seven sub-deacons, forty-two acolytes, fifty-two exorcists, lectors, and porters" — sufficient even by modern stand-

ards for a very solemn liturgical function (Euseb. *E.H.* 6.43.11).
But we do not know if these clerics ever came together at one
time to assist at a divine service, for the *domus ecclesiae*, or
private oratory, had existed at Rome from Apostolic times.
From the *domus ecclesiae* developed the *tituli*, or "titular
churches," which served as a basis for a division of both clergy
and laity into different liturgical groups.[5]

Certainly everything was much simpler than in later centuries.
There was an almost complete lack of liturgical pageantry.
Bishops and clerics wore the ordinary civil dress at Mass. There
were as yet no burning altar candles, no smoke of incense, no
special hymns. Only in the decoration of the room for the
divine service does any special care seem to have been taken.
Already in the *Acts of the Apostles* mention is made of "a
great number of lamps in the upper chamber" where Paul celebrated the breaking of the bread (Acts 20.8). There are frequent
references to precious vessels and other valuable church goods
in the accounts of Diocletian's persecution.

In the first centuries there was no Church law obliging all
the faithful to assist at Mass. This was rather taken as self-
evident. When in the year 303 the priest Saturninus with his
little community was arrested, the proconsul of Carthage asked
the lector Emeritus, in whose house the Mass had been celebrated: "Was the meeting held in your house despite the imperial prohibition?" To this Emeritus replied: "Yes, it was in
my house that we celebrated the Lord's feast." — "Why did you
let the people in?" — "Because they are my brothers, and I could
not close my doors to them." — "But you should have." — "I could
not, for we could not continue to exist without the Lord's feast"
(*Acta Saturn.* 11).

With the exception of those who were doing penance, all
who were present at Mass could receive Holy Communion.[6] As
we have already seen from Justin's *First Apology*, the deacons
carried the Blessed Sacrament to the homes of those who were
absent. The faithful, moreover, could reserve the consecrated

hosts in their homes, and on days when no Mass was offered, or when they were prevented from going to church, they gave Communion to themselves.

Grievous sinners were excluded from Communion, in certain circumstances for years. They had definite works of penance to perform, and assisted at Mass from a special place set apart for them. The penance was public in that the whole community saw that they were excluded from Holy Communion. Ecclesiastical absolution concurred with the permission to again receive the Eucharist. If a sinner became seriously ill before completing his penance, he was nonetheless given Communion as Viaticum. And with this he was absolved, even if he happened to recover. Many were of the opinion that such an absolution should not remain in force, but as Cyprian dryly remarked: "After the *pax* has been given to those in danger of death, we cannot crush or throttle them, . . . since the divine piety and fatherly forgiveness has been made manifest in them" (*Ep.* 55.13). In other words, if the penitents were absolved, they remained absolved.

In the third century certain bishops permitted the dying *poenitentes* to receive absolution and Viaticum only if they had already performed a long and rigorous penance. This excessive severity was zealously combated by the leading pastors, such as Pope Cornelius, Cyprian of Carthage, and Dionysius of Alexandria. In a letter to the bishop of Antioch, who was inclined to the more stringent view, Dionysius narrates an incident that had occurred a short time before in Alexandria. An old man named Serapion, who had previously been an exemplary Christian, apostatized during the Decian persecution, and was accordingly excluded from the sacraments. He fell ill, and for three days lay unconscious. When at last he came to himself, he sent his small grandson in the middle of the night to call a priest. The priest himself was sick, but since the bishop had given orders that no one should ever be permitted to die without Viaticum who asked for it, he gave "a small bit of the

Eucharist" to the boy to take to his grandfather. The boy hastened home and to the great joy of the old man gave him Holy Communion. A moment later he was dead (Euseb. *E.H.* 6.44.1–6).

The bishop of Alexandria saw in this preservation of the man's life a divine approbation of the milder practice. For us the telling of this nightly episode is a very clear indication of the role played by the Eucharist in the lives of the Christians during the centuries of persecution.

The long period of waiting which even the milder bishops imposed upon the penitents had the disadvantage of frequently depriving the faithful of their souls' nourishment at the very time when they most needed it. This was something which did not escape the watchful eye of Cyprian. After the Decian persecution, in accordance with the traditional ecclesiastical discipline, he had excluded from the sacraments all those who had fallen, and in Carthage these could be numbered by the thousands, nor was he moved by earnest entreaties to grant absolution before the prescribed time except in the case of sickness. In the winter 252–253 hardly a year had passed since the persecution, and Cyprian was of the opinion that he should prolong the penance of those who had lapsed from the faith. Rumors, however, now began to be spread that the new emperor Gallus was about to initiate another persecution. Cyprian therefore wrote to Pope Cornelius it was time that "we should gather into the army of the Lord each and every soldier of Christ who wishes to bear arms and asks for battle. . . . And we should not leave those whom we arouse to combat naked and defenseless, but we should strengthen them with the body and blood of Christ since the purpose of the Eucharist is to be a safeguard to those who receive it" (*Ep.* 67.1–2).

Since the Eucharist played such an important role in the lives of the early Christians, it should be a foregone conclusion that at least some traces of it should be found in the ancient cemeteries.

Among the most important of these references to the Eucharist are those connected with the famous martyr Tarsicius. His tomb was to be found in the mausoleum of Pope Zephyrinus, as is sufficiently indicated by the cult which was there given to him. The proximate circumstances of his martyrdom may be derived from the epigram which Damasus wrote for him. The story is so unique and so different from the legendary motifs of later times that we may confidently regard it as historical. According to Damasus, Tarsicius was carrying "the Sacrament of Christ. When the raging mob demanded that he show it to them, he chose to yield up his life under their blows rather than to betray the heavenly members to the rabid hounds."[7]

We should like to know who this Tarsicius was. Damasus compares him with the proto-martyr Stephen, who also was slain by a tumultuous mob. He attributes to both "an equal service," but the particular circumstances were different. Stephen was killed by the Jews; the occasion was his preaching of the faith to them. He was stoned; and thus, in a certain sense, his enemies themselves erected his memorial. He was the first of all the martyrs; he was a "true Levite." Damasus then draws the contrast between this martyrdom and that of Tarsicius: the particulars of his death were different, but his service was the same. So much for the general structure of the epigram.

From this it may be concluded that Tarsicius was no "Levite," but a layman. That a layman should carry the sacred mysteries was indeed something extraordinary, but it was not impossible as the story of Serapion as told by Dionysius of Alexandria clearly indicates. The *fermentum,* the consecrated particles used in the sacred liturgy in the titular churches, at least in the time of Pope Innocent I (401–417), were carried by the acolytes.[8] Both deacons and acolytes were grown men. Boys were admitted to the lectorate, but there is no evidence that the sacred mysteries were ever entrusted to the lectors.

The later legend, which appears to be nothing more than an elaboration of Damasus' inscription, has actually made of

Tarsicius a boy, and under this guise he has since become famous in Wiseman's *Fabiola* as the saintly server, the martyred minor seminarian. It is quite possible that this was actually the case. But whatever it may have been, there can be no doubt about the reality of this extraordinary martyrdom.

The inscription of Damasus plainly shows us that the ancient Christians believed in the real presence of Christ in the Blessed Sacrament, and not only at the moment of consecration or of communion. They were certain that the "heavenly members" of Christ, to use the expression of Damasus, were at all times hidden under the consecrated species.

A question of particular interest to visitors to the catacombs is whether or not, and if so, when and how, Mass was celebrated in the catacombs. It is a question of capital import for an understanding of early Christianity. Since the ordinary Eucharistic services during the first centuries were held within the city in what were later known as the "titular churches," the rites observed in the cemeteries could not have been the regular religious ceremonies of the community. They were rather a liturgical cult of the dead, or from the end of the third century, a memorial service for the martyrs, or possibly a secret Mass during a time of persecution.

From the fourth century on, when the great cemeterial basilicas were erected above ground, the Holy Sacrifice of the Mass was as a rule offered in them by priests particularly appointed for this purpose.[9] There are, however, in some cemeteries rooms which are frequently described as "underground basilicas." One of these is to be found in the *coemeterium Maius* on the Via Nomentana. On each side of a corridor near the steps leading down into the cemetery are double connecting rooms. Their walls are lined with tombs. There is a fifth room, or *cubiculum*, without any sepulchers at the end of the longitudinal axis of these four *cubicula*. In it there is a *cathedra*, or throne, and to the right and left of it, running along the wall, are benches which have been hewed out of the tufa. That this is a room in which the Eucharistic sacrifice was offered is very probable, but the whole construction comes only from the fourth century. Likewise, the altar in the crypt of St. Pamphilus on the Via Salaria Vetus belongs at the earliest to the fifth or sixth century.[10]

That altars are nowhere to be found in the crypts is no proof that Masses were never celebrated there. For a long time, it is true, it was believed that altars were to be found in the cemeteries. These were identified with the so-called *sepolcri a mensa*, or *arcosolia*, and it was believed that Mass was celebrated on the horizontal slab beneath the arch of such a tomb. But many of these tombs appear to be entirely unsuited for such a purpose since they are much too high or too low, and at times located in very narrow corridors. But it is perhaps unnecessary to look for altars since in ancient times a fixed altar for the consecration of the Eucharist was not essential.

Paul indeed speaks of "the table of the Lord," in contrast to "the table of devils" (1 Cor. 10.21), and Cyprian of "another altar" which the schismatics erected. Ignatius even uses the Greek word for "sacrificial altar." But these expressions at best indicate only the Eucharistic sacrifice and the Communion rite, not a definite piece of liturgical furniture. One of the very reasons why the Christians were called atheists was that they had neither temples nor altars.[11] Any kind of a support on which the linen cloth could be spread and the chalice placed sufficed. There was no missal to be carried from side to side, and no candles on the altar. Consequently, a small flat surface was all that was needed, a table of any sort, a pedestal, or a stone column. In the painting in "the Chapel of the Sacraments" in Callistus the *Ichthys*, or "Fish," lies with the bread upon a round, three-legged table of the same design as those which we so frequently meet in old Roman household furniture. In the Gnostic *Thomas' Acts* an incident is narrated during the course of which an ordinary household bench was used for celebrating the Eucharist.[12] In case of necessity, a flat supporting surface could be entirely dispensed with. The bishop Theodoret of Cyrus († 458) tells us that he once offered the Holy Sacrifice in the cell of a hermit which was completely lacking in furniture. He therefore had one of his deacons simply hold the sacred vessels in his hands (*Hist. relig.* 20). At Antioch the priest Lucian was bound to the floor of the prison, and he there celebrated "the tremendous sacrifice" of the Mass with the sacred vessels placed upon his own breast (Philostorgius 2.13). It is thus conceivable that the Eucharist was celebrated in the catacombs without it being necessary to find traces today of permanently fixed stone altars.

Mere possibility is, nevertheless, no proof that this was actually the case. We have no positive evidence for the celebration of the Eucharist in the catacombs prior to the erection of the cemeterial basilicas.

At a very early date the liturgy for the dead came into use. This was certainly celebrated as closely as possible to the tomb, but we do not know the rite, nor do we know what place the Eucharist had in it. It is probable that fixed memorial days were solemnized by the consecration of the Eucharist. In the apocryphal *Acts of John,* which belong perhaps to the second century, it is related that "at dawn on the third day" John came to the tomb of Drusianna with Andronicus and the brethren "in order that we might there break the bread."[13]

From the middle of the second century the state looked upon the cemeteries with suspicion. Undoubtedly this was connected with the cult of the martyrs which was evolving at this time, and which could be regarded as a protest against the edicts of persecution. Such an interpretation could have easily arisen if near the tombs of the martyrs real religious services were held, which would probably have been associated with the celebration of the Eucharist.

There is thus a definite probability that the Eucharist was offered for the dead in the catacombs, and later in honor of the martyrs. On the other hand, the fond opinion of former years that in times of persecution the regular liturgical services of the community were held in the subterranean cemeteries is to be entirely rejected. Nowhere in the catacombs are there rooms spacious enough for a fairly numerous congregation. There was no more security in the cemeteries than in the city churches, but rather less. The cemeteries were known to the police, but this was not necessarily the case with the city churches. These were rooms in private dwellings which differed exteriorly in no wise from other houses. An individual might hide himself in one of the cemeteries, but not a great multitude of the faithful, who had to make their way out and back through the gates of the city and along highways stretching across the open Campagna. A secret gathering could be much more easily held in a private house. If the police got wind of such a meeting place, Mass could be offered in another.

We have, then, no extant witness from antiquity that community services were held in the cemeteries. The only incident which perhaps points in this direction is that of the martyrdom of Pope Xystus. His arrest took place in "the cemetery" while he was preaching. There was usually a sermon in conjunction with the Eucharistic sacrifice, and it hardly seems probable that he would have been preaching in the country on a less solemn occasion. We do not know the circumstances which brought about the interruption of this service by the persecutors, but whatever they were, the gathering itself seems to have been something of an exception.

CHAPTER IX

BAPTISM

IT CANNOT properly be maintained that in Christian antiquity baptism played a more important role than it does today. The theological value of baptism as the sacrament of rebirth and incorporation into the Church is as real today as it was in the days of Tertullian and Cyprian. Within the family the day of a child's baptism is celebrated as a feast, and it is surrounded with tender and loving customs. Christians regard it as the height of impiety and irreligion to neglect the baptism of an infant.

There is a difference, however, in that the baptism of adults in antiquity was much more frequent than it is today. Still we must not imagine that the early Christian communities were composed almost exclusively of converts. Everywhere there were numerous Christians who had been born in Christian families and who had been baptized soon after birth. When Polycarp, the bishop of Smyrna, told the judge that he had already served his Lord for eighty-six years, this meant that he had been a Christian that long, and as a consequence that he had received baptism in his very early youth (Euseb. *E.H.* 4.15.20). The earliest church ordinances, such as the *Didascalia* from the beginning of the third century, mention the children who had their own place in church and were present for the whole divine service. They must thus have been baptized. In antiquity the Eucharist was given immediately after baptism even to very small children. Cyprian speaks of a *puella parvula*, a "little girl," who had not reached the use of reason, who refused the chalice when it was offered to her by a deacon (*De lapsis* 25). The same Cyprian opposed the strange opinion of some that baptism should only be given on the eighth day after birth since in the Old Testament that was time for circumcision. The bishop of Carthage saw no reason why Baptism could not be given on the second or third day after birth (*Ep.* 64.2).

In such circumstances the frequent mention of baptism in the inscriptions may cause a certain amount of surprise. For the most part these inscriptions come from the fourth century, when it was the custom even in Christian families to put off baptism as long as possible. We thus find such epitaphs as that of the infant Aristo who died as a neophyte at the age of eight months in 389, and also those of much older children such as that of the nine-year-old Romanus who died shortly after baptism in 371.[1]

The word *baptismus,* or *baptisma,* almost never appears in the catacombal inscriptions. Usually such expressions as *fidem accepit* ("he received the faith"), or *accepta gratia Dei* ("having received the grace of God") or more briefly *accepit* ("he received") or *consectus est* ("he obtained") were used. Still more frequent is the designation *neophytus,* literally the "newly-planted," or *neophotistus,* "the newly illuminated."

The faithful of the Pentecostal community in Jerusalem were, of course, immediately baptized; but as early as the years of St. Paul's preaching there seems to have been a fixed period of waiting for his proselytes. In the second century Justin records a rather long period of preparation for baptism, and in Tertullian the word *catechumeni* appears for the first time. Tertullian also mentions Easter and Pentecost as being days set aside for solemn baptism, but he adds that for the reception of the grace of the sacrament any day and any hour are the same as any others (*De bapt.* 19).

In the fourth century solemn preparation for baptism reached its peak. A distinction was now made between the ordinary catechumens and the *competentes,* or *photizomenoi,* who had presented themselves as candidates for the reception of baptism on the following Easter. Their special preparation began with *Quadragesima.* When the list of *competentes* had been drawn up, the scrutinies began in the presence of the bishop. These are already mentioned in the early third century by Hippolytus. Each individual was examined as to whether or not he was suitable, a special inquiry being made into his profession. Soothsayers, servants in the temples, and in fact all who had anything to do with the pagan cults were excluded, likewise all who took part in the public spectacles — actors, gladiators, and professional athletes. In the fourth century, however, a milder attitude was taken toward these latter. In his *Apostolic Tradition* Hippolytus states that school teachers could be baptized if they had no other means of livelihood (16.13). Husbands and wives had to have their marriages regularized.

Then the proximate preparation began. All had to appear daily for the catechetical instruction of the bishop. The Creed was learned by heart and had to be recited. Those who had been baptized earlier could assist at these catechetical instructions as auditors, and they did so with great earnestness, as we know from the account of Etheria, the pilgrim to Jerusalem.[2] At this time also repeated blessings, exorcisms, and other liturgical ceremonies were conducted for the aspirants for baptism. In the baptistery during the night of Holy Saturday, the bishop conferred the sacrament, and on Easter morning the newly baptized received their First Holy Communion. During the whole of Easter week they still had to remain together. Clothed in the white garment which they had put on after baptism, they received from the bishop the final "mystagogical" catechesis, during which they were instructed in the mysteries proper to their religion, especially with regard to the doctrine of the Eucharist, about which up to that time only passing references had been made.

This solemn instruction was, of course, meant for adults. As a matter of fact, the cessation of the bloody persecutions in the fourth century brought in a mighty influx of new Christians, but at this same time even within Christian families there came in the pernicious practice of postponing the baptism of children as long as possible. This was partially due to the ever increasing severity of public penance. The sacrament of penance was surrounded with the same type of solemn rites as baptism, so that it came to be regarded as a definite conclusion to a life of penance. The conviction arose that absolution, at least solemn absolution, could be received but once in a lifetime. There was thus a natural desire to receive it as near as possible to the end of life. In Cyprian's time no such opinion was prevalent. The many *lapsi* of the Decian persecution received absolution without great difficulty, even if they had completed a public penance before their latest fall. Later, when the use of the sacrament of penance was so greatly restricted, catechumens were anxious to put off baptism until ripe old age to escape at least the necessity of obtaining absolution in the sacrament of penance for the sins of their youth. There thus arose the evil custom of permanent catechumens who regarded themselves as Christians, but who hesitated from year to year to present themselves as candidates for baptism. With astonishment we hear how even fervent Christian parents acquiesced in this abuse. St. Augustine tells us that as a boy he fell into a serious illness and longed for baptism. He earnestly begged this favor from his mother "and from the mother of us all, the Church." Monica was on the point of yielding to his request, and would have done so if he had not suddenly recovered (*Conf.* 1.11). Perhaps Augustine would have been spared all the errors of his later life if he had been baptized at this time. Other saints of this period, such as Basil and Chrysostom, both of whom had saintly mothers, also received baptism only as adults. A special case was that of Ambrose who was baptized only after he had been elected bishop.

There are numerous instances, especially of individuals of high rank, who put off their baptism until old age, if not even to their very deathbed. The emperor Constantine received baptism only a few days before he died, and the same is true of his son Constantius. The prefect of the city, Junius Bassus, whose beautiful sarcophagus is to be found in the Vatican grottoes, also died as a neophyte in 359 at the age of forty-two, as his inscription indicates. Many of these permanent catechumens must have been overtaken by death before they could receive the sacrament. Of these also the catacombal inscriptions furnish sad examples: a Boniface who died in the year 397 at the age of forty as a catechumen; a Greek Andragathos, a thirty-five-year-old catechumen; a Sozomena, who was overtaken by death as an *audiens*, that is, a catechumen who had not received baptismal instructions; and there are others.[3]

This unwarranted postponement of baptism was a grave abuse, and we are surprised that even zealous and prudent pastors failed to oppose it energetically. On the other hand, it cannot be denied that this abuse also had its wholesome effects. There was hardly ever a time when such an earnest and careful preparation was made for baptism, and when the sacrament itself was so devoutly received, as in the fourth century. Some of the most precious writings of the Fathers, for example, the *catecheses* of Cyril of Jerusalem, Ambrose, and Gregory of Nyssa, would perhaps never have been written if the majority of Christians of the time had been baptized as children. We have a comparable case for this in the unwarrantedly long delay for the reception of First Holy Communion in the nineteenth century, which similarly brought with it an extraordinarily earnest and profound preparation for this sacrament.

Liturgical sources, especially the *Ordo Romanus VII* and the *Gelasian Sacramentary,* enable us to reconstruct in detail the baptismal ceremonies which took place during "the great night" in the Lateran basilica. To be sure, we have to deal here with the ceremonies of the fifth and sixth centuries, and thus of the period of highest liturgical development at Rome. In the preceding centuries, we may presume, many of the details were simpler.

The Easter baptisms attracted a great concourse of people from all over Christian Rome to the Lateran, where at the same time the papal station was being observed.[4] On no other day or night did the Lateran basilica embrace in its aisles so many people as on the occasion of the reverent keeping of the vigil, the baptisms, and the Solemn Mass of Easter. The Christian poet Prudentius, who visited Rome in the first years of the fifth century, describes the long files of faithful who hastened past the former temples of the gods to the Lateran to receive "the sacred sign of royal chrism" (*Contra Symmach.* 1.586). By the word "chrism" is meant the sacrament of confirmation, which the neophytes received immediately after baptism.

On the evening of Holy Saturday the pope, the entire clergy, and those who were to be baptized and their sponsors made their entrance into the basilica. In Constantinople some three thousand catechumens were baptized on Easter in the year 404 (Palladius, *Dialog. de vita S. Joh. Chrys.* 9). We may presume that there was a similar number at Rome at this time. After the procession had entered, a deacon ascended the ambon and began the *Praeconium Paschale,* today's *Exultet.* The *lumen Christi,* or "light of Christ," was already in the sixth century symbolized by the Easter candle. All of the lamps in the crowded church were then lit. It was a dramatic representation of the light brought by Christ into the world. In the splendid Lateran basilica it was all the more impressive, since the rich marble columns, the walls covered with polished stone, the gilded ceiling of the nave, the gold and silver vessels on the high altar, and the seven richly adorned side altars used only on this day shone with the light of the lamps, and reflecting the beams shot them racing again about the crowded church. There next followed the blessing of the baptismal water, during the course of which the Easter candle was dipped into it. This symbolically expressed the fact that the divine light of grace kindled in each neophyte ought not to be extinguished before death. The use of light throughout the ceremonies was a reminder of the Lord's resurrection and of the acceptance of the faith by those regenerated in the sacrament of rebirth.

After long passages from the Old Testament had been read, those who were to be baptized left the basilica, probably through an exit in the apse, with the pope and clerics for the neighboring baptistery. One after the other the archdeacon presented the candidates to the pope, who asked each of them brief questions about their faith, which they answered in a word or two. The one to be baptized then descended into the baptismal water, which was only high enough to cover his feet. Three times water was poured over him while the words of baptism were being pronounced. Guided by the hand of his sponsor, he then came out of the water and put on the white garment which he would wear until the following Sunday, *Dominica in Albis*. Baptism was followed by confirmation, which from the time of Pope Hilary (461–468) was conferred in the adjacent oratory of the Holy Cross which had been specifically erected for this purpose.

By this time it was early morning, and the procession returned to the basilica where Mass was celebrated and the newly baptized received their First Holy Communion. With this, the ceremonies, which closely correspond to the new liturgy of Holy Saturday, came to an end at the Lateran. The only Easter Sunday Mass was celebrated in Santa Maria Maggiore.[5]

The Lateran baptistery stands today in substantially the same condition as it was when it was erected by Pope Xystus III (432–440). The upper portions of it and the cupola were renovated by the Renaissance popes, but the eight beautiful porphyry columns over the baptismal font are original. Xystus III built the octagon upon earlier foundations, namely, those of the baptistery dating from the time of Constantine, a rotunda with the same diameter as the later eight-sided structure. The latest investigations, which were carried through by J. B. Giovenale, have further demonstrated that this baptistery erected under Pope Silvester (314–336) was not the earliest on this site.[6] The foundations of still another round edifice of a much smaller diameter were found beneath it. This pre-Constantinian baptistery was built into one of the baths of the Lateran palace. When was it erected?

We know that Pope Melchiades (311–314) held a council in 314 in the Lateran palace. It is presumed that by this time Constantine had already given the palace to the pope. Constantine's wife Fausta had inherited it from her father, the emperor Maximian Herculeus. Melchiades may have built there the first baptistery, which his successor Silvester replaced with the larger building. Still it is not impossible that the pre-Constantinian baptistery was erected even earlier. The ancient Aedes Lateranorum had become an extensive complex of different buildings loosely connected together. Septimius Severus (193–211) had erected there a barracks for the imperial equestrian bodyguard, the *Equites Singulares*. Later Constantine, after the battle of the Milvian bridge, disbanded the corps and built on the site formerly occupied by the barracks the great Lateran basilica.[7] In the long period of peace before the persecution of 303, when the Christians were on good terms with the imperial court, they could have obtained possession of a part of the elaborate complex for a place of worship. This would also explain why Constantine later gave the whole palace to the Christians, and why he built the great basilica on this particular site. However this may be, it is at least certain that from the year 313 at the very latest, the papal baptistery has been located here. The tradition has never been broken, and the baptistery is still used today.

We do not know whether or not baptism was ever administered in the catacombs. In several places in the cemeteries there are wells from which spring water may be drawn, but this does not necessarily imply that the water was used for baptism. The

only known subterrranean baptistery is found in the cemetery
of Pontianus on the Via Portuensis, but it was built in the fifth
or sixth century in a pre-existing room for the use of the people
dwelling on the Campagna, and was probably connected with
the cemeterial church.[8]

CHAPTER X

THE PEOPLE OF GOD

In an ordinary tour of the catacombs a pilgrim to Rome sees hardly more than a few dozen inscriptions. He therefore obtains no adequate notion of the amount and meaning of the extant epigraphical material. In the past century De Rossi estimated that there were around fifteen thousand Christian inscriptions coming from the environs of Rome. The number today must be considerably more than twenty thousand. By far the greater number of these come from the cemeteries, but only a small fraction of them are now found there. The rest are preserved in Rome and other Italian cities, and also in museums outside of Italy. In Rome many of the inscriptions were cemented to the walls in the vestibules of the old basilicas and hence are easily to be seen, for example, in Santa Maria in Trastevere, San Silvestro, and in the cloisters of San Paolo, San Lorenzo, and Santi Quattro Coronati, which have become regular museums of Christian antiquity. Many inscriptions, however, even after their discovery have been again lost and are only preserved in transcripts.

Unfortunately there does not yet exist a complete corpus of Christian inscriptions. Of the more recent publications, the collection begun by De Rossi and continued by Gatti and Silvagni is fundamental. More accessible is the collection of Diehl, which also takes into account Christian inscriptions outside of Rome, but it does not include Greek inscriptions.[1] Apart from these works we have only monographs at our disposal.

Most Christian inscriptions are easily read (pl. 2), though from the fourth century on they decline in quality, not only in spelling and grammar, but also stylistically. But even the later inscriptions are not so poorly written as to be indecipherable even to the laity. An exception, however, must be made for the cursive Greek *graffiti,* which require special study.

Latin is by far the more common language for the Christian inscriptions of Rome. Noteworthy is the fact that Latin inscriptions written in Greek characters are not rarely found. As an example of one of these we may cite the following from the year 269: ΛΕΥΚΕΣ ΦΕΛΕΙΕ ΣΕΒΗΡΕ ΚΑΡΕΣΣΕΜΕ ΠΟΣΟΥΕΤΕ, which reads when transliterated: *Lucius filiae Severae carissimae posuit.* . . .[2] Such inscriptions are important for philologists since they indicate the change that took place in the pronunciation of Latin. The reason for this strange usage of Greek letters for Latin words is to be sought less in the fact that the particular individuals may have been Greeks than in the fact that the Greek script which they had learned in school was more familiar to them. Roman children at times first learned the Greek alphabet, and only afterward the Latin. The reason why many of the inscriptions were written entirely in Greek may, of course, be due to the fact that the individuals were Greeks by birth, but this was not exclusively the case. It seems that Christians liked to use Greek in their inscriptions because it was the old language of the liturgy. The papal inscriptions up to the end of the third century were written in Greek, though certainly not all of these popes were Greeks.

In antiquity Christian proper names were no different from those of their pagan countrymen. Biblical names are late and rare, as are also such strange religious appellations as *Quodvultdeus* or *Habetdeus.* No objection was made to names with a mythological origin. Christian parents named their children Aphrodisia, Dionysius, and Apollonius without scruple.

Because of the great number of Greek proper names among both pagans and Christians, it must not be concluded, as sometimes happens, that at certain epochs Rome was a Greek-speaking community. It is true that at every period of Roman history except the very earliest very many Greeks lived in Rome, but so did many others from every other part of the empire. But in spite of this, the great majority of the community was always Latin. When parents gave their children Greek names, they were either merely following the fashion, or they simply did not regard such common names as "Dionysius," "Agapitus," and "Sebastianus" as being foreign. Thus we find very frequently within the same family both Latin and Greek names.

"Barbarian" names are rare, though at least from the fourth century a constantly increasing number of foreigners, especially from the North, flowed into Rome. But they quickly adopted Roman manners and Roman names. Thus, when an inscription with such a name as "Adabrandus" is discovered, it can be dated from the sixth century or even later.[3]

The city of Rome, like our modern metropolises, grew in size as a result of migrations to the city. In the late empire there were only a very few families which had lived in Rome for generations. Ancient Rome, no less than our large modern cities, was a melting pot in which the various elements took on a certain uniform culture, in this case Latin and Roman.

The ordinary spoken language of all these old and new Latins was, of course, no longer the speech of Cicero. This is definitely shown by the inscriptions. From the second century after Christ at the latest, the pronunciation of Latin underwent a profound change. The case endings were no longer pronounced in their entirety. Grammar as a consequence fell into a state of confusion. The uneducated simply wrote phonetically, for example, *in aeternu dolore,* without knowing whether this should indicate *in aeternum dolorem* or *in aeterno dolore.*[4] Many consonants were softened, and it was no longer known how they should be written. There thus came into existence such forms as *quesquet* for *quiescit, baptidiare* for *baptizare, Zesus* for *Jesus.* "B" and "V," and "E" and "I" were constantly being interchanged. *Staviles* was written instead of *stabilis, bibet* instead of *vivit*. On the other hand, since there were always people who had received a formal education, in every century we come across Christian inscriptions composed in more or less good hexameters.

In the year 300, toward the end of the persecutions, Rome must still have had half a million inhabitants, of which only a fraction, hardly a seventh were Christians. In the later period of peace this proportion constantly increased in favor of the Christians. Hence the majority of Christian inscriptions are from the fourth and fifth centuries. In the sixth century Rome was finally a Christian city, but the population had so decreased that for the reign of Gregory the Great, around 600, the inhabitants could be numbered at most in tens of thousands. From this time on the inscriptions practically cease.

Even when the Christians still formed only a small minority in the community, they lived scattered throughout the city like the rest of the citizens, and not in a ghetto or in subterranean caves.

As early as the turn of the second century Tertullian objected to the accusation that the Christians were unsocial and formed a cast apart: "How is it that we are called a burden to the community, we who live with you, who eat the same food, wear the same clothing, have the same furniture and other necessities of life? We are not Brahmans or Indian yogis, dwellers in the woods, and exiles from civil life. . . . We live in this world with you, making use of your forum, meatmarket, baths, inns, shops, fares, markets, and every other commercial venture. We sail, serve in the army, go on vacations, and trade with you. We mix with you and even publish our works for you to use" (*Apol.* 42.1–3).

All of this is confirmed in the fullest manner by the inscriptions. Every conceivable civil avocation appears there. We find among the Christians a baker from the *XII Regio Piscina Publica* (the environs of San Saba and the Baths of Caracalla), who died in the year 401 at the age of forty-five; a smith from the Subura; a linen-weaver also from the Subura; a tanner buried in Commodilla; a seamstress buried in Callistus; a painter; a stone mason; a *quadratarius*, or one who carved inscriptions; a *montanarius*, that is, a professional miner, who as it seems did not belong to the ecclesiastical corporation of the *fossores*, or "diggers," but who still, as is recorded on his epitaph, "had worked in all the cemeteries."[5]

In Commodilla was the tomb of an *elephantarius*, that is, a dealer or worker in ivory. From Hermes comes the inscription of a *pastillarius*, one who was by profession a druggist or perfumer. Like other artisans, the *pastillarii* formed a corporation, and we have the inscription of Marcellus, the president of a druggists' union, who died in 435. Inscriptions of confectioners, barbers, and veterinarians are also found, to mention only a few of the other professions represented.[6]

Activities usually associated with a farm also had a limited sphere within the city. In the inscriptions reference is made to a gardener, a fruit grower, and even to a swineherd.[7]

There were others who occupied positions in the state as magistrates or as minor officials. Cucumio, who during his lifetime had the great inscription, which is still admired by visitors to Domitilla, made for himself and his wife Victoria, was employed as a clothes-keeper in the Baths of Caracalla. Another was a secretary to the *praefectus vigilum*. The *vigiles* were the members of the city fire department, but they formed at the same time a kind of police force. Sallustius Severianus was secretary to the highest official in the city, the *praefectus urbi* — the prefect of the city. This was a position which could easily have led to further advancement had he not died in 402 at the age of twenty-two. Among the officials there was also an *horrearius*, who was probably the administrator of the public granaries. In the imperial palace on the Palatine there were always high officials, though the emperor seldom lived there any more. Thus we find a Christian buried in 404 who had been the *vestitor imperatoris*, or emperor's valet.[8]

The offices of notary, teacher, and doctor are frequently represented in the Christian inscriptions. From the *coemeterium ad Catacumbas* comes the sarcophagus of a doctor who was not only renowned for his talent, but also kind, and not eager for the goods of the poor. Doctors from foreign lands seem to have been particularly trusted. We find among the Christian physicians a Spaniard with the barbarian name of "Rapetiga," who died in 388, and another with the genuine African name of "Miggin." Lawyers and advocates are also found.[9]

Christian soldiers of every grade in the army are very numerous. An Aurelianus, whose inscription is now in the Lateran museum, was for thirty years a centurion. How rarely the extraction of an individual can be determined from his name is shown by the inscription of a high Christian officer, which is also to be found in the Lateran museum. His father bore the Latin name "Lupicinus," he himself the Greek name "Heraclius," yet his native country was Raetia Secunda, which is now lower Bavaria.[10]

If one walks through the famous cemetery of Staglieno in Genoa and admires the precious monuments of wealthy families, he will surely come upon the finely wrought marble flower vendor who all her life saved up her money in order to be able to erect such an expensive memorial. More than a thousand years earlier this ambition of the Genoese flower vendor had already inspired a Roman vegetable woman. Her tomb, which comes from the middle of the fourth century, is still to be seen in the catacomb of Callistus. She did not, indeed, go so far as to erect a marble statue for herself, but she nonetheless succeeded in obtaining what could only have been granted to rather well-to-do Christians, that is, her own *arcosolium*. On the rear wall is painted her picture as she stands between two tables laden with different kinds of vegetables, and in front of her is another basket with more of the same. Unfortunately, the upper part of the figure has been destroyed. In the vault of the arch are birds and flowers, an easily understandable allusion to paradise.

Another sepulchral fresco leads us away from the humble life of a vegetable vendor into the turbulent activity of the ancient circus performers. The tomb is in a catacomb under the Vigna Massimo on the Via Salaria Nuova. Because of the secular character of the tombs in this area, it was long held that this was a pagan catacomb. However, through the discovery of a new part of this same catacomb, the tireless investigations of Wilpert have succeeded in showing its indubitable Christian character.

Our *arcosolium* is from the fourth century, and its paintings are in a sad state of preservation. Nevertheless, with the help of old copies of the paintings, the extant parts can be completed with certainty. The lunette in the rear of the *arcosolium* contains within a circle the portrait bust of a young man, obviously of the one who was buried there. The other pictures indicate his profession. On the front wall of the sepulcher are two Victories with palms and crowns. In the vault of the arch, a charioteer with a span of four horses is twice represented. In his right hand he holds a crown and in his left a palm. Palm and crown were the trophies which were bestowed upon the victor in a chariot race. We thus have here the tomb of a young charioteer who had won crowns and palms in the races. From the green feather on the head of one of the horses, it may rightly be deduced that the dead charioteer was in the service of the Greens, or at least that he had won for them his most glorious victories.

The ancient charioteers may be compared in many ways with the jockeys of today. Often coming from the lower strata of society, they could achieve fame and fortune in their vocation. In ancient Rome there were four parties of charioteers which competed against each other. Just as today football and basketball teams are distinguished by the colors they wear, so also the four parties of charioteers had their different colors. They were divided into the Whites, Reds, Blues, and Greens. The enthusiasm for this sport and the general interest of the Roman populace was so great that these parties divided up not only the fans among the youths of Rome, but even the empire. The solidarity of the parties and their influence was extraordinary and entered deeply into politics. Not infrequently the emperors themselves were adherents of one or other of these parties, and were consequently at odds with the others. The Blues and Greens were the strongest, and later united. According to a rumor of the times, the emperor Caligula, a fanatic follower of the Greens, had the horses and drivers of the opposing parties put to death. He personally entered the races as a charioteer, as did Nero, Commodus, and Caracalla in later years. Nero wore the colors of the Greens; the emperor Vitellius, on the other hand, alligned himself with the Blues and had this party to thank for his elevation to the principate. The fanaticism of the throngs was so great that on one occasion, according to Pliny, when the body of one of the heroes of the Reds was being cremated, one of the fans hurled himself into the flames and was there burned with the dead charioteer. Statues of the most renowned victors were erected all over Rome, and even famous poets were not ashamed to sing the praises of the heroes of the circus. The income of the most popular charioteers can only be compared with that of our greatest movie stars. Juvenal estimated that the income of a star of the Reds was equal to the income of a hundred advocates. Even if this conjecture is exaggerated, it still must have been a fantastic sum.[11]

Only from our grave under the Vigna Massimo do we know that there were Christian charioteers. Rome of the fourth and fifth centuries was substantially Christian just like its mighty rival on the Bosphorus, yet the rivalry among the charioteers and the partisanship of their followers persisted without a letup. That it still persisted in the sixth century is known from the famous revolution of Nika in Constantinople.

It can easily be imagined that the Church did not look with favor upon the games in the circus with their excesses and the boundless rivalry of the various factions. Pope Leo the Great complained bitterly that the spectacles attracted more people than the stations of the martyrs. But the circus-mad Christians did not care to give them up, and brought to their defense the example of Elias who was carried into heaven on a chariot.

We perhaps do no great injustice to our Christian charioteer if we do not count him among the most fervent Christians. Or is it an accident that on this Christian tomb there is no particular indication of Christian beliefs, but only the portrayal of a very worldly profession? Near the tomb of the charioteer is located another of a soldier and his family. Here also there is lacking any sign of Christianity. In the lunette of the *arcosolium* the soldier is represented with his spear and round shield, and dressed in a long tunic and chlamys, or mantle. Next to him stands a boy, probably his son. In the vault is a portrait bust of the soldier, and on the right side of the tomb he appears for a third time, but here dressed in a *tunica succincta*, or short tunic, with a drawn sword. This picture is balanced on the left by the portrait of a woman with a child, doubtlessly mother and son.

Quite near the entrance to the catacomb of Priscilla there is a beautiful little burial chamber with an unusual, crudely executed painting that has given rise to various interpretations (pl. 29). Thus, for example, it has been taken for a picture of eight martyrs condemned to draw water. Let us take a closer look at it. On the left are two large barrels lying next to each other upon the ground. On the right are two groups of four men each who with poles slung upon their shoulders are moving a third large barrel. Wilpert has rightly recognized the fact that this picture does not represent a religious theme but is the sepulchral portrait of a small coopers' union. This little group of workmen, who, as so frequently happened, possessed a common burial place, had themselves painted at their daily occupation just as the vegetable vendor and the charioteer.

Like the coopers in Priscilla, a group of Roman bakers owned a burial chamber in the catacomb of Domitilla. This is adorned with more accurate and richer paintings than the former. In the center stands the figure of the master baker dressed in his work clothes with a bushel filled with grain behind him. Underneath

186

Pl. 29. Fresco in the crypt of the coopers in the cemetery of Priscilla. The *graffiti* above the painting are more recent. The name of Antonius Bosius (✝ 1629) is plainly to be seen.

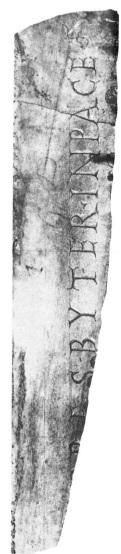

Pl. 30. An inscription, *presbyter in pace*, "a priest at peace," from Callistus.

runs a frieze which cleverly depicts the importation and transport of grain. At the time bakers not only had to take care of the preparation of the bread, but they also had to grind the grain.

The grain first came to Ostia, the ancient port of Rome, from the great granaries of the city such as Sicily, Sardinia, and Egypt. Here it was transferred to smaller boats and brought up the Tiber to the neighborhood of Aventine, where it was unloaded and brought into the warehouses of the *annona*, the bureau in charge of the wheat imported into Rome. From here it was then taken to the bakers. In our catacomb cycle we find represented on the left the transportation of grain from the ships to the public granaries. Three boats loaded with grain are anchored just off the bank of the Tiber. Ten workmen, who are supervised by two officials of the *annona*, carry the sacks from the boats to the warehouse. Some have sacks upon their shoulders. Others behind them are about to pick up other sacks. On the right side of the picture we see four workmen wearily tugging at poles, like the coopers in the catacomb of Priscilla, as they carry a heavily laden barrow of grain to the bakers. These latter are represented by a group of seven men earnestly engaged in conversation.

The bakers who commissioned the decoration of this crypt did not neglect to have their Christianity indicated in a very telling way. To the right next to the main picture, they had portrayed the miracle of the multiplication of the loaves.

Two more sepulchers belonging to this cycle of crafts and trades deserve to be noticed. In the neighborhood of the bakers' crypt is an *arcosolium* with the portrait of a wholesaler working with six assistants in his store. The marketing of oil and wine is to be seen in a fresco painted in the lunette of another *arcosolium* in the catacomb of Pontianus. In it a sailboat loaded with amphorae is depicted. A sailor is at the oars, while another holds the tiller. The owner of the tomb could thus have been a dealer in oil and wine or a boatman engaged in the transportation of goods on the Tiber.

There is no reason for believing that the occupations and professions of the Christians in the years of persecution were essentially different from those of the fourth and fifth centuries. Even if we had no dated inscriptions for this period, other sources would furnish the same picture. The Christian Minucius Felix, who about the year 200 wrote an apologetic work, the *Octavius,* was an advocate at Rome. Sextus Julius Africanus was appointed librarian for the Pantheon by the emperor Alexander Severus (222–235). He seems, however, to have professed a rather worldly type of Christianity. No Christian doctor is known for the earliest period of the Church at Rome. This is probably due to chance since there was one among the martyrs of Lyons in 177. There is considerable evidence for Christians in high and low positions in the imperial court, especially in the court of Valerian before he began the great persecution of 257. Six Christians were executed with Justin about 165, and of these, two were imperial slaves. Carpophorus, as we have already seen in the *Philosophumena* of Hippolytus, was an imperial freedman and patron of Callistus. Callistus himself, before his election to the papacy, had been a banker near the *piscina publica.* The numerous soldier martyrs are a proof that at all times there were Christians in the army.

In his treatise *De idololatria* Tertullian describes a whole series of professions and the difficulties which from his point of view they furnished a Christian who wished to avoid every semblance of idolatry. There can be no doubt that there actually were such difficulties since the whole of public and private life was shot through with religious ceremonies. Only Tertullian, in his fear of idolatry, goes much too far. He will not, for example, permit Christians to be artists or craftsmen engaged in the production of works of art because they would all too easily find themselves in the position of being actually employed in the manufacture of pagan cult objects. The necessity of acquiring an education is a sufficient excuse for a Christian's attendance at a pagan school, but Tertullian does not see how a Christian can teach pagan literature without approving the idolatry portrayed in it. He even considers the profession of a merchant as being hazardous, not only because of the dangers from avarice and cheating, but also because many of the goods sold in the shops, such as incense, would be used in pagan rites. He permits slaves, freedmen, and minor officials to be passively present at sacrifices offered by their superiors, but they must in no way co-operate in the ceremonies, for example, by presenting them with wine for a libation or assisting them to pronounce the sacrificial formulae. He admits the theoretical possibility of a Christian occuping a high public office, but since such a position would require the offering of sacrifices, the taking of oaths, the care of the temples, the staging of public games, and other duties forbidden to a Christian, it is practically impossible. He absolutely rejects military service. After describing the dangers confronting a Christian he concludes: "Faith guided by the Spirit of God sails between these rocks and bays, between these straits and shallows of idolatry, safely if it is careful, free from care if it is not frightened" (*De idol.* 24).

This treatise of Tertullian was written when as a Montanist he had given himself over to an intolerable rigorism. Though it does not at all represent the official attitude of the Church at this time, it is nevertheless highly instructive, for it shows that there were really great difficulties for Christians in public life, and also that there were many Christians who endeavored to master these difficulties.

We have a very remarkable inscription from the year 217. It is on a great sarcophagus from a sepulcher on the Via Labicana which is now preserved in the park of the Villa Borghese:

"To Marcus Aurelius Prosenes, freedman of the two emperors (Marcus Aurelius and Lucius Verus, or Marcus Aurelius and

Commodus), official of the imperial household, superintendent of the treasury, superintendent of the imperial patrimony, superintendent of the public spectacles, superintendent of wines, appointed by the divine Commodus to administer the barracks, to their most devoted and well-deserving patron, his freedmen from their own means have dedicated this sarcophagus."

This inscription is like that of many another high imperial official, and there is nothing particular in it to attract any special attention. But on the side of the sarcophagus, carved in small letters as if it were a timid postscript, may be read:

"Prosenes was taken up to God . . . (the day of the month and probably a place name are illegible) . . . in the consulship of Praesens and Extricatus for the second time (A.D. 217) while he was returning to Rome from the campaigns. His freedman Ampelius has written this."[12]

The phrase *receptus ad Deum* ("taken up to God") clearly indicates that Prosenes was a Christian. At the time of his death he was an old man since he had been emancipated before 180, if not before 169. Under five emperors, Marcus Aurelius, Commodus, Pertinax, Severus, and Caracalla, he had served in confidential posts of the highest order which brought him into constant contact with the emperors. He was certainly very wealthy, but at the time of his death he no longer had any living relatives. Probably he had accompanied the emperor Caracalla to Mesopotamia, and when the emperor was murdered April 8, 217, he had started home but was himself overtaken by death on the way. His body was brought to Rome by members of his household and solemnly buried in the usual pagan way. It is probable that only one of his freedmen knew that he was a Christian, but this one, whose name was Ampelius, and who was certainly himself a Christian, could not tolerate the thought that the tomb of his revered patron bore no indication of his Christian faith. He therefore carved the postscript on the stone.

What a difficult position must this prominent man have held in the imperial court with the daily danger of a conflict between his faith and his duty toward his emperor! Prosenes as *procurator munerum* was in charge of the imperial games, the baiting of wild beasts in the amphitheater, and the gladiatorial combats which marked the Roman feasts. During his whole career there was indeed no great persecution of the Christians at Rome, but he would certainly have known that in the year 202 his colleague in Carthage was compelled to loose the wild beasts upon Perpetua and Felicitas. On the other hand, Prosenes may have been in a position to do much service for the Church, not only with his great wealth, but also through his influence at court. He may have lent a helping hand to Marcia in the pardon which through her intercession Pope Victor obtained from Commodus for the Christians banished to Sardinia (Hippol. *Philosoph.* 9.12).

And yet this man must have led a lonely life. Even his death in a foreign land was lonely. None of his brethren could comfort him. Had he died at Rome, the priest Hippolytus would perhaps have edified him with learned quotations from Scripture; the deacon Callistus would have brought him Viaticum; and the bishop Zephyrinus would have anointed him with holy chrism. But as it was, he had to console himself on his lonely deathbed with the thought which his faithful Ampelius scratched in after times upon his sarcophagus: *Prosenes receptus ad Deum.*

In antiquity not only the names of the departed were immortalized upon their tombstones, but frequently the relatives who had erected the memorial were named as well. This has enabled us to obtain an intimate view into many a family circle.

The eulogies which the relatives engraved upon the tombstones are as a rule somewhat stereotyped, beginning with the very common *bene merenti* ("to the well-deserving"), which even appears on the graves of infants. The same is true in the constantly repeated protestations of husbands and wives that they had lived together *sine querela* ("without dissension"). On the other hand, these laudatory formulae, which are also found on non-Christian tombs, give the impression of a certain culture and refinement which is often in strange contrast with the barbaric orthography and grammar.

Surely it is more than an empty formula when a Christian affirms of his dead wife: "To a woman of singular modesty who always surrounded her husband with special affection"; or when another writes: "To a woman of admirable goodness and incomparable sanctity and exemplary chastity. Her life was marked by kindness, propriety, piety, and was in all things worthy of praise. She lived for thirty-three years, of which fifteen were with me, and never did she grieve me. She bore seven children, of whom four are with her near the Lord."[13]

When it is stated that a four-year-old child had been "marvelously innocent and wise," it seems to us to be somewhat exaggerated. But a father was obviously sincere when he wrote: "To my sweet son Dalmatius, a lad of great talent and wisdom. His unlucky father could not enjoy him for even seven full years. He learned to write Greek, and without any help taught himself how to write Latin."[14]

If such personal details are not precisely what we look for or what chiefly attract us in the catacombal inscriptions, they still reveal the humanity of the early Christians. They bring us closer to these men and women in showing us their family customs, their daily occupations, and their place within the community. We see that they lived in the midst of a world which despite all its differences was still the same as ours, that they tasted the joys and sorrows of life just as we do. But that which speaks loudest to our hearts from these stones is the common faith, the common hope in the hereafter which we share with all these forgotten little people, men, women, and children, and which actually enable us to stretch out our hands to them as to our true brothers and sisters.

Above all there is the formula repeated thousands of times — *in pace* (pl. 30). It is much more than a mere formula. It is an expression borrowed originally from the Jews, but which was used so extensively by the Christians that it became a mark of Christian burial almost as certain as the later monogram of Christ.[15] The profound content of this simple saying was keenly felt by the early Christians, as is shown by the many variations of the formula: *in pace Domini, in pace Dei, in pace Christi, in pace aeterna.*

This "peace" is much more than a mere rest, an absence of strife and pain. It is most properly the union with God, the enjoyment of God's company. The souls of the departed live a real life in this "peace." Thus it is well said: "May you sleep in the peace of the Lord!" "Live always in peace!" "Rejoice always in peace!" "May you live in the peace of God!"[16] Moreover, this "peace of God" in which the soul lives is not something which begins only with death. Its perfection, of course, comes only hereafter, but already on earth the Christian lives in peace. Hence we find frequently the formulae: "He died as a believer in peace." "He lived in peace as a believer." *Pax* can thus directly signify communion with the Church. A Roman inscription of the year 357 tells us that Quintianus was buried *in pace legitima.*[17] There was at this time in Rome the schism between Liberius and Felix. Thus, *in pace legitima* here means: "in union with the lawful Church."

This exactly corresponds with the terms employed by the early Christian writers, in whom there is found a frequent connection between *pax* and *communio.*[18] Even today the two are associated in the formula of the solemn papal encyclicals which are addressed to all those *pacem et communionem cum Apostolica Sede habentes* ("having peace and communion with the Apostolic See"). This does not mean, "Not being at odds!" but rather, "Being united with the pope in a supernatural society!" In a letter to Jerome, Augustine describes a young man as *Catholica pace frater* ("a brother in Catholic peace").[19] With that he wished to say, "He belongs to the Catholic Church, he is not a schismatic." Among the Greeks instead of *pax et communio* we find not rarely κοινωνία καὶ ἀγάπη ("communion and love" – Athanasius *Apol. c.*

Arianos 20). And even in Latin inscriptions instead of *in pace* we find *in agape*[20] — ἐν ἀγάπῃ.

The peace which the faithful departed find in God is a real life. Very frequently instead of "May you live in peace!" there is simply, "May you live in God!" On an inscription in the Lateran museum is engraved: *Semper in Deo vivas, dulcis anima* ("May you always live in God, sweet soul!"). Analogous turns are: "May you live in the Lord!" "May you live in the name of Christ!" "May you live in Christ!" "May you live in the Lord Jesus!" "May you live in the Holy Spirit!" and even "May you live among the saints!" "Your spirit be among the saints!"[21]

It is a life of happiness. "In peace and paradise" is found in an inscription from Carthage; "in peace and refreshment" is in another from the catacomb of Hermes. Often it appears as a life of light in contrast to the darkness on earth. An inscription in St. Praxedes from the year 397 reads: "Severianus here sleeps in the sleep of peace. . . . His soul has been taken into the light of the Lord." And one from the Lateran museum states: "Hermaeiskus, you live a light in God."[22]

In this afterlife the blessed are, moreover, in an excellent position to be mindful of, and to assist their brethren, left behind on earth.

A father writes upon the grave of his seven-year-old son: "Your soul rests in God. Pray for your sister." Apparently the man was a widower, and of his children only a girl survived, who was now his whole concern. Another writes: "Januaria, enjoy your happiness and pray for us!" On a long, partially destroyed inscription from Callistus may be seen: "I do not deserve to be united with God. Through your intercession obtain for me that God pardons my sins." Another prayer is recorded on an inscription now preserved on the Capitol: "Atticus, sleep in peace. Thy salvation is secure; but be mindful of us and pray for our sins!"[23]

But in their turn the survivors prayed for their dead, convinced that these prayers could still assist them. They believed in purgatory. All the pious desires on the tombstones, even the simple, "May you rest in peace!" or, "May the souls of all the saints receive you in peace!" are prayers for the good of the soul, just as much as: "Lord Jesus, be mindful of our child!" A husband writes on the tombstone of his wife: "May every one of the brethren who reads this pray to God that He may receive her holy and innocent soul!"[24]

We cannot expect to find the whole of Christian doctrine and every phase of Christian life expressly indicated in the inscriptions of the catacombs, which are after all simply tombstones. Such information may be found in rich measure in the contemporaneous writings of the Church Fathers. But that which finds clearer expression in the inscriptions than in any classical work of theology is the depth to which the truths of faith penetrated these early Christians. For all of these men and women, for those who were educated, and for those who could scarcely read and write, the world of faith was the fullest reality. God, Christ, immortality, everlasting beatitude, the communion of saints, were for them as real and positive as the daily life that surrounded them. But with all its reality, it is a pure belief, completely free from all that crass materiality which, even with respect to a belief and hope in the hereafter, always adheres in a greater or less degree to non-Christian popular religions.

CHAPTER XI

THE ART OF THE CATACOMBS

WHAT is extant of early Christian art comes almost exclusively from the catacombs. Our knowledge of it is therefore largely restricted to funereal art. From this it does not follow that there was no Christian art apart from that connected with tombs, but only that our knowledge is one-sided, being derived from the works which chanced to survive.

To tell the truth, we might even be surprised that there was any Christian art at all so early, for it cannot be denied that many spiritual leaders of the first centuries were averse to it. This came in part from the prevalent rejection in the Old Testament of any kind of pictorial representation, but in part it was also due to a not ungrounded fear of abuse and lapse into idolatry. Even as late as the early fourth century, the Council of Elvira in Spain issued a decree against the use of pictures in churches.[1]

This spiritual current, however, cannot have been too strong, for an actual restraint on art is hardly noticeable. The people, who from earlier times had been accustomed to pictures, desired them, and this attachment of the ordinary Christians eventually triumphed over all scruples. We know today that even in Judaism, which strictly forbade their use, this prohibition was not enforced in the diaspora, that is, in the area outside of Palestine.[2] In Dura Europos, besides the Christian church already mentioned, there was also uncovered a synagog whose walls were covered with pictures.

Frescoes and sarcophagal reliefs are the major types of art represented in the catacombs. Among the minor arts we have in particular the so-called *fondi d'oro,* known in English as "gold glasses." These consist in pictures cut out of gold foil and sealed between two pieces of glass (pl. 9). The greatest collection of these *fondi d'oro* from the catacombs is to be found in the Museo Cristiano in the Vatican. Besides these, there are a number of objects wrought in terra cotta or bronze from the catacombs still extant, and finally, thousands of terra-cotta lamps, most of which have a decorative, but others also a pictorial motif.[3]

In the art of the catacombs we have the first beginnings of Christian art before us. There is none earlier. It is therefore worth asking where this art originated, whether in its formal expression it is a new creation of Christianity, or whether it is only an extension of the already existing artistic tradition of antiquity. Advocates are found for both opinions. It seems to us that the content is for the most part certainly new, but that the form does not at first differ from that which was employed in contemporary pagan art. Some have seen in the pictures of the catacombs a dissolution of classical form which exactly corresponded to the new spiritual tendencies of the Christian way of life. But this does not seem to have been the case. There was at this time in Roman art itself a strong impressionistic movement ready to be adapted to the new spirit. In the course of time the classical style, which had already disintegrated into a kind of impressionism, under the influence of the new Christian mentality and its preoccupation with the afterworld, evolved into a heavily expressionistic Byzantine idealism. But this evolution was completed only in the sixth century. In the middle of the fourth there was a brief revival of classicism in Christian art which led to a kind of Renaissance, and of which the most beautiful witness is the famous sarcophagus in St. Peter's grottoes of the prefect of the city Junius Bassus. This movement may still be traced in the mosaic of the apse of St. Pudentiana, and there is nothing more instructive or impressive than a comparison between the Jupiter-like head of Christ in St. Pudentiana and the essentially Byzantine transcendent Christ of Sts. Cosmas and Damian or St. Paul outside the walls.

A second and still much more controverted question is that connected with the origin of early Christian art: Is it to be sought in the East or in Rome. Strzygowski and Wilpert may be named as the chief advocates of these two opposite opinions.[4] But we should immediately note that we do not agree with the question as it is posed. The general culture of the Roman empire was Hellenistic, which was in turn a composite of many different elements. Between Rome and the East there was a constant exchange of religion, customs, and art. The mingling of the East and West was so thorough that the question of priority can hardly be raised. If indeed one only intends to say that something or other in Roman art reflects the Oriental spirit and somehow or other derives from it, without immediately speaking of an Oriental import, and vice versa, then the proposition is valid since the primitive mental attitudes of Rome and the East were of course widely different, and found expression in correspondingly divergent artistic forms.

If we are to maintain that early Christian art was a continuation of the art of antiquity, then by this must be meant the whole Hellenistic culture which arose from an amalgamation of Graeco-Roman and Oriental elements. In the latter must, of course, be included the contributions of the Jews. Since the discovery of synagog paintings, something which was once thought to be impossible, we may reasonably expect to find in them the exemplars of certain types of Old Testament pictures. Many such illustrations in the catacombs do in fact betray in the deftness and stability of their form a connection with an earlier, fully-developed type.

This leads us to believe that there was in early Christian art a certain dependence on Jewish art in both form and content. How far it went in particulars cannot now be determined. If we are content to restrict ourselves to essentials, we can say something to this effect: with regard to its form, the art of the catacombs is dependent upon the contemporary non-Christian art, but with regard to its content, it is essentially independent and autonomous. Apart from purely decorative motifs, Christianity borrowed only a few pictorial themes from contemporary pagan art, and from the very beginning it gave to these representations a new Christian meaning. The best known example of this is the adoption of the figure of Orpheus for Christ. A further motif of the same sort is to be found in the story of Amor and Psyche. Other representations, on the other hand, anything, for example, which suggests a happy life in the hereafter, express ideas which are common to mankind and are thus immediately intelligible to pagans as well as Christians. At times it is impossible to decide whether or not a certain motif is simply used as a decoration or whether it has some special significance.

The essential content of early Christian art, however, came from the Sacred Scriptures and from the truths of faith preserved in a living tradition. Stories from the Old Testament and, in particular, those from the New connected with the life and miracles of Christ are what animate the surfaces of the marble sarcophagi and the painted walls of the catacombs. We find on them the story of the prophet Jonas narrated again and again in all its phases — how he was thrown into the sea and was swallowed by the whale, how he was cast forth, and how he finally rested in the shade of the ivy which God had prepared for him. There also we find the story of Susanna, who was calumniated by the elders and delivered by Daniel, of Daniel in the lions' den, of Noah in the Ark, of Abraham who offers his son Isaac, of Moses striking water from the rock (pl. 31). These are some of the themes from the history of

200

Pl. 31. Paintings on an arcosolium in Domitilla. Above and to the left is represented the resurrection of Lazarus, below is the paralytic with his bed. To the right and above is the adoration of the Magi; below is Moses striking water from the rock.

the Old Testament which constantly recur. The most popular incidents depicted from the New Testament are the miracle of the multiplication of the loaves, the resurrection of Lazarus (pl. 31), the healing of the paralytic, the adoration of the three kings, the cure of the blind man, the healing of the woman with the issue of blood, the marriage feast of Cana, and the baptism of Jesus.

Besides these scenes taken from Scripture we find other representations borrowed from the world of faith, for example, those dealing with the Eucharist, baptism, marriage, and catechetical instruction. To this latter type belong two of the most important and common themes of this early period, the Good Shepherd and the Orant, to which we must return in the next chapter. In the pictorial cycle must also be included one or other motif taken from the so-called apocryphal writings. Many pictures, on the other hand, are inspired by life itself, such as those which are portraits of the dead or which represent them at their former occupations.

As a rule, a visitor to the catacombs is particularly interested in knowing the age of the frescoes, sarcophagi, and inscriptions which he sees there. Above all he would like to know which is the oldest of the many things brought to his attention, and next he would like to learn as closely as he can its exact age. Here, as in so many other matters in the field of Christian archaeology, the opinions of scholars vary considerably. Earlier investigators, such as De Rossi, Marucchi, and Wilpert, believed that the oldest parts of the cemeteries could be dated from post-Apostolic times, that is, from the end of the first century. The present generation of scholars, on the other hand, prefers to set their beginnings in the first half of the second century. From this it can be clearly seen that the dating of the oldest parts of the catacombs and their frescoes is not absolute, or in other words, one which can be supported by concrete dates actually found on the sites. The dates must be calculated from various types of evidence, and hence it should be no surprise that there is at times a variation of several decades with regard to the same object. One method of determining the years in which a section of a cemetery was constructed is to study it in relation to the general plan of the cemetery and with respect to other parts definitely known through dated inscriptions. Another means of dating is to study the trademarks with which bricks in antiquity were frequently stamped. Finally, a comparison may be made between the oldest paintings of the catacombs and the contemporaneous pagan art.[5] If the origins of Christian art are to be sought in the first century, then the earliest Christian paintings should manifest an essential conformity with the fourth, and last style of Pompeian paintings, but this is not the case. The fourth Pompeian style is a kind of compromise between decorative and three-dimensional composition. It is characterized by architectural motifs overlaid with baroque embellishments.[6] No trace of such a style is found in the catacombs. On the contrary, the decoration is largely limited to a few fine red and green lines on a white background. Since this is the style which characterizes pagan paintings of the first half of the second century, and since there are no compelling reasons for assigning an earlier date to the catacombal paintings, the later date is to be preferred. Using, then, the first half of the second century as our point of departure, we may trace without fear the further developments of Christian art. The renunciation of forty or fifty years provides, moreover, no basis for a feeling of disillusionment, since it will ever remain a striking experience to come face to face with pictures which illustrate the belief of second century Christians in the same truths which we have ourselves received from our parents and teachers.

We must now take up a problem which is perhaps the most controverted of all those connected with the art of the catacombs, namely, the question as to what is the true and proper meaning of the paintings and sarcophagal reliefs in the catacombs. To be more precise, it is not so much a matter of the significance of individual works, but rather of the central idea dominating early Christian art. According to one school of thought, all of the various representations are inspired by a single concept which serves as the key for understanding and interpreting each separate object. According to this school, early Christian art is essentially symbolic in that the different scenes, Jonas, for example, and Daniel, the paralytic, Lazarus, and the rest, are only symbols for a fundamental concept which underlies all of the various representations. But the exact content of this idea is also disputed. According to some it is the resurrection of the dead, according to others it is the triumph over death. Other opinions could also be cited, but it is sufficient to note, and this is of capital import, that all of them see in the representations of the catacombs a symbolic relationship with the dead.

The outstanding champion of this symbolic interpretation of the art of the catacombs was Wilpert. His rejection of an historical interpretation of the biblical scenes was later opposed by Paul Styger who supported precisely this interpretation in his work on early Christian sepulchral art.[7] Styger was able to show that none of the basic ideas which had been proposed as the key to the interpretation of all the various scenes could be satisfactorily applied to the extant material. In support of their position, the defenders of a symbolic interpretation of the art of the catacombs had introduced an illicit comparison with early liturgical prayers in which a series of incidents from Scripture such as those in the catacombal cycles were interpreted in a symbolic sense. Styger has shown that these formulae were actually later than the paintings in the catacombs and that the various cycles do not admit such a simple and harmonious interpretation. On the other hand, the historical interpretation of early Christian art which was favored by Styger maintains that the pictures are of a purely narrative character without any reference to the dead. The same pictures would thus be as appropriate in a Christian home as in the catacombs since according to him this is where they had their origin.

The fundamental error of this latter theory is the same as that under which the former labors. They both oversimplify the problem and try to explain everything in the same way. Actually, the matter is not so simple, and there is no single aspect under which the whole material can be ordered. Let us consider again, as we have already done several times before, a modern cemetery, since in the final analysis the catacombs are nothing but cemeteries. If today, for example, we walk about the Roman Agro Verano, we see a variety of objects represented on the tombstones. Here there is a crucifix over a grave, over there an angel of the resurrection, and further on an angel of sorrow strewing roses. On another grave is a figure of death or of Christ's resurrection. There are busts of the deceased, and photographs of both the living and the dead. Often a statue of our Lord or His Blessed Mother meets our eyes, often too only a bare cross, a truncated pillar, or a simple stone slab with an inscription. It would certainly be impossible to find a single dominant idea for all of these various objects. Death, sorrow of separation, belief in the resurrection there find expression, but also truths of the Christian faith which have no express connection with death. If we now make the comparison between what is to be seen in a modern cemetery and what is to be seen in the catacombs, we can easily see that the situation is largely the same, except that in the ancient subterranean cemeteries religion had a more important role and there was less ostentation in death. But even in the catacombs there are many tombs which bear no marks of religious beliefs, and some also only those of a worldly character. Among the religious representations of the catacombs there are some which refer to death and resurrection, such as the raising of Lazarus from the dead. But there are others, such as the adoration of the Magi and the annunciation to Mary, which cannot with the best of will be pressed into such a relationship. There are again others, as for example, the Good Shepherd, which have a symbolic meaning.

We might here sum up our opinion by saying that we cannot subscribe to either of the proposed theories since they do violence to the facts and to their natural interpretation. The representations are neither exclusively symbolic nor exclusively historical, but may be either one or the other. The symbolism itself is not limited to a single truth but expresses different ideas. But this does not mean that the different concepts represented are not conformable to the character of the place in which they are found.

An objection which can be raised against the parallel drawn with modern cemeteries is that current concepts and sensibilities should not be used to interpret and explain anything so historically remote as the Roman catacombs. This is certainly a valid objection, and it would be a great error to explain their precise content merely from a contemporary point of view. But first, the comparison made between the catacombs and modern cemeteries is meant only as a comparison, and not as a proof; and further, this comparison does not extend to particulars, but only to certain general areas in which human reactions are always fundamentally the same.

From what has hitherto been said it should be clear that the interpretation of early Christian pictorial art is not so simple and self-evident as might first appear. Otherwise there would not be such lively controversies among scholars. For a fuller appreciation of the problem, it may be useful to describe briefly the means used to attack it. A necessary condition for successful scientific work in any field of archaeology is the publication of the material which has been found in as complete and accurate a manner as possible. For the Christian archaeologist such publication permits the study of the remains outside the catacombs and provides a broader basis for comparison. Old works on the catacombs have a special value since they frequently contain pictures of objects which have since been lost or destroyed. Of the newer publications, those of Raffaele Garrucci, S.J., and Monsignor Joseph Wilpert are to be particularly commended for their completeness. The six-volume history of Christian art written by Garrucci is a true corpus of early Christian art embracing everything known at the time with regard to the mosaics, frescoes, sarcophagi, statues, gilded glasses, works of metal, wood and ivory carvings, miniatures, and coins. From the standpoint of completeness, this work is still unsurpassed, but the technique employed in the illustrations leaves much to be desired by modern standards, since neither colors nor photographs were used. Wilpert has the honor of brilliantly remedying this defect. After fresh studies he published in costly and monumental folios the paintings of the Roman catacombs, the extant paintings and mosaics of the Christian churches from the fourth to the thirteenth century, and the entire remains of early Christian sarcophagi.[8]

The reproduction of the paintings of the catacombs involved some very difficult problems. The photographs had to be made with artificial light and often in extremely awkward places, as in the case of those pictures found within the vault of an *arcosolium* hardly a yard high. After the photographs had been taken and enlarged, a painter applied the colors to them on the spot under Wilpert's supervision.

In his memoirs Wilpert records difficulties of another kind:

At last I only lacked the important paintings of a room and *arcosolium* in the catacomb of Praetextatus which lies in a vineyard, at that time belonging to the lawyer N. For many years he had engaged in litigation with the commission in charge of the catacombs. He finally lost his suit. The court declared that the catacombs as religious centers belonged to the commission representing the interests of the Church. "The catacomb belongs to you," the lawyer thereupon told De Rossi, "but the vineyard belongs to me, and as long as I live no one will set foot in the catacomb." He kept his word. The first one he chased from the vineyard was De Rossi himself. . . .

Over twenty years had since passed. "The lawyer will certainly have calmed down by this time," I thought to myself, and went with a letter of recommendation from one of his friends to ask for an entry into the catacombs. It was a complete fiasco. He flew off as if he had been bitten by a tarantula when I mentioned the word "catacomb." I saw at once that all entreaties would be useless, so I returned home with nothing accomplished.

But just as I was tricked by the lawyer, so he was by me. Since I could not finish my work without the paintings under his vineyard, there remained only one other possibility. I had to secure an approach under ground, and this I did with the assistance of three young and courageous theologians without anyone suspecting it. The catacomb of Praetextatus has two entrances, one under the vineyard of the lawyer, and another in the neighboring property separated by a low hedge belonging to Prince Torlonia. Through this second entrance one could go for a considerable distance under the lawyer's vineyard until the passage was blocked by a cave-in extending for eleven yards. The passage had to be reopened. The students had picks and shovels. . . . After four months the job was finished. On Easter Tuesday I held my triumphal entry into the reconquered part of the catacomb; that is, I crawled on all fours through the opening, which was large enough to permit a man to pass through if he were not too fat. Through this opening the painter and the photographer with his equipment had to creep. The frescoes were of course immediately copied. As a reward for this particular exploit, I was nominated for a membership in the commission in charge of the catacombal excavations.[9]

This incident from Wilpert's autobiography gives some idea of the ardent toil and unconquerable tenacity which such work entails. And yet this is only the material side of the undertaking. More difficult and galling is the intellectual labor involved. An archaeologist, for example, finds himself confronted with a picture of which only faint traces remain or of which only a portion is extant. Or he may have in his hands a fragment of a sarcophagus. These are constantly recurring problems, and he must employ every means at his disposal to identify the objects, or if this is not possible, at least to restrict as far as he can the number of objects which they might represent. Such identification is usually made by a comparison with other paintings and sarcophagi whose contents are known. Sometimes a small part of a scene is sufficient for a positive identification of the whole. Thus, for example, a star is in most instances a sure indication of the adoration of the Magi. Feet of man-sized birds belong to the Sirens, and these in turn have reference to Odysseus bound to the mast. In the art of the early Christian sarcophagi this legendary Greek hero represents Christ, who, bound to the mast of the cross on the little ship of the Church, overcomes the false teachings of heretics and the wicked allurements of the world. A cock almost always points to the prophecy of Peter's denial, a lion as a rule to Daniel in the lions' den, and a basket of bread to the miracle of the multiplication of the loaves. These are facile instances which present no difficulty to anyone somewhat familiar with early Christian art. But not every fragment of a sarcophagus or fresco is so considerate as to furnish archaeologists with such characteristic features. Most of the time what is found are a pair of feet, a piece of a clothed figure, or some object that is hardly identifiable. In such cases further investigation is often precluded, and any attempt to discover the meaning of, and to reconstruct, the original object would be more in the nature of a clumsy joke than a serious scientific endeavor. But there are many cases which lie between these two extremes, and for them there is need of great learning, much experience, and endless patience — qualities which often lead to astonishing discoveries.

But even then an archaeologist is still far from the end of his difficulties. When he has determined the material object, for example, that here a definite scene from Scripture is portrayed, he must still examine whether or not this scene

209

Pl. 32. Painting, from Praetextatus showing a lamb between two wolves. Over the lamb is written "Susanna," and over one of the wolves *senioris*, "elders," a clear indication that this is a symbolic representation of the story of Susanna.

Pl. 33.   A *fossor* with a pickax and lamp, from Callistus.

is to be taken in a symbolic sense, and thus has a much deeper content than appears at first sight. This brings us back again to the controversies about the proper meaning of early Christian art. With regard to this problem we have concluded that there is no single dominant idea pervading all the various representations, but that it can differ from case to case. Thus each object must be examined to see if it contains a symbolic meaning or not, and if it does, of what. From this it may easily be imagined that there is need of much study and research. Up to the present, particular investigations of this type have been carried through only to a very limited extent. Moreover, it frequently happens that we have lost the key for unlocking these pictures. Only in a few instances have the artists themselves given us the necessary key, as for example, in the interesting picture on the *arcosolium* of a certain Celerina in the catacomb of Praetextatus. It shows a lamb standing between two wolves. Over the lamb is written "Susanna," and over one of the wolves, "Senioris." The three animals thus represent Susanna and the two elders who tried to seduce, and who later accused her (pl. 32). In other cases the only thing left to do is to examine the writings of the Fathers of the time, especially their sermons, in order to determine what the early Christians understood by certain images. It is not enough to find one or two texts which would seem to clarify a certain pictorial type, but it must be demonstrated that it is a known and accepted symbol. An example of the successful employment of this method of investigation was the deciphering of the symbolic meaning of the great cluster of grapes from the Promised Land which the two spies carried back to the Israelites on a pole. It may confidently be maintained that the grapes suspended from the pole represent Christ upon the cross, and the two spies, the Church and the Synagog. Such conclusions make it highly desirable that efforts should be made to discover the original significance of the greatest possible number of early Christian paintings and sculptures. This would furnish us with a deeper insight into the rich life of faith lived by these Christians of the first centuries.

We cannot fully appreciate the catacombs and their humble art unless we know a little about those who laid them out and who decorated their walls and graves, and the conditions in which they toiled and lived. This was the work of the *fossores,* or "diggers." In the minds of the early Christians these men were so intimately connected with the catacombs that at times they had *fossores* painted on the walls of their crypts who represented no particular individuals but merely the office itself. There are other representations, of course, which belong properly to the tomb of a *fossor* and which represent the dead man at his profession, as was commonly done in the fourth century (pl. 33).

One of the best known pictures of this latter type was that of the *fossor* Diogenes in Domitilla. The fresco formed the rear wall of an *arcosolium,* whose sarcophagus has unfortunately disappeared. Diogenes could be seen in front of a group of buildings surrounded by his tools — mattock, pickax, hammer, and lamp. The picture itself was destroyed in an attempt to remove it, but drawings of it are still extant. In other pictures the *fossores* are seen at the entrance to a crypt or engaged in their toilsome work under the light of a little lamp.

The *fossores* belonged to the lesser clerics and were assigned to a determined cemetery. Besides their particular task of hewing out the corridors and tombs in the tufa and keeping them in repair, they also held in later times the office of *ostiarius,* or sexton, in the cemeterial basilicas. Since the whole subterranean system was entrusted to their care, they, or at least their foreman, must have had a certain amount of technical knowledge. That Diogenes could have been laid to rest in a tomb with a sarcophagus indicates some measure of affluence.

The *fossores* had to conclude the contracts with individual Christians or families and receive payment for the sepulchers. This is attested by many inscriptions, such, for example, as the one from Commodilla of the year 380: "I, Flavius Victor, have during my lifetime bought with my wife a grave from the *fossor* ——— (the name is illegible);" or another from Cyriaca of the year 400: "Soteris has in her lifetime bought (this tomb) from the *fossor* Celerinus for herself and her husband Vernaculus"; or another of the fourth or fifth century: "Constantius and Sosanna have bought in their lifetime a place for themselves in the presence of all the *fossores*." An inscription from 426 carries also the price: one *solidus* and a half in gold.[10] We do not know if all the graves were so expensive. The *fossores* did not, of course, sell the graves for their own personal gain but for the administration of the cemetery, which in its turn was subject to a priest of one of the city churches. Thus, for example, Domitilla was dependent upon the church known as the *titulus Fasciolae*, the modern Sts. Nereus and Achilleus.

Even today there is a band of men employed in the Roman catacombs known as the *fossores*. They also are busy with the tombs, but their task is not to lay out new corridors and crypts but to clean out and straighten up what was once dug there beneath the ground by their colleagues fifteen hundred years ago. This is naturally a work of great scientific importance. It is therefore carried on under the direction and supervision of professional archaeologists. For many years these excavations have been directed by Professor Enrico Josi, who is recognized as the greatest living authority on the catacombs and their problems. Today's *fossores* are frequently the heirs of a tradition which has been developed and handed down through generations. Thus, for example, one of the workmen in the catacombs is a descendant of that Zinobili who more than a hundred and ten years ago discovered the tomb of the martyr Hyacinth and reported his discovery to the then superintendent of the catacombs, Father Marchi.

Painters and sculptors also belonged to the ancient *fossores*. We must not imagine them to have been great artists. For the most part they were modest workmen whose productions seldom surpassed mediocrity and often failed to achieve it. There are, indeed, among the paintings of the catacombs and the sarcophagal reliefs works of great formal beauty and extraordinary vitality, but on the whole, these are the exception. The possibility of a wealthy family employing an artist of unusual talent is also not to be excluded. Among the sculptors a careful distinction must therefore be made between those who belonged to the *fossores* and who fashioned the simple marble coverings for the tombs with their inscriptions and little symbols, and those who had their own workshops in which the sarcophagi were made. We must look for such shops, just as we do today, along the great streets leading to the cemeteries. Today, for example, along the street that leads to the Roman Agro Verano, we find that the closer we get to the cemetery, the more shops we see offering tombstones for sale and taking orders for them. We must imagine that there were similar shops in ancient Rome on the Via Salaria, the Via Appia, and on the other roads which led to the great centers of burial. Not infrequently ancient sarcophagi are found on which the features of the dead person are only traced in general outline. These portraits were never finished, but have remained just as the buyers found them in the shops. They should, of course, have been completed according to the directions of the purchaser, since this was the reason why they were left in the rough. The stylistic similarity found in various sarcophagi from a particular region betrays the fact that they must have been produced in the same shop, or by the same person. An analogous conclusion may be drawn for the paintings of the catacombs wherever in the same cemetery the same style and technique are frequently employed.

Tools portrayed on an epitaph in Callistus — two brushes, a compass, and a sharpened pencil — clearly manifest the occupation of the person buried there. It was a young painter named Felix, who died at the age of twenty-three. From the catacomb of Peter and Marcellinus there is a covering for a tomb on which a sculptor is shown at his work. A son, according to the inscription, engraved the slab for his father, "the holy and pious Eutropius." He represented his father at his profession, sitting on a high stool working on a sarcophagus which rests upon two supports. It is a strigilated coffin, that is, one scored with vertical undulating lines, with two lion heads. A partner, perhaps the son himself, helps with the work. To the right there is a finished sarcophagus with the designation "Eutropius." To the left is a large portrait of Eutropius, this time with his hands uplifted in the typical manner of an Orant. In his left hand he holds a cup, the symbol of beatitude.

The ancient Romans, despite their love of art, had no special esteem for painters and sculptors since they were manual laborers. Only slaves and freedmen were engaged in such work, and their pay was correspondingly poor. Nevertheless, painters were always regarded a little more highly, and paid a bit better, than sculptors. Sculptors occupied the same social level as the mosaicists. The emperor Constantine was the first to attempt to raise the professional level of the artists by granting them special privileges.[11]

It is by no means certain that all the paintings, sculptures, and products of the minor arts, such as terra-cotta lamps and gold glasses, which are of a Christian character were always executed by Christian artists. Particularly in the earliest period can doubts be raised with regard to this matter. From where would such a large number of Christian artists and artisans have come in so short a time? It seems much more likely that pagan workshops must have frequently executed commissions in accordance with the directions furnished by their Christian patrons. Christian artists, on the contrary, must often enough have found themselves in the position of being asked to execute works for pagan customers. As long as there was only a question of indifferent motifs, such as the portrait of a dead person or decorative scenes containing cherubs and the hunting of wild beasts, there was no difficulty. But if the client demanded pictures of a specifically pagan character, the Christian artist was faced with a conflict of conscience. It is understandable, then, why the exercise of this profession in the first centuries was regarded with suspicion and held to be dangerous for Christians. A rigorist like Tertullian would have nothing to do with it at all. But as the Christian communities became increasingly larger, this difficulty sank into the background.

But there still remains another interesting problem. How could the earliest artists, whether pagans or Christians, so quickly happen upon the appropriate artistic forms in which to embody the new truths of Christianity? This difficulty is the more real in that most of the works in the catacombs, as we have seen, are not the products of creative geniuses but of very ordinary workmen. It is obvious that these simple souls must have been inspired by others who had a deeper insight into the Christian mysteries than they themselves. Hence no mistake will be made in postulating the spiritual help of clerics in the execution of the more complicated works, as frequently happened in Christian art well into the Middle Ages. But this does not settle the problem of the artistic forms to be used in expressing these spiritual concepts. As a rule, simple, easily depicted subjects were preferred, while others of a more difficult character were reduced to their minimum essentials. The scenes were thus portrayed as simply as possible: a man between two lions is Daniel in the lions' den; one who strikes a rock with his staff is Moses procuring the miraculous water; another touching a basket with his staff represents the miraculous multiplication of the loaves (pls. 9, 34); a man who carries a four-cornered object on his shoulders is the paralytic who was commanded by our Lord to take up his bed and walk (pl. 31); and a man standing in a chest is Noah in the Ark (pl. 35). In these historical scenes it is clear that the contents of the pictures are limited to what is absolutely necessary. Even the most un-learned painter could achieve this much. Nevertheless there still remains a series of more difficult paintings, for example,

Pl. 34.   The multiplication of the loaves, from Jordani.

Pl. 35. Noah and the dove, from Peter and Marcellinus.

the story of Jonas and the adoration of the Magi. Here the artists occasionally drew their inspiration from earlier paintings which provided an externally analogous form, and which with a few modifications could be adopted for a new use. A certain treasury of types was thus slowly but surely acquired which in time became the common patrimony of the early Christian artists.

CHAPTER XII

THE CREED OF CATACOMBAL ART

EVEN a Christian who is only superficially instructed in his faith is fully aware of the fact that the Christian faith is the same today as it was in the first century, and that the primitive Christians believed in the same truths that we do. Nevertheless a careful and attentive study of the catacombs and their artistic contents cannot fail to make a deep impression. Indeed, one is even surprised as he perceives with his own eyes the continuity of the faith in the paintings and sarcophagi of the early Christian cemeteries.

In the following paragraphs we shall discuss a few interesting items from the totality of those which illustrate the creed of the early Christians, without, however, intending "to prove" anything by them. The Christian faith needs neither the paintings of the catacombs, nor the reliefs of the sarcophagi, nor any other imaginative representations of antiquity to prove its age. It is entirely independent of such proof, and rests upon much richer and surer sources. Nevertheless these artistic creations put us in immediate contact with the spiritual and religious world of primitive Christianity. There is hardly anything so fresh and vital as the old pictures of the catacombs, which though faded with age and damaged by the damp tell us directly of the ideals and sentiments of the early Christians and are not like so many written documents which only retell what they have learned from others.

Pl. 36. Corner of a sarcophagus from St. Sebastian's with a representation
of the Good Shepherd.

Pl. 37. Typical ceiling of a *cubiculum*, in Peter and Marcellinus. In the center is the Good Shepherd. The story of Jonas is told within the semicircles separated by Orants: thrown into the sea; cast up by the whale; under the calabash tree. The fourth scene has not survived.

The classical figure of the catacombs and of ancient art in general is the Good Shepherd. One does not have to walk far through the catacombs to run across this image (pls. 7, 36, 37). It appears much more frequently than any of the others. Styger has counted one hundred and twenty paintings and one hundred and eighty plastic representations of this figure.[1] Very frequently it is found in the center of a decorated vault or in the lunette of an arcosolium. In most cases the Good Shepherd carries a sheep upon His shoulders. At times He is merely standing in the midst of His flock. For us, a shepherd with a lamb upon his shoulder is primarily the symbol of one who has the charge of souls, of the Saviour who goes in search of sinners and forgives them, just as Christ has told us in His beautiful parable (Lk. 15:1–7). But for the early Christians, the figure of the Good Shepherd contained much more than the mere narrative in our Lord's parable. As we know from the writings of the Fathers they associated it with a series of profound theological concepts which are not so current today when we think of the Good Shepherd.[2] The Saviour as Shepherd is the Teacher who leads the faithful into the true pastures. He is moreover the great King who rules over His people. The office of shepherd as a symbol of royalty is found in the whole of classical antiquity. As early as Homer, Agamemnon appears as "shepherd of the people" (Il. 2.243). In the writings of the Old Testament, God is represented even more properly as a Shepherd (Isa. 40:11; Ezech. 34:12). Thus in the guise of a shepherd carrying a lamb, Christ is to be understood as God, as the eternal Logos, and not merely in His historical epiphany as man. The lamb which the Shepherd carries is consequently not the individual sinner, though it is possible to think of the man or woman upon whose grave the figure happens to be found, but human nature which the divine Logos assumed, and in which all men are embraced. However, in order to appreciate more perfectly the deep significance of this picture, we must take into account the common notion in antiquity of the dangers which the soul separated from the body had to confront on its way to heaven through the upper regions inhabited by demons. The divine Logos-shepherd, who carries mankind upon His shoulders, has redeemed men through His death and leads them home through every danger to the Father. This may be illustrated by a terra-cotta lamp which contains the figure of the Good Shepherd beneath seven stars, that is, the seven planets whose spheres were considered to be the great danger zones for souls. Beyond the stars in the radiant ether was heaven.[3] It is thus understandable why the figure of the Good Shepherd was so dear to the early Christians, especially in the face of death, since it symbolized so many and such consoling truths of their faith.

We may perhaps be surprised that these early Christians should have possessed such deep and weighty concepts, but we must not forget the influence of their spiritual guides, whose sermons and writings were replete with such modes of thought. They were accustomed to consider themselves not so much as individuals but rather as members of the Church and of mankind redeemed in her. Thus even a scholar like Gregory of Nyssa did not transcend the world of Christian ideas when he wrote in his commentary on the *Canticle of Canticles* in the person of the bride: "O Good Shepherd, where do you pasture Your sheep, you carry the whole flock upon Your shoulders? For a single lamb is the whole of human nature which you have taken upon your shoulders. Show me the verdant land, let me find the font of refreshment, lead me to Your rich meadows and call me by my name, so that I may hear Your voice, for I am your lamb. And with the call of Your voice give me everlasting life" (*Homil.* 2).

According to the well-known explanation given by St. Augustine and others, the word "fish" was used for Christ since the initial letter of the phrase "Jesus Christ, Son of God, Redeemer" spell out the Greek word for fish, ΙΧΘΥΣ (*De civ. Dei* 18.23). The origin of the symbol is thus not to be sought in the

225

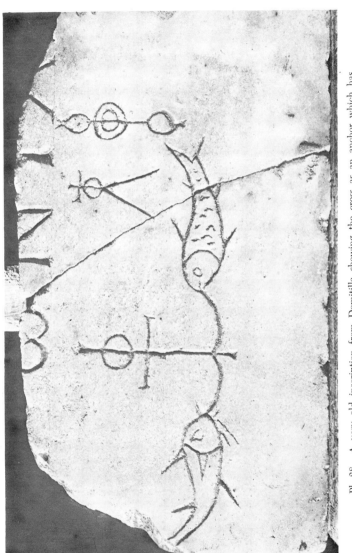

Pl. 38. A very old inscription from Domitilla showing the cross as an anchor which has caught two *pisciculi*, or "little fish," which represent the faithful.

representation of a *fish* but in the Greek *word* for fish. On one of the earliest extant Christian tombstones, belonging certainly to the second century, it is found in the combination "Fish of the Living," life-giving Fish.[4] But then the allegory was further developed: Christ is the Fish, the faithful are the *pisciculi,* or little fish; we are born in the waters of baptism, and we cannot be saved if we depart from them (Tert. *De bapt.* 1). Ambrose explains this symbol in yet another way: Men are the fish caught by the fisherman Peter (pl. 38); his hook does not kill, but sanctifies them (*Exameron* 5.6.16). According to Wilpert this concept of Peter as the fisher of men is represented on several of the sarcophagi. On the left side of the frontal relief of the famous sarcophagus of La Gayolle, which belongs to the middle of the third century, a bearded fisherman draws a fish out of the water with his hook. To his right stands an Orant.

The Good Shepherd and the Fish are two symbolic representations of Christ. But besides these we often find our Lord represented realistically as a wonder-worker. These miracle scenes may, of course, contain a further symbolic meaning. Those miracles which manifest our Lord's salvific will and power may be regarded as variations of the Good Shepherd theme. Taken together with similar scenes from the Old Testament which reveal the same salvific will of God, for example, incidents from the lives of Susanna, Jonas, Daniel, Abraham, Noah, and the three Babylonian youths, they indicate the confidence which the dead have had, and which the living still have, in the help of God at the difficult and decisive hour of parting from this world.

The constant repetition of different scenes from Sacred Scripture show us how much these early Christians were in love with the written word of God. In the so-called "Cappella Greca" of Priscilla there is a painting of the resurrection of Lazarus, which despite its faded colors is clearly discernible against the red background. It was painted about the year 150, and thus only fifty or sixty years after the composition of St.

John's Gospel, which alone narrates this miracle. One can hardly come into closer contact with primitive Christianity.

Much of the early Christians' knowledge of the faith came from the eager reading of the Old and New Testaments, but much also of their spiritual attainments came from oral instruction. Hence there is a real reason for the popularity in early Christian art, especially in the sarcophagi, of the figure of Christ teaching and of the Christian catechist. Our Lord is often to be seen in the midst of His disciples instructing them. Often too a catechist is represented seated upon a stool with a scroll in his hands and in front of him a pupil. The fact that this scene was considered serious enough to be represented upon the sarcophagi is a clear indication that there is question here of instruction in the faith and not of youthful hours spent in school.

The attitude of early Christian art to the passion of our Lord is singular. The greatest reserve was shown toward it, and open reference to it was carefully avoided. Only very late do we find clear representations of the crucifixion. One of the first of these is to be seen in the fifth century cyprus door of the church of St. Sabina in Rome. The cross was used much earlier, but not the crucifix. The sufferings of Christ were represented in symbols or metaphors. We have already noted a symbolic representation of the passion in the great cluster of grapes which the two spies carried upon a pole. A metaphorical representation may be seen in the so-called "jeweled cross," a cross richly adorned with precious stones, but without a corpus. But even these representations of the cross are late.

In the catacomb of Praetextatus is a very old picture which may represent a veiled crowning with thorns. A man holds a reed over the head of another who is lightly crowned with leaves or twigs. From the treasury of types in early Christian art no other meaning can be given to this scene except that of a veiled crowning with thorns. This same kind of image is also found on the sarcophagi. Thus the so-called "Passion Sar-

Pl. 39. The Passion Sarcophagus in the Lateran museum, of about the year 340. 〉
left to right we have: Simon the Cyrenian carrying the cross; the crowning with thorns
resurrection (symbolically portrayed); Christ before Pilate. Worth noting is the transform
of the passion into a triumph.

Pl. 40. Fourth-century relief from the catacomb of St. Agnes. now found in the wall
to the steps leading down into the basilica. The saint is represented as an Orant stan
in the *fenestella* of the altar over her tomb.

cophagus" has a scene in which a soldier holds a laurel wreath over the head of Christ (pl. 39). On the same sarcophagus we find the way of the cross and Christ before Pilate, so there can be no doubt as to its meaning as a crowning with thorns. Christ is not represented on the way to Calvary. Simon of Cyrene alone carries the cross. At the center of this sarcophagus toward the top may be seen the arched and fluted rim of a large shell on which has been carved an eagle's head holding in its beak a large laurel wreath. Framed within this victory crown is a cross, symbolic of the resurrection, surmounted by the monogram of Christ. Two doves are resting on its crossbeam, and at its foot the guardians of the tomb are asleep. The passion of our Lord is thus seen entirely transformed into the triumph of the resurrection, and the *via dolorosa* has become a triumphal procession.

This veiling of the passion was due in part to a prudent regard for the prejudices of the Jews and pagans, for "Christ crucified," was "unto the Jews indeed a stumbling block, and unto the Gentiles foolishness" (1 *Cor.* 1:23). As a proof of this we need only think of the famous mocking crucifix from the Palatine.[5] On the other hand, this seeing of all things in the light of the great truths is characteristic of the early Christians, who were more taken up with the divinity of our Lord than with His humanity. They looked upon the sufferings of Christ as His victory over sin and the prelude to His triumphant resurrection. The loving immersion in the secrets of the earthly life of Jesus, particularly those of His childhood and passion, belongs more properly to the Middle Ages, which were animated by the spirit of Bernard and Francis.

One of the most common and, at the same time, most controverted figures of early Christian art is the Orant, a male or female figure with hands lifted up to heaven, the typical gesture for prayer in antiquity (pls. 35, 37, 40, 41, 44). With the passage of time, this image, which is among the earliest products of Christian art may have taken on a new meaning. Without doubt

Pl. 41. The martyr Petronilla leads Veneranda into paradise, in Domitilla.

the figure of the Orant in most instances has reference to the
dead. This can, as a matter of fact, be proved at times by some
mark of identification such as a name written near the painting.
But the controversy is with regard to the Orant's attitude of
prayer. Some maintain that it represents the prayers of the
dead for those who are left behind, others that it depicts the
dead in the act of adoring God, and still others that it expresses the happiness of the glorified soul. But what is there
to prevent us from believing that in one instance the Orant
had one meaning, and in another, another? or that the Christians
looked upon this attitude of prayer as one of the most telling
images of life hereafter? In this matter also there is the danger
of oversimplification, of applying to everything the same universal
concept which in itself is much too narrow and concrete.

The Orant as a picture of the soul in heaven appears in two
forms. It may appear in the first place as a portrait of the
deceased. There are pictures of families in which the father,
mother, and children stand next to each other as Orants. Many
of these paintings are of striking beauty or give a vivid character-
ization of the dead, as for example the so-called "Veiled Virgin"
in the catacomb of Priscilla. The greater number, however, give
more evidence of good will than skill. A second type represents
the soul as a feminine Orant, and thus deprived of the in-
dividuality of a portrait. Whether this figure represents the soul
of the deceased or not is an open question, for there are a
sufficient number of cases in which the Orant cannot be related
to a particular soul.

This is especially the case when the Orant is used as a
decorative device in the four wedges of a vault, or when it
emerges as an ornamental figure from a great stylized blossom,
or when it is alternately repeated with the figure of the Good
Shepherd, with which it is placed in intimate connection. Both
forms are here clearly removed from the realm of actuality and
placed in the abstract sphere of symbolism. It is further remarkable that representations of this type are among the earliest. In

such instances, what is the meaning of the Orant? It is certain, first of all, that it cannot represent a specific individual who has died. But then does it merely indicate the happiness of the soul saved by the Good Shepherd? The fact, moreover, is not to be overlooked that also on the sarcophagi the Orant is frequently placed in connection with the Good Shepherd, so that an allegorical meaning for both can rightly be sought. It has been suggested that a symbolic representation of the Church may be seen in the Orant, the counterpart to the divine Bridegroom. It would be premature to maintain one opinion at the expense of others since the specialized research necessary to clarify the problem has not as yet been made. Nevertheless, it may safely be said that the earlier investigators of the catacombs, like De Rossi and Garrucci, were right in looking for a symbolic figure of the Church in early Christian art. Their profound knowledge of the Fathers of the Church led them to such a search. From the very beginning Christian writers were preoccupied with questions dealing with the Church, and their teaching with regard to it was much more popular than is imagined today.[6] It is, therefore, quite possible that religious concepts which seem to us to be about as remote as the speculations of professional theologians found at a very early date a popular artistic expression.

The Orant is also an indication of a belief in the communion of saints, just as it is an indication of a belief in a better life hereafter. The figures themselves are at times accompanied by expressions of good will for the dead, or of the survivors recommending themselves to their prayers in heaven. Among the sepulchral inscriptions there are many examples of this reciprocal union in prayer with those beyond the grave. To cite but one example, an epitaph from the catacomb of Callistus contains the prayer: "Atticus, your spirit is in a state of bliss, pray for your parents!"[7]

A particularly significant representation of the *communio sanctorum* is the introduction of the dead into heaven by the saints. In the sarcophagi and gold glasses, it is frequently the apostles Peter and Paul who receive the departed into their midst. A very beautiful picture is to be found in the catacomb of Domitilla (pl. 41). In the center stands a matron named Veneranda in the attitude of an Orant. She faces a young woman standing close by, and who is identified by a written title as the martyr Petronilla. The left side of the fresco has sadly deteriorated, but it can still clearly be seen that flowers were painted there as a symbol of paradise. Above and to the right is an open book, and under it, an open chest filled with scrolls. The meaning is clear: the martyr Petronilla accompanies the matron Veneranda into paradise.

This living consciousness of the union of all Christians with one another in the communion of saints is only a special facet of the profound realization of the union of all the faithful in one Church. This same awareness of the Christians is also useful for understanding another favorite image of early Christianity, namely, the adoration of the Magi.

The history of the Magi is represented eighty-five times in early Christian paintings and sculptures, and consequently belongs to the most important scenes of early Christian art (pl. 31).[8] A few years ago, during the excavations under the grottoes of St. Peter's, the covering of a great sarcophagus was found having on its right side the adoration of the Magi. This representation is particularly noteworthy in that behind the throne of the Mother of God stands a large cross as a kind of background — another proof that the thought content of this scene should not be interpreted in a superficial manner. On this cover there are three Magi who render homage to the Christ Child. As we know, this number three is not given in Sacred Scripture, though three gifts were offered. Accordingly, we do not always find three Magi in early Christian art. Where the space was too small for three, there are fewer. At times, for the sake of symmetry, the number is increased to four. The earliest representation of the Magi, which goes back at least to the middle of the second century, is found in

Pl. 42. The prophet Balaam in the presence of Mary and her Child points to the star (Num. 24:17). This painting in Priscilla is certainly one of the earliest of the Madonna. It probably belongs to the end of the second century and is one of the best in the catacombs.

the Cappella Greca of Priscilla. It is probably the earliest picture of Mary that we possess. The meaning of this picture, as may well be imagined, is not exhausted with the mere telling of the story. Moreover, it is not directly concerned with the Mother of God, who in the catacombs is hardly ever pictured by herself, but always in conjunction with her divine Son and His work of redemption.

In this context we must mention another famous picture of Mary in this same catacomb (pl. 42). The painting is usually interpreted as Mary with the prophet Isaias as he predicts the virgin birth of Christ. Mary is seen seated with the Child on her breast. Before her stands a man dressed as a philosopher who points to a star which shines above her head. Artistically, this picture is one of the best in the catacombs.

The prophet here represented is not Isaias but Balaam. This is clearly indicated by the star at which he is pointing. Only Balaam prophesied the birth of the Redeemer in connection with a star: "A star shall rise out of Jacob, and a scepter shall spring up from Israel" (Num. 24:17). This same prophet is portrayed in other paintings of the catacombs. In the writings of the Fathers, the prophet Balaam belongs to the race and profession of the Magi. Origen, for example, clearly states that the Magi were descendants of Balaam either through direct lineage or through the tradition of their calling (*In Num. hom.* 15.4). The same idea is found in other ecclesiastical writers. St. Jerome observes: "To confound the Jews, a star arose in the East. They were to learn of the birth of Christ from the Gentiles who knew it from the prophecy of Balaam, from whom they were descended" (*In Matth.* 1, cap. 2.2). This connection between the star, the Magi, and Balaam is further confirmed by the epitaph of a certain Severa.[9] On the left side of the slab is a portrait of the deceased with the acclamation: *Severa in Deo vivas.* ("Severa, may you live in God!") On the right, the adoration of the Magi is portrayed. Behind Mary's throne stands a prophet who points to the star. As we have seen from the Fathers, it must be the prophet Balaam. The relation of the star and Balaam to the Madonna is thus rendered more intelligible. The scene belongs to the Magian cycle.

But why were the Magi so esteemed? Their feast, the feast of the Epiphany, is one of the oldest in the Church, and is celebrated with more solemnity in the East than Christmas itself. St. Augustine may furnish us with the answer in one of his Epiphany sermons: "The Magi, the first fruits of the Gentiles, came to see and adore Christ; and they not only merited their own personal salvation, but they also symbolized the salvation of all nations" (*Sermo* 203: *In Epiph.* 5.3). In the representations of the Magi the *ecclesia ex gentibus* proclaimed its great title to renown: the first fruits of the Gentiles adored the Lord before the Jews. This also explains the early Christian predilection for the prophet Balaam, a seer not of the Jews but of the Gentiles.

It would be strange indeed if the strong consciousness of belonging to the Church possessed by the early Christians, as well as some of its more conspicuous manifestations, did not find some expression in early Christian art. An explanation would certainly have to be sought if such an important event as baptism, for example, was not found represented. As it is, we need not look for such an explanation since baptism is portrayed in sepulchral art in many different ways. The most obvious of these is without doubt the baptism of a catechumen, as for example is found in one of the so-called "Sacrament Chapels" in the catacomb of Callistus (pl. 43). By preference the person to be baptized is represented as a child, although it was frequently an adult who received the sacrament. In this an artistic convention of the time may have played a role: the size of the individual portrayed was made to correspond to his intrinsic dignity. Thus we frequently find that the people cured by our Lord are represented on a much smaller scale than the person of Christ Himself. In this particular matter we may also consider the notion of rebirth, which in His conversation with Nicodemus our Lord connected with the sacrament of baptism.

Pl. 43. Baptismal scene from Callistus.

This concept was self-evident to the Christians who had been indoctrinated with it through reading the epistles of St. Paul (*Tit.* 3.5; *Col.* 2.12). The small figure of the person to be baptized thus contains an allusion to the inner grace of the sacrament of baptism, and consequently goes far beyond the realistic representation of the visible rite.

More frequent even than this representation of the sacrament of baptism in early Christian art is the baptism of Christ by John the Baptist. This scene can as a rule be easily distinguished from the former in that John is clothed only in a loincloth, but even more particularly by the fact that as in the gospel narrative the Holy Ghost is seen above our Lord in the form of a dove. No mistake would, of course, be made in recognizing in this scene from our Lord's life a reference to the sacrament of baptism. In addition to these two pictorial types there is a series of symbolic representations of baptism. Among these there are, for example, the picture of Moses striking water from the rock, and in particular a very common scene portrayed on the sarcophagi, that of Peter who, like Moses, strikes water from a rock. The meaning of this last incident is still quite obscure since it is not recorded in the Gospels. There is here some connection with the apocrypha, but just what it is and where it has its origins is difficult to say. Only a very careful and minute investigation of the sources could lead us to a further solution of the problem. From what we now know of the scope and spirit of early Christian art the symbolism of baptism must actually have been more extensive than can as yet be proved.

As we have already indicated, the fish, whose life element is water, also belongs to the cycle of symbolic representations of baptism. Still the highly favored fish symbol of Christian antiquity played its most important role in representing not baptism but the Eucharist.

Christ as a *fish* was employed in a special sense for Christ as *food,* and thus for the Eucharist. The classical proof for this is the inscription of Abercius. A large fragment of the stone bearing this inscription, which probably comes from the latter part of the second century and which is certainly to be dated before 216, was found in Asia Minor in 1883 by the English scholar William Ramsay. In 1892 it was given by the Sultan to Pope Leo XIII. It now adorns the Lateran museum.

In this inscription, which is written in Greek hexameters, Abercius states that he was "a pupil of a chaste Shepherd . . . whose great eyes see in all directions." This Shepherd had taught him "the faithful Scriptures" and had sent him to Rome. There he saw a people "having a resplendent seal" (σφραγίς, "seal," is a common expression for baptism). Of his journey thither he remarks: "Everywhere I found companions. . . . Faith was my guide wherever I went and everywhere furnished me with food, a very large and pure Fish from a spring, which a chaste Virgin had caught, and this she (probably, the Church) gave constantly to her friends to eat, having excellent wine mixed with water which she gave with bread."[10]

The description of the Eucharist can be recognized at a glance: the faithful ever and again receive wine mixed with water and bread as food, but faith tells them that it is the great, pure Fish, that is, Christ born of the Virgin.

In one of the Sacrament Chapels in Callistus there is a picture of a man dressed as a philosopher stretching out his hands over a small three-footed table on which bread and fish are laid (pl. 44). To the right of it stands a woman with her hands uplifted in prayer. There can be little doubt that this is a representation of the Eucharist. Whether the man who stretches out his hands is Christ, or whether it is a priest in the act of consecration may be left undecided. Certain it is that fish and bread were symbols of the Eucharist. And it is also certain that the altar in Christian antiquity normally had the shape of a table, so much so in fact, that the altar was simply called a "table." Even today *mensa* ("table"), is the term used to designate the flat surface at the top of the altar.

There is still another painting which should be discussed here.

Pl. 44. Three-legged table with bread and fish found in Callistus. To the right is Orant. The scene probably represents the Sacrifice of the Mass.

It is found on the vault of a ceiling in Callistus. A fish lies on a table very much like the one already described. To the side of the table are several baskets of bread. Both are probably from the end of the second, or the beginning of the third century. The baskets of bread are an allusion to the second miraculous multiplication of loaves, of which seven baskets were left over after the disciples had obtained for our Lord seven loaves and a few small fish (Mt. 15:32–37; Mk. 8:5–8). Also from about this same early period come the two Eucharistic pictures from the so-called "crypt of Lucina" in Callistus. To the right and left of a lost central piece, a large fish is painted with a basket of bread, in the middle of which is a red blur, which likely indicates the Eucharistic species of wine. Whatever may be the interpretation of this latter, there can be no doubt about the fundamental Eucharistic signification of the whole.

To the cycle of Eucharistic representations certainly belong the banquet scenes. These scenes, which are also found in pagan art, are quite common in the catacombs. Here again different fundamental concepts enter into the various frescoes which are not always easily distinguished today. Such fundamental concepts which come into play are the Eucharistic meal itself, the *refrigerium,* or banquet for the dead, and finally the heavenly banquet of the blessed. These different concepts must all be taken into account in explaining the pictures. The miraculous multiplication of the loaves with the fish and the baskets of bread must also be considered.

At times the banquet of the blessed is the easiest to disengage from this complicated cycle of pictures and to identify as such. In the catacomb of Peter and Marcellinus there are two scenes in which the saints address Agape and Irene as if they were celestial servants: "Irene, some hot water!" "Agape, stir it for me!" "Agape, mix us some wine!" "Irene, pour some hot water!"[11] "Agape" and "Irene" are likewise expressions for the happiness of heaven just as *"pax"* and *"in Christo."*

In pictures in which seven baskets of bread and fish are to be seen, the Eucharistic interpretation is, of course, quite obvious. Nevertheless, in particular cases it is difficult to advance any positive proof because of the mutual dependence of one scene upon another. Of all the Eucharistic banquet scenes, the most famous, and possibly the oldest, is that which was discovered by Wilpert in the Cappella Greca of Priscilla, and which he christened the *Fractio Panis.*

We may here make a brief reference to a third sacrament of the Church represented in early Christian sepulchral art, the sacrament of matrimony. There are not many of these, and what there are, are found only on the sarcophagi. Rather remarkable is the fact that the pagan goddess of marriage, *Juno pronuba,* is occasionally found. In other works, however, the figure of Christ was substituted for it. In a fragment of a sarcophagus of the Villa Albani, Christ is seen behind the bride and groom, who have joined their hands together. Over the head of each of them our Lord holds a crown. In the large sarcophagus of Flavius Julius Catervius and Septimia Severa in the cathedral of Tolentino the hand of God appears above the pair holding the crown. An inscription on the sarcophagus expressly states: "Equal in merit, almighty God bound them together in sweet matrimony."[12]

We began our treatment of the creed as illustrated in the art of the catacombs with a discussion of the most important figure, the divine Logos-shepherd. We shall close it with a glance at the second most important, Peter. It is indeed surprising to learn how often the figure of the Prince of the Apostles stands in the foreground of primitive Christian art, and we may rightly conclude from it the position which he occupied in the conscious faith of the early Christians.

Paintings, and especially the sarcophagal reliefs, give many details of his life: our Lord's prophecy of his denial, the conferring of the keys, his liberation from prison, the resurrection of Tabitha; and his going to execution. These scenes from the life of Peter were further enlarged by others taken from the apocryphal writings: the miracle of the spring, for example, his flight, and the cure of his daughter. Together with Paul he frequently appears as a companion of Christ or as a guide for a soul entering into paradise. Wilpert has also shown that he is represented as a fisherman and shepherd. Without counting the scenes from the apocrypha, Wilpert identified twenty-seven different incidents taken from Peter's life, and he calculated the sum total of the representations of the saint to be over three hundred.[13] At any rate, the number of times that Peter is portrayed in early Christian art and the variety of incidents recorded of his life are most extraordinary. Only the pictorial cycles dealing with the life of Christ are found more frequently.

The most popular of all the Petrine scenes, which is only surpassed numerically by the representation of the Good Shepherd, is the so-called "miracle of the spring." Styger counted twenty-six paintings and one hundred and twenty sculptures of this incident.[14] Authorities are at variance with regard to its interpretation. Wilpert sees in it the baptism of Cornelius. Others regard it as representing the baptism of the martyrs Processus and Marcianus, who according to legend were the guards of St. Peter in the Mamertine prison and were there baptized by him. Whatever may be the interpretation, the parallel with Moses' miracle of the spring cannot be overlooked. This parallel does not consist in the mere adaptation of an incident in the life of Moses for that of Peter, but rather in a comparison of persons. In a fresco in the catacomb of Callistus, Moses is represented on the left as he removes his sandals from his feet; near him to the right, but still in the same picture, Peter is seen striking water from the rock. Since Moses is always portrayed beardless and Peter always with a beard, there can be no doubt as to the diversity of persons. This Moses-Peter parallel turns up again in another series of pictures, that is, in the twofold consignment of the law. This is a very common scene and is known as the *Dominus legem dat* ("The Lord gives the law"). The name is derived from the words which are frequently seen on the scroll which Christ hands to Peter. The latter as a rule receives the law with veiled hands, a token of respect shown in the reception of an object. This same gesture may be seen on the silver shield of the emperor Theodosius. The emperor is handing over the *imperium,* that is, the right to govern in the name of the emperor, to a new provincial prefect. Theodosius is seated upon a throne and is handing over the law, which the official receives with veiled hands.[15] This was the rite observed in the appointment of a new governor.

The tradition of the law has only one meaning. Christ entrusts the custody of the law, the administration of the kingdom to Peter. Only Peter receives the law, never Paul, though he is hardly ever missing from this scene. The unique position of Peter is still further emphasized by the parallelism between this tradition of the law and the earlier tradition of the law to Moses. The parallelism between Moses and Peter under various aspects cannot be questioned in early Christian art. But this parallel can signify only one thing: just as God entrusted His people to Moses in the Old Testament, so in the New He handed over the direction of His people to Peter.

If we wished to discuss the creed of the catacombs at greater length, we would have to continue our journey through them, for quite obviously not everything which we may learn from the paintings and reliefs has been brought to light. Much has been passed over, for example, the forgiveness of sins and the last judgment. Other truths were barely touched upon. Still others which belong to the early Christian creed are not found in the catacombs, which are after all only cemeteries. Despite this, enough has been said to prove the original proposition, namely, that the *Credo* of the primitive Christians was the same as the *Credo* in which we Christians believe today.

> *Jesus Christus heri et hodie, ipse et in saecula!*
> "Jesus Christ, yesterday, and today: and the same forever!" (*Hebr.* 13:8)

NOTES

ASS   *Acta Sanctorum*

AB   *Analecta Bollandiana*

CIL   *Corpus Inscriptionum Latinarum*

DACL   *Dictionnaire d'Archéologie Chrétienne et de Liturgie*

Diehl   E. Diehl, *Inscriptiones Latinae Christianae Veteres* (3 vols., Berlin: 1925–31)

EnC   *Enciclopedia Cattolica*

Ferrua   A. Ferrua, S.I., *Epigrammata Damasiana* (Vatican City: 1942)

HThR   *Harvard Theological Review*

Kirschbaum   E. Kirschbaum, S.J., *The Tombs of St. Peter and St. Paul* (trans. J. Murray, S.J., London: 1959)

LP   L. Duchesne, *Le Liber Pontificalis* 1 (Paris: 1886)

NBAC   *Nuovo Bulletino di Archeologia Cristiana*

RAC   *Rivista di Archeologia Cristiana*

RE   *Real-Encyclopädie der Klassischen Altertumswissenschaft*

RHE   *Revue d'Histoire Ecclésiastique*

De Rossi   G. B. de Rossi, *Inscriptiones Christianae Urbis Romae* (Vol. 1, Rome: 1857; Vol. 2.1, Rome: 1888)

Silvagni   A. Silvagni, *Inscriptiones Christianae Urbis Romae* N.S. (Vol. 1, Rome: 1922; Vol. 2, Rome: 1935)

ST   *Studi e Testi*

ThS   *Theological Studies*

      ○   ○   ○   ○

Abbreviated titles are given to books and articles after they have been once cited in full. With the exception of the *Acta Saturnini* all of the quotations from the *acta* and *passiones martyrum* are translated from R. Knopf and G. Krüger, *Ausgewählte Märtyrerakten* (Tübingen: 1929[3]).

NOTES

Chapter I

1. O. Marucchi, NBAC 18 (1912) 180; E. Josi, RAC 13 (1936) 231–236; 16 (1939) 320-322; Ferrua, pp. 170-171. For the recent rediscovery of a fragment of an inscription of Pope Damasus in a former pigpen over the catacomb of Domitilla, see A. Ferrua, RAC 33 (1957) 70-72.

2. L. von Pastor, *History of the Popes* 19 (ed. R. Kerr, St. Louis: 1930) 266.

3. G. Ferretto, *Note storico-bibliografiche di archeologia cristiana* (Vatican City: 1942) 132–161.

4. *Hic fugiens persecutionem Diocletiani in criptis habitando, martyrio coronatur post annos VIII* (LP, p. 161; see also pp. xcviii–xcix and p. 70). This notice in the *Liber pontificalis* is derived from the *Vita Caii*, which has been taken from the elaborate *Legend of Susanna*. See ASS, April 22 (3rd vol. for April, Antwerp: 1675) 13–14.

5. L. Hertling, "Die Zahl der Christen zu Beginn des vierten Jahrhunderts," *Zeitschrift für katholische Theologie* 58 (1934) 247. Since there is no exact evidence for the number of Christians at Rome during the first centuries, any figures which may be suggested are a matter of some conjecture. Adolf Harnack, for example, in *The Expansion of Christianity in the First Three Centuries* 2 (trans. J. Moffatt, New York: 1905) 459 estimates the number of Christians at Rome at the beginning of the fourth century as somewhere between 60,000 and 120,000.

6. P. Baumgarten, *G. B. de Rossi* (Italian version by G. Bonavenia, Rome: 1892²) 44.

7. H. Leclercq, "Itinéraires romains," DACL 7.2 (1927) 1902–22; R. Valentini, "Itinerari," EnC 7 (1951) 518–525; O. Marucchi, *Manual of Christian Archaeology* (trans. G. Belvederi, Paterson: 1935) 115–143.

8. H. Leclercq, "Kalendaria," DACL 8.1 (1928) 634–640; A. Ferrua, "Cronografo dell' a. 354," EnC 4 (1950) 1007–09.

9. Ferrua 18.

10. Gregory's attitude toward the relics of the martyrs may be known from a letter which he addressed to the empress Constantia. He refused her request for the head or some other part of the body of St. Paul on the grounds that it was contrary to Roman custom to touch the bodies of the saints and unworthy of the respect that was due to them. He promised to send her instead filings from the chains worn by St. Paul during his captivity (*Ep.* 4.30).

11. Marucchi, *Manual*, pp. 120–121; H. Leclercq, "Le papyrus de Monza," DACL 11.2 (1934) 2753–56.

12. The only reliable data which is contained in many of the late legends of the martyrs is that connected with the tombs. See H. Delehaye, *Étude sur le légendier romain* (Brussels: 1936) 40–41.

13. Diehl 3332b.

14. P. Styger, *Die römischen Katakomben* (Berlin: 1933) 14–18.

15. *Ibid.*, pp. 5–8.

16. *Acta Apostolicae Sedis* 21 (1929) 289–290.

17. A. Ferrua, "Une nouvelle catacombe," *Études* (June, 1956) 396–403.

Chapter II

1. Cic. *De leg.* 2.58: *Hominem mortuum, inquit lex in XII, in urbe ne sepelito;* Paul *Sent.* 1.21.3: *Intra muros civitatis corpus sepulturae dari non potest;* Dig. 47.12.3.5 (*Ulpianus ad edictum praetoris*): *Divus Hadrianus rescripto poenam statuit quadraginta aureorum in eos qui in civitate sepeliunt.*

2. A. Amore, "Catacumbas, Cimitero di," EnC 3 (1949) 1058–59.

3. During the past few decades there has been a great deal of controversy with regard to Church property during the second and third centuries. G. Bovini in *La proprietà ecclesiastica e la condizione giuridica della Chiesa in età precostantiniana* (Milan: 1949) has collected together the data referring to such ownership and has summarized the numerous theories which have been proposed to explain its legality. For a criticism of Bovini's own solution to the problem see F. De Visscher, "Le régime juridique des plus anciens cimetières chrétiens à Rome," AB 69 (1951) 39–54.

4. CIL 6.16246: *ex indulgentia Flaviae Domitillae;* see also 6.8942.

5. Stein, "Flavius Clemens," RE 6.2 (1909) 2536–39.

6. Dio 67.14.2: "The same year Domitian slew the consul Flavius Clemens along with many others although he was a cousin and had as his wife Flavia Domitilla, who was also a relative of the emperor. The charge brought against both of them was that of atheism, a charge on which many others who drifted into Jewish ways were condemned." By itself, the charge of "atheism" brought against Clemens and Domitilla is no sure indication of their Christian faith. Accusations of "impiety" were common in the latter years of Domitian's reign when the emperor demanded that divine honors should be given to him (Suet. *Domit.* 13.2; Dio 67.4.7). If we can trust Pliny the Younger in the matter, such accusations were even brought against those who failed to give the same honors to the emperor's favorite gladiators (*Panegyr.* 33). In writing of Clemens and Domitilla, however, Dio qualifies the "atheism" with the adoption of "Jewish ways." Suetonius,

moreover, notes that Clemens was a man of "despicable indolence" (Suet. *Domit.* 15.1: *contemptissimae inertiae*). This may indicate a reticence on the part of Clemens to take part in the many religious ceremonies connected with public life. A further problem, however, still remains. In his description of Clemens, did Dio wish to convey the information that Clemens was actually a Jewish proselyte, or did he fail to distinguish between the Jews and the Christians and regarded the latter merely as a sect of the older religion? Relying upon the text of Dio and a few enigmatic passages in the Talmud, a number of scholars have maintained that Clemens was not a convert to Christianity but to Judaism. See, for example, S. Krauss, "Flavia Domitilla," *Jewish Encyclopedia* 5 (1903) 406–407; K. Friedmann, "Ancora sulla persecuzione di Domiziano," *Atene e Roma N.S.* 12 (1931) 82; E. Smallwood, "Domitian's Attitude toward the Jews and Judaism," *Classical Philology* 51 (1956) 7. The argument that Clemens was not recognized as a Christian martyr until the eighth century (Smallwood, *art. cit.*, p. 7) proves nothing in the matter. At Rome there seems to have been no special cult of the martyrs before the middle of the third century. As a consequence, such a well-known martyr as St. Justin, who was executed about the year 165, received the honors of a Mass and an Office only during the reign of Leo XIII. Clemens' conversion is involved in a number of difficulties, but the cumulative evidence is certainly in favor of his conversion to Christianity rather than to Judaism.

7. There is some question as to what was the primitive name of this cemetery. The earliest itineraries seem to indicate that it was named after the martyrs Nereus and Achilleus who were buried there. A somewhat later document, which is derived from a seventh century or earlier source, the *Index coemeteriorum* in the *Notitiae regionum Urbis Romae*, however, describes it as the *coemeterium Domitillae Nerei et Achillei* (Marucchi, *Manual,* p. 136). Styger maintained that there are good reasons for believing that the cemetery was originally named after Domitilla (*Katakomben,* p. 63), but Josi is of the opinion that the name was derived from the *Acta Ss. Nerei et Achillei,* a legend of the fifth or sixth century which states that these two saints were buried on the estate (*praedium*) of Domitilla ("Domitilla, Cimitero di," EnC 4 [1950] 1842).

8. Styger, *Katakomben,* p. 86. Leclercq, "Aristocratiques: les Flaviens," DACL 1.2 (1924) 2853–54, holds to the earlier opinion that the large slab bearing the inscription was a cover for one of the tombs in the catacomb.

9. P. Styger, "*L'origine del cimitero di Domitilla sull'* Ardeatina," *Atti della pontificia Accademia romana di archeologia. Serie III. Rendiconti* 5 (1926–27) 131–134; *id., Katakomben,* p. 99; A. Schneider, "Der Eingang zum 'Hypogaeum Flaviorum,'" *Mitteilungen des deutschen archäologischen Instituts. Römische Abteilung* 43 (1928) 11. Since writing this important article Schneider has modified his opinion with regard to the origin of

this cemetery. He now believes that it is impossible to establish a connection between it and the Flavians. See *Theologische Literaturzeitung* 75 (1950) 743.

10. H. Achelis, *Acta Ss. Nerei et Achillei* (Texte und Untersuchungen 11.2: Leipzig: 1893). 43–44, 65 n.1.

11. In a letter to the virgin Eustochium, Jerome reminds her of the fact that her mother had visited the little rooms on the island of Pontia, *quam clarissimae quondam feminarum sub Domitiano Principe pro confessione nominis Christiani Flaviae Domitillae nobilitavit exilium* (*Ep.* 108.7). In his translation of the *Chronicon* of Eusebius (218th Olympiad), Jerome further specifies that the Flavia Domitilla exiled to the island of Pontia was the niece of Flavius Clemens. Dio, on the other hand, states that Domitian banished the wife of Flavius Clemens to the island of Pandateria (67.14). Despite the diversity of the relationship with Clemens and the place of exile, it has frequently been maintained that there was but one Flavia Domitilla. See, for example, Styger, *Katakomben*, p. 66. There is more reason however for believing that there were two Christian women who were exiled at this time, both having the same name. See O. Marucchi, *Le catacombe romane* (Rome: 1934) 139; E. Josi, "Domitilla, Cimitero di," EnC 4 (1950) 1842–43.

12. Dio 67.14.

13. The *hypogeum* consists of a fairly large room, or crypt, a flight of stairs, and a large corridor at right angles to the crypt. Most of the inscriptions referring to the Acilians were discovered in the corridor or neighboring crypts. Since they were found at a rather high level in the earth which filled the *hypogeum* and crypts, they may have been thrown down into the catacomb from an abandoned cemetery that once existed on the surface. See Styger, *Katakomben*, pp. 109–110.

14. For the genealogical table of the *Acilii Glabriones* see Von Rohden, RE 1 (1894) 258.

15. Styger, *Katakomben*, p. 145.

16. It is not certain that the husband of Arria Priscilla was the consul of 152, for another inscription seems to indicate that his wife was named Faustina; nor is it likely that this Priscilla was a Christian since she was a *flaminica* (Von Rohden, RE 1 [1894] 258, No. 42).

17. M'. ACILIUS V[erus] /C. V./ PRISCILLA C. [*Femina* or *Puella*]. Cf. Styger, *Katakomben*, p. 107.

18. In the *Index coemeteriorum* of the *Notitia regionum Urbis Romae* this catacomb is called the *coemeterium Priscillae* (Marucchi, *Manual*, p. 126). This indicates that at least in the fifth century the catacomb was designated by this name. An even earlier witness for this title is given by a *graffito* which is probably to be dated in the fourth century. It was found not far from the much-discussed *hypogeum* with an invocation to *Domna Priscilla*. Though it is impossible to trace the exact relation between the cemetery and the Acilians, some such connection must have existed. See

P. Styger, *L'origine del cimitero di Priscilla sulla via Salaria* (Lwów: 1931) 20–21; *id., Katakomben*, p. 110.

19. H. Leclercq, "Aristocratiques: Pomponia Graecina," DACL 1 (1907) 2847–48.

20. L. Fillion, "Pierre (Saint)," in F. Vigouroux, *Dictionnaire de la Bible* 5.1 (1912) 373–374; M. Calbucci, *Il primo viaggio di S. Pietro a Roma* (Quaderni "Verbum" 2: Rome: 1942) 18–19.

21. Hippol. *Philosoph.* 9.12.

22. *Multas fabricas per cimiteria fieri iussit* (LP, p. 4).

23. *Cubiculum duplex cum arcisoliis et luminare*
iussu pp. sui Marcellini diaconus iste
Severus fecit mansionem in pace quietam
sibi suisque memor . . . (Diehl 3458).

24. *Multa corpora sanctorum, effodiens eorum sacra cymiteria, . . . abstulit* (LP, pp. 451–452).

25. See J. Guiraud, "Le commerce des reliques au commencement du IXᵉ siècle," *Mélanges G. B. de Rossi: Suppl. aux Mélanges d'archéologie et d'histoire* 12 (1892) 74–95; H. Delehaye, *Cinq leçons sur la méthode hagiographique* (Brussels: 1934) 87–91.

Chapter III

1. A formula frequently found in the biographies of the early popes in the *Liber pontificalis* are the words *iuxta corpus beati Petri* ("near the body of the blessed Peter") to indicate the place of their burial. A number of archaeologists have maintained that this actually represents a practice in the early Church. See, for example, A. Barnes, *The Martyrdom of St. Peter and St. Paul* (New York: 1933) 164–169. During the course of the excavations beneath St. Peter's, eleven graves (not including the early grave of a child) were discovered near the Apostle's tomb. J. Ruysschaert, "Réflexions sur les fouilles Vaticanes," RHE 49 (1954) 21–37, has suggested that these might be the tombs of the eleven popes who according to the *Liber pontificalis* were buried near St. Peter. This rather tenuous hypothesis has been exploded by further excavations which have uncovered nearly thirty more individual tombs or ossuaries in the same general area. See J. Ruysschaert, "The Tomb of St. Peter: the Archaelogical Evidence," *Thought* 34 (1959) 12.

2. Marucchi, *Manual*, p. 134.

3. O. Marucchi, "La questione del sepolcro del Papa Zefferino e del martire Tarsicio in seguito ad un' ultima scoperta," NBAC 16 (1910) 205–225.

4. J. Wilpert, "Das Mausoleum des hl. Zephyrin," *Römische Quartalschrift* 22 (1908) 183–195. There is, of course, the possibility that Pope Zephyrinus was buried in a mausoleum no longer extant, as has been noted by Pio Franchi de' Cavalieri, "Del sepolcro di S. Zefirino," *Note agiografiche*

4 (ST 24: Rome: 1912) 69–76. See also E. Josi, "Zeferino," EnC 12 (1954) 1785–86.

5. H. Leclercq, "Calliste, Pape," DACL 2.2 (1910) 1660.

6. G. Wilpert, *La cripta dei papi e la cappella di Santa Cecilia nel cimitero di Callisto* (Rome: 1910) 3.

7. F. Cabrol, "Hippolyte," DACL 6.2 (1925) 2409–19; G. Bovini, *Sant' Ippolito dottore e martire del III secolo* (Rome: 1943). Though Hippolytus is traditionally regarded as an antipope, there is nothing in his writings which would indicate that he himself believed that he was the rightful bishop of Rome. See A. Wand, "St. Hippolytus," ThS 8 (1947) 280–281. Pierre Nautin's attempts to show that a certain Josipe was the author of the *Philosophumena* and *World Chronicle* rather than Hippolytus has met with little favor. See B. Capelle, "Hippolyte de Rome," *Recherches de théologie ancienne et médiévale* 17 (1950) 145–174.

8. *Eodem tempore Pontianus episcopus et Yppolitus presbiter exilio sunt deportati ab Alexandro in Sardinia insula Bucina Severo et Quintiano consulibus* (A.D. 235 — LP, p. 145).

9. For the resignation of Pontianus see H. Leclercq, "Pontien," DACL 14.1 (1939) 1411–12.

10. *Hippolytus fertur . . .*
    Catholicam dixisse fidem sequerentur ut omnes.
    Sic noster meruit confessus martyr ut esset.
                                                        (Ferrua 35)

11. Cyprian *Ep.* 30.5: *post excessum nobilissimae memoriae viri Fabiani.*

12. Marucchi, *Catacombe,* p. 230; J. Wilpert, *Die Malereien der Katakomben Roms* 1 (Freiburg im Breisgau: 1903) 502.

13. Ferrua 17; Marucchi, *Catacombe,* p. 199.

14. Cyprian *Ep.* 80.1: . . . *rescripsisse Valerianum ad senatum ut episcopi et presbyteri et diacones in continenti animadvertantur.*

15. Ferrua 16; Marucchi, *Catacombe,* p. 198. See plate 27.

16. Where Cyprian tells us that four deacons were executed with Xystus, the *Liber pontificalis* gives the names of six who were executed with him: Januarius, Magnus, Vincent, Stephen, Felicissimus, and Agapitus (LP, p. 155). For the little that is known about these last two saints see A. Amore, "Felicissimo e Agapito," EnC 5 (1950) 1138–39. In the same context the *Liber pontificalis* records the martyrdom of St. Laurence a few days later with the subdeacon Claudius, the priest. Severus, the lector Crescentio, and the porter Romanus. See A. Frutaz, "Lorenzo," EnC 7 (1951) 1538–542.

17. See Chapter II, note 23, p. 201.

18. Ferrua 40.

19. *Hic fateor Damasus volui mea condere membra*
    sed cineres timui sanctos vexare piorum.
                                                        (Ferrua 16)

Chapter IV

1. O. Marucchi, *Notizie degli scavi*, 1901, pp. 489–495; *id.*, NBAC 7 (1901) 297–298; *id.*, *Catacombe*, p. 396.

2. G. Marchi, *Monumenti delle arti cristiane primitive nella metropoli del cristianesimo* (Rome: 1844) 238–240.

3. The cemetery of Novatian consists of two levels. The first of these was discovered in 1926, the second in 1929. Some scholars have objected to the identification of this Novatian with the third century heresiarch on the following grounds: (1) the title of "bishop" is not included on the inscription; (2) the gallery in which the tomb was found seems to have been constructed later than A.D. 270; (3) there is no indication of any Novatian doctrines in the catacomb. An attempt has been made to identify this "martyr" with an obscure Novatian mentioned in the *Martyrologium Hieronymianum* for June 27. It is still an open question. See A. Frutaz, "Noviziano, Cimitero detto di," EnC 8 (1952) 1975–76.

4. According to the *Liber pontificalis*, the presbyter, later pope, Marcellus buried Marcellinus with three other martyrs near the tomb of St. Crescentio: *Corpora . . . sepelivit in via Salaria in cymiterio Priscille, in cubiculum qui patet usque in odiernum diem, in cripta iuxta corpus sancti Criscentionis* (LP, p. 162). For the itineraries see Marucchi, *Manual*, pp. 126–127. For the inscription and the *graffito* referring to Crescentio see Marucchi, *Catacombe*, pp. 505–507. For the various attempts to identify the tombs of Marcellinus and Crescentio see H. Leclercq, "Marcellin," DACL 10.2 (1932) 1764–73.

5. Cyprian relates of the martyrs Celerina, Laurence, and Egnatius: *Sacrificia pro eis semper ut meministis, offerimus, quotiens martyrum passiones et dies anniversaria commemoratione celebramus* (*Ep.* 39.3). Elsewhere, however, he insists upon the commemorative character of these services. With reference to the confessors who died in prison he writes: *Dies eorum quibus excedunt adnotate, ut commemorationes eorum inter memorias martyrum celebrare possimus* (*Ep.* 12.2). For the annual celebration at the tombs of the martyrs see H. Delehaye, *Les origines du culte des martyrs* (Brussels: 1933²) 24–49.

6. J. Kirsch, *Der stadtrömische christliche Festkalender im Altertum* (Münster: 1924) 221–237.

7. Ferrua 47; Marucchi, *Catacombe*, p. 575.

8. Marucchi, *Catacombe*, p. 577.

9. Ferrua 28.

10. E. Schäfer, *Die Bedeutung der Epigramme des Papstes Damasus für die Geschichte der Heiligenverehrung* (Rome: 1932) 99.

11. Aug. *Conf.* 9.7; *De civ. Dei* 22.8.2; Paulinus of Milan, *Vita Ambrosii* 14; Gaudentius *Sermo* 17; Paulinus of Nola *Ep.* 32.17. Delehaye, *Origines*, p. 76, suggests that a special revelation may not have been necessary for the discovery. See also, P. Courcelle, "L'invention et la translation des

Saints Gervais et Protais," in *Recherches sur les Confessions de Saint Augustin* (Paris, 1950) 139–153.

12. Optatus 1.16: *Ante spiritalem cibum et potum os nescio cuius martyris, si tamen martyris, libare dicebatur, et cum praeponeret calici salutari os nescio cuius hominis mortui et si martyris sed necdum vindicati, correpta cum confusione irrata discessit.*

13. Cyprian *Ep.* 12.1: *Corporibus etiam omnium, qui etsi torti non sunt, in carcere tamen glorioso exitu mortis excedunt, impertiatur et vigilantia et cura propensior. Neque enim virtus eorum aut honor minor est quo minus ipsi quoque inter beatos martyras adgregentur.* See E. Malone, *The Monk and the Martyr* (Washington: 1950) 37–40.

14. Marucchi, *Manual*, pp. 132 and 124.

15. De Rossi 1:4.

16. With respect to individuals, this may well have been the case. The Spanish poet Prudentius who visited Rome in A.D. 402 or 403 apparently thought that the numbers written on the tombs represented the numbers of those buried within them:

> *Plurima litterulis signata sepulcra loquuntur*
> *martyris aut nomen aut epigramma aliquod,*
> *sunt et multa tamen tacitas claudentia tumbas*
> *marmora, quae solum significant numerum.*
> *Quanta virum iaceant congestis corpora acervis,*
> *nosse licet, quorum nomina nulla legas.*
>
> (*Peristephanon* 11.7–12)

Cf. H. Delehaye, *Sanctus* (Brussels, 1927) 143; A. Ferrua, RAC 33 (1957) 34-36.

17. Ferrua 43, 42.

18. Twelve Christians were executed at Smyrna in 155 or 156; eight (Justin and his companions) at Rome in 163/165; about forty at Lyons in 177; twelve at Scilli in Africa in 180; forty-five (Saturninus, Dativus, and their companions) from Abitina in Africa in 303; the bishop Silvanus and forty others at Gaza in 304, but not all of these were executed at the same time; forty at Sebaste in the persecution of Licinius about the year 320. See L. Hertling, "Die Zahl der Martyrer bis 313," *Gregorianum* 25 (1944) 125.

19. Delehaye, *Origenes*, p. 402: "Il y a donc eu beaucoup plus de martyrs, qu'il n'y eut d'anniversaires institués."

Chapter V

1. Marucchi, *Manual*, p. 114.

2. Diehl 1753.

3. H. Grisar, *Analecta Romana* 1 (Rome: 1899) 259.

4. The pallium is a circular band of wool with pendants worn over the chasuble by metropolitan archbishops and the pope on certain feasts as a

sign of dignity and jurisdiction. The pallia are made from the wool of lambs blessed in the basilica of St. Agnes on January 21. During First Vespers of the feast of Sts. Peter and Paul, June 29, the pallia are blessed by the pope. They are then reserved in a silver casket in the "niche of the pallia" until their distribution to the newly created archbishops. See H. Leclercq, "Pallium," DACL 13.1 (1937) 931–940; P. Siffrin, "Pallio," EnC 9 (1952) 646–647.

5. See C. Respighi, "La tomba apostolica del Vaticano," RAC 19 (1942) 9.

6. De Rossi 2.1: p. 237.

7. H. Lietzmann, *Petrus und Paulus in Rom* (Bonn: 1927²) 196–203.

8. B. M. Appollonj-Ghetti, A. Ferrua, S.I., E. Josi, E. Kirschbaum, S.I., *Esplorazioni sotto la confessione di San Pietro in Vaticano eseguite negli anni 1940–1949* (2 vols., Vatican City: 1951); J. Ruysschaert, "Réflexions sur les fouilles Vaticanes," RHE 48 (1953) 573–631; 49 (1954) 5–58; J. Toynbee and J. Perkins, *The Shrine of St. Peter and the Vatican Excavations* (London: 1956). For further bibliography see the 289 books and articles listed by J. Ruysschaert in *Triplice omaggio a Sua Santità Pio XII* 2 (Vatican City, 1958) 33–47.

9. J. Perkins, "The Shrine of St. Peter and its Twelve Spiral Columns," *Journal of Roman Studies* 42 (1952) 21–33.

9a. Four more mid-second century dated tiles have been found in other tombs since the official report of the excavations was issued. Ruysschaert, *Thought* 34 (1959) 12; cf. Kirschbaum, pp. 138-139.

10. These two *graffiti* were not noted in time to be included in the official report. The first four letters of the Apostle's name in Greek, ΠΕΤΡ, are found a bit to the north of the central niche over the tomb of St. Peter. Since they were scratched upon the red wall before the erection of the retaining wall on which most of the *graffiti* are found, they are probably to be dated from the early third century. See A. Ferrua, "La storia del sepolcro di San Pietro," *Civiltà Cattolica* 103.1 (Dec. 29, 1951) 25–26; E. Kirschbaum, "Das Petrusgrab," *Stimmen der Zeit* 150 (1952) 330. The Latin inscription in the mausoleum of the Valerii has been published by M. Guarducci, *Cristo è San Pietro in un documento preconstantiniano della*

necropoli Vaticana (Rome: 1953) 18: *Petrus, roga T̊ XS H̊S pro sanctis hominibus Chrestianis [ad] corpus tuum sepultis* ("Peter, beseech your Christ Jesus for the holy Christians buried near your body"). Cf. Ruysschaert, RHE 49 (1954) 6-18. Since only a very small fraction of the original plaster on the red wall is extant and visible, it is quite probable that many more *graffiti* containing the name of Peter were once scratched upon it. See Kirschbaum, pp. 138-139.

11. LP, p. 176: *Ipsum loculum undique ex aere cypro conclusit, quod est inmobile: ad caput pedes V; ad pedes, pedes V; ad latus dextrum, pedes V; ad latus sinistrum, pedes V; subter, pedes V; supra, pedes V; sic inclusit corpus beati Petri apostoli et recondit.* For the problems which this

text created for earlier archaeologists see Barnes, *Peter and Paul,* pp. 173–175.

12. A. von Gerkan, "Die christliche Anlagen unter San Sebastiano," in Lietzmann, *Petrus und Paulus,* p. 292. E. Kirschbaum, "'Petri ad Catacumbas.'" *Miscellanea Mohlberg* (Rome: 1948) 221–229.

13. For the *graffiti* see Marucchi, *Catacombe,* pp. 261–265. For the rite see H. Leclercq, "Refrigerium," DACL 14.2 (1948) 2179–90. The funeral repasts of the pagans were inspired by an attitude toward death that was in essential contrast with the spiritual outlook of the Christians. The fact that these repasts were actually adapted for Christian use has been described as a "masterpiece of accommodation," by J. Quasten in "'Vetus Superstitio et Nova Religio' — the Problem of *Refrigerium* in the Ancient Church of North Africa," HThR 33 (1940) 256.

14. R. Marichal maintains that a consular date of Aug. 9, 260, may be found among these *graffiti.* See "Les dates des *graffiti* de Saint-Sébastian," *Comptes rendus des séances de l'Académie des Inscriptions et Belles-Lettres,* 1953, p. 64.

15. Ferrua 20; Marucchi, *Catacombe,* p. 254.

16. LP, p. 150.

17. *Passio Ss. Apost. Petri et Pauli* 66: *in loco qui dicitur Catacumba via Appia miliario tertio* (R. Lipsius and M. Bonnet, *Acta Apostolorum apocrypha* 1 [Leipzig, 1891] 175). See Lietzmann, *Petrus und Paulus,* pp. 170–171.

18. Marucchi, *Manual,* p. 132: *Ibi sunt sepulcra apostolorum Petri et Pauli, in quibus XL annorum requiescebant.*

19. H. Grisar, *Römische Quartalschrift* 9 (1895) 455; Lietzmann, *Petrus und Paulus,* pp. 155–156.

20. G. Wilpert, *La tomba di S. Pietro* (Rome: 1922) 19; Barnes, *Peter and Paul,* pp. 98–99.

21. L. Duchesne, "La 'Memoria Apostolorum' de la Via Appia," *Memorie della Pontificia Accademia Romana di Archeologia* 1 (1923) 1–22. G. Belvederi, *Le tombe apostoliche* (Vatican City: 1948) 54–59, holds that the translation took place shortly before 258. J. Carcopino in *De Pythagore aux Apôtres: Etudes sur la conversion du Monde Romain* (Paris: 1956) 262-277 has attempted to show through a study of the four liturgical feasts of Sts. Peter and Paul that the bodies of the two saints were brought to the Appian Way on February 22, 258, and that the remains of St. Peter were were returned to the Vatican on January 18, 336, and those of St. Paul to the Ostian Way on January 25 of the same year. But see J. Toynbee's criticism of his arguments in *Gnomon* 29 (1957) 266-267.

22. Lietzmann, *Petrus und Paulus,* pp. 114–122.

23. Pliny *Ep.* 10.68 (to the emperor Trajan): *Petentibus quibusdam ut sibi reliquias suorum . . . transferre permitterem, quia sciebam in urbe nostra ex eius modi causis collegium pontificum adiri solere, te, domine, maximum pontificem consulendum putavi quid observare me velis.*

24. Franchi, *Note* 5 (ST 27: Rome: 1915) 124. H. Chadwick in "St. Peter and St. Paul in Rome: The Problem of the *Memoria Apostolorum ad Catacumbas*," *Journal of Theological Studies* N.S. 8 (1957) 31-52 suggests that there was no certainty in the early Church as to the actual location of the graves of the apostles since during the persecution of Nero it had been impossible to recover their bodies. On June 29, 258, there could have been an "invention," or discovery, of their remains near the Via Appia as the result of a special revelation. This discovery gave rise to a private cult and the erection of the *memoria*. The suggestion, however, seems to do violence to the literary and archaeological evidence at our disposal.

25. ASS, Sept. 29 (8th vol. for Sept., Antwerp: 1762) 61: *Ego enim sum Michaël archangelus, qui in conspectu Domini semper adsisto: locumque hunc in terris incolere, tutumque servare instituens, hoc volui probare indicio, omnium, quae ibi geruntur, ipsiusque loci me esse inspectorem atque custodem.*

26. R. Lanciani, "La 'Memoria Apostolorum' al III miglio dell' Appia e gli scavi di San Sebastiano," *Atti della Pontificia Accademia Romana di Archeologia. Dissertazioni 2ª Ser.* 14 (1920) 57–111; H. Delehaye, "Le sanctuaire des Apôtres sur la voie Appienne," AB 45 (1927) 305; *id., Origenes,* pp. 263–267.

27. Council of Carthage, A.D. 401, Canon 14: Omnino nulla memoria martyrum probabiliter accipetur, nisi ubi corpus aut aliquae reliquiae sunt aut origo alicuius habitationis vel possessionis vel passionis fidelissima origine traditur (J. Mansi, *Sacrorum conciliorum . . . collectio* 3 [Florence, 1759] 971).

28. L. Mohlberg, "Historisch-kritische Bemerkungen zum Ursprung der sogenannten 'Memoria Apostolorum' an der Appischen Strasse," *Colligere fragmenta. Festschrift A. Dold* (ed. B. Fischer and V. Fiala, Beuron: 1952) 52–74.

29. Cf. Paulus *Dig.* 11.7.44.

30. E. Josi, RAC 29 (1953) 94-95.

31. P. Testini, "Le presunte reliquie dell'apostolo Pietro e la traslazione 'ad Catacumbas'," *"Actes de Vᵉ Congrès international d'Archéologie chrétienne* (Paris: 1957) 529-538.

32. Kirschbaum, pp. 199-212.

Chapter VI

1. Tertull. *Apol.* 5.3; *Ad nat.* I 7.9. See J. Borleffs, "Institutum Neronianum," *Vigiliae Christianae* 6 (1952) 129–145.

2. For the various theories with regard to the legality of the persecutions see H. Leclercq, "Droit persécuteur," DACL 4.2 (1921) 1564–1648; A. Sherwin-White, "The Early Persecutions and Roman Law Again," *Journal of Theological Studies* N.S. 3 (1952) 199–213; H. Last, "Christenverfolgung II (juristisch)," *Reallexikon für Antike und Christentum* 2

(1954) 1208–28. Mommsen's explanation of the legality of the persecutions was based on his own dogmatic reconstruction of Roman criminal law. He attempted to distinguish between condemnations which were of a really "juridical" character and those which were only "coercive" on the general principle *nulla poena sine lege.* But this is a modern principle which was never accepted as a general norm at Rome. Only in the *quaestiones perpetuae,* which flourished in the last century of the Republic and gradually disappeared in the Early Empire, was there any adequate definition of penalties by law. For the arbitrary powers of the Roman criminal courts apart from the *quaestiones perpetuae* see F. Schulz, *Principles of Roman Law* (Oxford: 1936) 175–176 and E. Levy, "Statute and Judge in Roman Criminal Law," *Bulletino dell' Istituto di Diritto Romano* N. S. 4 (1938) 396–406. For a recent résumé of the persecutions see J. Moreau, *La persécution du christianisme dans l'Empire romain* (Paris: 1956).

3. The Latin original of this rescript was given by Justin at the end of his *First Apology.* In the manuscript, however, which furnishes us with the text of this work, the Latin has been replaced by the Greek translation made by Eusebius (*E.H.* 4.9.1–3). Eusebius also gives the text of a similar rescript of Antoninus Pius (*E.H.* 4.13.1–7). But this is so favorable to the Christians that it is generally considered to be spurious. Harnack, on the other hand, believed that it represented a genuine document with Christian interpolations. See *Das Edict des Antoninus Pius* (Texte und Untersuchungen 13.4: Leipzig: 1895) 37–60.

4. The *Martyrdom of Polycarp,* which is still extant, consists in a letter written by the Christians of Smyrna to the church at Philomelium. A shortened version of this narrative is given by Eusebius (*E.H.* 4.15.3–45). The date of Polycarp's death has been much discussed in recent years. After examining the various hypotheses, P. Meinhold comes to the conclusion that the traditional date of 155/156 is still the most probable. See "Polykarpos," *RE* 21.2 (1952) 1680.

5. L. Hertling, "Die Zahl der Martyrer bis 313," *Gregorianum* 25 (1944) 103–129; É. de Moreau, "Le nombre des martyres des persécutions romaines," *Nouvelle revue théologique* 73 (1951) 812–832.

6. J. Knipfing, "The Libelli of the Decian Persecution," *HThR* 16 (1923) 363.

7. Cyprian *De lapsis* 7–9. Dionysius' description of the persecution is quoted by Euseb. *E.H.* 6.41.9–42.6. The legendary *Martyrdom of Trypho* seems to contain a very fragmentary but authentic account of the persecution at Rome. See Franchi, *Note* 3 (ST 22: Rome, 1909) 75–87.

8. Cf. Sueton. *Div. Iulius* 41: *Recensum populi nec more nec loco solito, sed vicatim per dominos insularum egit.*

9. The prominent apostates are described by Cyprian as *insignes personae* (*Ep.* 8.2). Dionysius' account of the sacrifices at Alexandria is preserved in Euseb. *E.H.* 6.41.11. For the readiness of some of the Christians to comply with the edict, see Cyprian *De lapsis* 8: *Quot illic a*

magistratibus vespere urgente dilati sunt, quot ne eorum differretur interitus et rogaverunt!

10. Cyprian *De lapsis* 2: *Explorandae fidei praefiniebantur dies.*

11. Knipfing, "Libelli," pp. 383–384: ". . . now in your presence, I, together with my wife, Taos (?), my sons Ammonius and Ammonianus, and my daughter, Thecla, acting through me (δι' ἐμοῦ) have offered sacrifice, poured a libation, and partaken of the sacred victims."

12. Cf. H. Grégoire, *Les persécutions dans l'empire romain* (Brussels: 1951) 46: "La persécution de Dèce est beaucoup plus remarquable, en effet, par les défaillances que par les martyres." A more accurate description of the persecution is given by J. Lebreton and J. Zeiller in *The History of the Primitive Church* 3.1 (trans. E. Messenger, London: 1946) 653: "The practical result of the persecution was almost nil." See also K. Bihlmeyer, "Die Christenverfolgung des Kaisers Decius," *Theologische Quartalschrift* 92 (1910) 49: "So war denn die grosse Aktion des Decius gescheitert."

13. The *Acta Proconsularia Cypriani* are probably derived from four distinct documents, but there is no reason for doubting the essential accuracy of the *acta* in their present form. The official court record of his own trial was cited by Dionysius in his description of the Valerian persecution (Euseb. *E.H.* 7.11.6–11). For the history of this persecution see P. Healy, *The Valerian Persecution* (Boston: 1905).

14. The various measures taken against the Christians have been discussed by G. de Ste. Croix in "Aspects of the 'Great' Persecution," HThR 47 (1954) 75–113, but he needlessly minimizes the severity of the persecution.

15. *Gesta apud Zenophilum* (Corpus Scriptorum Ecclesiasticorum Latinorum 26, pp. 186–188).

16. *Acta Purgationis Felicis Episcopi Autumnitani* (*ibid.* p. 198): *Nam cum persecutio esset indicta Christianis, id est, ut sacrificarent aut quascumque scripturas haberent, incendio traderent, Felix . . . consensum adtulerat ut de manu Galati scripturae traderentur.* Whether Felix actually surrendered the writings, as the Donatists alleged, is beside the point. See also *Acta Saturn.* 1 (Patrologia Latina 8, col. 705): *Fas enim non fuerat ut in Ecclesia Dei simul essent martyres et traditores.*

17. Aug. *Brevi. collat. cum Donat.* 3.34. In their accusations the Donatists also included Pope Marcellinus and the priests, later popes, Marcellus and Silvester (Aug. *De unico bapt.* 27). As pope, Melchiades was commissioned by Constantine to settle the disputes between Cecilianus, the bishop of Carthage, and Donatus (Euseb. *E.H.* 10.5.18–20). He decided in favor of Cecilianus and thus won the lasting enmity of the Donatists (Aug. *De unico bapt.* 28; Optatus 1.23–24.)

18. See "Silvester," LP, p. 182.

19. G. B. de Rossi, *La Roma sotteranea cristiana* 2.2 (Rome: 1867) 52–58; P. Allard, *La persécution de Dioclétien* 1 (Paris: 1908³) 186–187.

20. LP, p. 72: *Ipse Marcellinus ad sacrificium ductus est, ut turificaret, quod et fecit. Et post dies poenitentiam ductus ab eodem Diocletiano fide Christi cum Claudio et Quirino et Antonino capite sunt truncati et martyrio coronatur.* The accusations made by the Donatists against Marcellinus were vigorously denied by St. Augustine (*Contra litt. Petiliani* 2.203–208, *De unico bapt.* 26–28). The fact, however, that the *Depositio martyrum*, the *Depositio episcoporum*, and the *Martyrologium Hieronymianum* do not mention his name may indicate that there were Christians who did not approve of his manner of acting during the persecution. If he had apostatized, it would certainly have been mentioned by Eusebius, who was in a position to know and who had no reason to suppress such a fact. See H. Leclercq, "Marcellin," DACL 10.2 (1932) 1762–64; V. Monachino, "Marcellino," EnC 8 (1952) 10–11.

21. The epigrams which Pope Damasus wrote for Marcellus and Eusebius indicate that the reasons for their banishment were the *seditio, caedes* (Ferrua 40), and the *bellum, discordia, lites* (*ibid.* 18) stirred up by the less fervent Christians as a result of the penances imposed upon the *lapsi.*

22. Lactantius *De mort. persecut.* 34; Aug. *Brevi. collat. cum Donat.* 3.34.

Chapter VII

1. For a critical appraisal of the *acta* and *legenda martyrum* see H. Delehaye, *Les passions des martyrs et les genres littéraires* (Brussels: 1921); *id., Les légendes hagiographiques* (Brussels: 1927³).

2. H. Jordan and C. Huelsen, *Topographie der Stadt Rom im Alterthum* 1.3 (Berlin: 1907) 389.

3. Acts 28.16; cf. G. Ricciotti, *Paul the Apostle* (trans. A. Zizzamia, Milwaukee: 1953) 425, 454.

4. Jordan, Huelsen, *Topographie* 1.3, p. 514.

5. Cyprian *Ep.* 12.1. Cf. E. Hummel, *The Concept of Martyrdom according to St. Cyprian of Carthage* (Washington: 1946) 14–33.

6. Pontius *Vita Cypriani* 14. Cf. Franchi, *Note* 4 (ST 24: Rome: 1912) 122–123.

7. *Acta Euplii* 2.3–6. These acts may have been considerably reworked by the Christians who edited them. See Franchi, *Note* 7 (ST 49: Rome: 1928) 1–46.

8. Contardo Ferrini, *Diritto penale romano* (Milan: 1902) 149.

9. F. Clementi, *Roma imperiale nelle XIV Regioni Augustee secondo gli scavi e le ultime scoperte* 1 (Rome: 1935) 143.

Chapter VIII

1. Ignatius *Ephes*. 20.2: ". . . breaking one Bread, which is the medicine for immortality and the antidote to death."

2. Hippol. *Apostolic Tradition* 4.3; 10.5. See G. Dix, *The Treatise on the Apostolic Tradition of St. Hippolytus of Rome* (London: 1937) 7, 19, for an English translation of the pertinent passages.

3. *Didascalia Apostolorum* 12 (trans. R. Connolly, Oxford: 1929, p. 120).

4. *Acta Saturnini* 2 (*Patrologia Latina* 8, cols. 705–706). See P. Monceaux, *Histoire littéraire de l'Afrique chrétienne* 3 (Paris: 1905) 140–142.

5. Marucchi, *Manual*, pp. 380–384.

6. The frequency with which Holy Communion was received in the early Church differed considerably with respect to time and place. For the Apostolic and sub-Apostolic times there is no clear indication that Mass was celebrated every day. Perhaps the first reference to the daily reception of the Eucharist is to be found in the *De idololatria* of Tertullian written toward the end of the second century. In this work he refers to the Christians who in accordance with the discipline of the time *quotidie* received the *corpus Domini* into their hands (*De idol.* 7). St. John Chrysostom in one of his homilies given in the late fourth century refers to the "daily sacrifice" (θυσία καθημερινή — *In Epist. ad Ephes. hom.* 3.4), but in this sermon as well as elsewhere he expresses his sorrow over the fact that many failed to receive the sacrament frequently: "Many partake of this sacrifice once a year, others twice, others frequently" (*In Epist. ad Hebraeos hom.* 17.4). St. Ambrose exhorted his flock to receive Holy Communion daily and not to imitate the negligence of the Greeks: *Si quotidianus est panis, cur post annum illum sumis, quemadmodum Graeci in Oriente facere consuerunt. Accipe quotidie, quod quotidie tibi prosit* (*De sacramentis* 5.25). See E. Dublanchy, "Communion Eucharistique," *Dictionnaire de théologie catholique* 3.1 (1923) 515–519; C. Testore, "Communione Eucaristia," EnC 4 (1950) 135.

7.   *Tarsicium sanctum Christi sacramenta gerentem*
       cum male sana manus premeret vulgare profanis,
       ipse animam potius voluit demittere caesus prodere
       quam canibus rabidis caelestia membra. (Ferrua 15)

8. Innocent *Ep.* 25.8: *Presbyteri . . . fermentum a nobis confectum per acolythos accipiunt.* For this beautiful rite see P. Cabrol, "Fermentum," DACL 5.1 (1922) 1371–73; J. Jungmann, "Fermentum. Ein Symbol kirchlicher Einheit und sein Nachleben im Mittelalter," *Colligere fragmenta*, pp. 185–190.

9. Innocent *Ep.* 25.8: *per coemeteria diversa constituti presbyteri.*

10. G. Kirsch, *The Catacombs of Rome* (Rome: 1946) 46–48.

11. Arnobius *Adv. gentes* 6.1: *In hac enim consuestis parte crimen*

nobis maximum impietatis adfigere, quod neque sedes sacras venerationis ad officia construamus, non deorum alicuius simulacrum constituamus aut formam, non altaria fabricemus, non aras.

12. *Acts of Thomas* 49 (M. James, *The Apocryphal New Testament* [Oxford: 1924] 388).

13. *Acts of John* 72 (James, p. 245). See J. Braun, *Der christliche Altar in seiner geschichtlichen Entwicklung* 1 (Munich: 1924) 48.

Chapter IX

1. *Aristo* (Silvagni 2771); *Romanus neofitus* (De Rossi 1:226).

2. Aetheria *Peregrin.* 46.1–4. See A. Stephenson, "The Lenten Catechetical Syllabus in Fourth-Century Jerusalem," ThS 15 (1954) 103–116.

3. *Bassus* (Diehl 90); *Bonifatius* (De Rossi 1:446); *Andragathos* (Silvagni 1856); *Sozomeneti alumnae audienti patronus fidelis* (Silvagni 2759).

4. In the early Church the term *statio* was practically synonymous with the partial fast which was observed by the Christians on Wednesdays and Fridays (cf. Tertull. *De orat.* 19). From the beginning of the fifth century the term was applied to the solemn concourse of people, clergy, and bishop to a particular church to celebrate the Eucharist on days of fast or particular solemnity. In an altered form the beautiful custom of the Stations is observed in Rome on eighty-six days of the year. These are all marked in the Roman Missal. See H. Leclercq, "Stations liturgiques," DACL 15.2 (1953) 1653–57; C. Mohrmann, "Statio," *Vigiliae Christianae* 7 (1953) 221–245.

5. H. Grisar, *Geschichte Roms und die Päpste im Mittelalter* 1 (Freiburg im Breisgau: 1900) 800.

6. G. Giovenale, *Il battistero Lateranense nelle recenti indagini della Pontificia Commissione di Archeologia Sacra* (Rome: 1929) 62–66.

7. E. Josi, "La visita agli scavi di San Giovanni in Laterano," *Atti del IV Congresso internationale di Archeologia Christiana* 1 (Rome: 1940) 53.

8. Kirsch, *Catacombs*, p. 182.

Chapter X

1. For the titles of these collections see the List of Abbreviations. A useful collection of early Christian inscriptions may be found in E. Kirschbaum, E. Junyent, J. Vives, *La Tumba de San Pedro y las Catacumbas Romanas* (Madrid: 1954) 409–570.

2. De Rossi 1:11.

3. Diehl 484.

4. Silvagni 1637.

5. *Pistor* (Marucchi, *Catacombe*, p. 105); *ferrarius* (Diehl 635); *lintearius* (Diehl 682); *corarius* (Diehl 638); *sarcinatrix* (Diehl 644); *pictor* (Diehl 669a); *marmorius* (Diehl 656); *quadratarius* (De Rossi 1:256); *montanarius qui laboravit per omnium climiterium* (Diehl 651).

6. *Elefentarius* (Diehl 680); *pastilarius* (Diehl 628); *patronus corporis pastillariorum* (Diehl 629); *dulciarius* (Diehl 626); *tussor* ("*tonsor*" — Diehl 604); *mulomedicus* (Diehl 616).

7. *Hortulanus* (Diehl 592); *pomararius* (Diehl 683); *porcinarius* (Diehl 689).

8. *Capsarius* (Diehl 603); *exceptor praefecti vigilum* (Diehl 450); *exceptor praefecti urbi* (Diehl 451a); *horrearius* (Diehl 591); *vestitor imperatoris* (Diehl 354).

9. *Hic iacet amicus et caru[s omnibus . . .], medicus ingeniosus, pru[dens . . . pau]peribus non cupidus . . .* (Diehl 609); *Rapetiga medicus* (Diehl 610); *Miggin medicus* (Diehl 608); *iuris consultor* (Diehl 748).

10. *Aurelianus, qui militavit centurio an. XXX* (Diehl 397); *Hic iacet Heraclius civis Secundus Retus filius Lupicini ex presidibus qui fuit praepositus militum Fotensium et vixit annis XXXV. Dep. XII Kal. Augustas* (Silvagni 1640).

11. For the Roman horse races see L. Friedlaender, "Die circensischen Spiele," in J. Marquardt and G. Wissowa, *"Römische Staatsverwaltung 6"* (Leipzig: 1885²) 504–524; Bussemaker and E. Saglio, "Circus," *Dictionnaire des antiquités grecques et romaines* 1.2 (Paris: 1887) 1187–1201.

12. Diehl 3332a–b; CIL 6.8498.

13. *Castitatis unice femine cuius semper circa maritum amor singularis apparuit* (Marucchi, *Catacombe*, p. 72). *Mire bonitatis adque inemitabili sanctitatis totius castitatis ràri exempli femine caste bone bite et pieose et in omnibus clorio se brattie* (?) *dicnitate que vixit annos XXXIII que sine lesione animi mei vixi mecum annos XV. Filios autem procreavit VII ex quibus sicum abet ad Dominum IIII* (Silvagni 1550).

14. *Mirae innocentiae ac sapientiae puero Marciano qui vixit ann. IIII et menses IIII dies II. Quiescet in pace* (De Rossi 1:125). *Dalmatio filio dulcissimo totius ingeniositatis ac sapientiae, puero quem plenis septem annis perfrui patri infelici non licuit, qui studens litteras Graecas non monstratas sibi Latinas adripuit et in triduo ereptus est rebus humanis* (Silvagni 1978).

15. Cf. H. Leclercq, "Paix," DACL 13.1 (1937) 465–466.

16. *In pace Domini dormias* (Diehl 2288)! *Semper vive in pace* (Diehl 2291)! *Semper in pace gaude* (Diehl 2292)! *Bibas* ("*vivas*") *in pace Dei* (Diehl 2212)!

17. *Fidelis recessit in pace* (Diehl 1358). *Vixit in pace fidelis* (Diehl 1351). *In pace legitima* (De Rossi 1:132).

18. Tertull. *De praescrip.* 32: *Haeretici nec recipiuntur in paçem et communicationem ab ecclesiis quoque modo apostolicis.*

19. Jerome *Ep.* 131.2 (Augustine to Jerome); see L. Hertling, "Communio und Primat," *Miscellanea Historiae Pontificiae* 7 (Rome: 1943) 4.
20. Diehl 2724.
21. *Bibas in Domino* (Diehl 2213)! *Vive in nomine* (Diehl 2219A)! *Vivas in Christo* (Diehl 2220A)! *Vibas in Domino Zesu* (Diehl 2225)! *Vibas in Spirito Sancto* (Diehl 2230)! *Vivatis inter xanctos* (Diehl 2231)! *Spiritum tuum inter sanctos* (Marucchi, *Catacombe*, p. 208)!
22. *In pace et paradissu* (Diehl 3451). *In pace et in refrigerium* (Diehl 2722).‾ *Dulcis et innoces hic dormit Severianus in somno pacis* (Silvagni 941). ΕΡΜΑΕΙΣΚΕ (Silvagni 1867).
23. *Anatolius filio benemerenti fecit qui vixit annis VII mensis VII diebus XXI. Spiritus tuus bene requiescat in Deo; petas pro sorore tua* (Marucchi, *Catacombe*, p. 557)! *Januaria, bene refrigera et roga pro nos* (*ibid.* p. 208)! *Non mereor uniter Dominum* [. . .] *re prestes in orationis tuis, ut possit amartias meas indulgere* (Diehl 1558). *Attice, dormi in pace de tua incolumitate securus et pro nostris peccatis pete sollicitus* (Silvagni 1283)!
24. *Paulo filio merenti in pacem.* . . . *Te suscipian omnium ispirita sanctorum* (Silvagni 2703)! *Meruit titulum inscribi ut quisque de fratribus legerit roget deu* [. . .] *ut sancto et innocenti spirito ad Deum suscipiatur* (*ibid.* 1677).

Chapter XI

1. Canon 36: *Placuit picturas in ecclesia esse non debere ne quod colitur et adoratur in parietibus depingatur* (J. Mansi, *Sacrorum conciliorum . . . collectio* 2 [Florence: 1759] 11).
2. E. Goodenough, *Jewish Symbols in the Greco-Roman Period* (4 vols., New York: 1953-58).
3. Marucchi, *Manual*, pp. 341–349.
4. J. Strzygowski, *Orient oder Rom* (Leipzig: 1901). In later years Strzygowski was less insistent upon the dominating influence of the East upon Christian art. See, for example, his *Origins of Christian Church Art* (trans. O. Dalton and H. Braunholz, Oxford:˙ 1923) 1–5. He still maintained, however, that "at the beginning of Christian art the Semites played a decisive part" (*ibid.*, p. 31). The opposite opinion of Wilpert may be found in *I sarcofagi cristiani antichi* 2 (Rome: 1932) 355: "L'arte cristiana antica di Roma . . . ha una origine propria, independente da qualsiasi influsso estraneo, . . . anche lo sviliupo è independente." See also E. Swift, *Roman Sources of Christian Art* (New York: 1951) 5–7.
5. Styger, *Katakomben*, pp. 14–17.
6. A. Maiuri, *Roman Painting* (trans. S. Gilbert, Geneva: 1953) 47–49.
7. J. Wilpert, *Die Malereien der Katakomben Roms* 1 (Freiburg im Breisgau: 1903) 150: "Die Symbolik bleibt einzig und allein Sache des

Verstandes." Styger, *Katakomben*, p. 359: "Allein die Bilder sind von Anfang an rein erzählerisch und nie zu Zwecken einer sepulkralen Symbolik entworfen worden." *Id., Die altchristliche Grabeskunst. Eine Versuch der einheitlichen Auslegung* (Munich: 1927) 75–119.

8. R. Garrucci, *Storia della arte cristiana nei primi otto secoli della Chiesa* (6 vols., Prato: 1872–81). J. Wilpert, *Die Malereien der Katakomben Roms* (2 vols., Freiburg im Breisgau: 1903); *id., I sarcofagi cristiani antichi* (5 vols., Rome: 1929–32); *id., Die römischen Mosaiken und Malereien der kirchlichen Bauten vom IV bis XIII Jahrhundert* (4 vols., Freiburg im Breisgau: 1916).

9. J. Wilpert, *Erlebnisse und Ergebnisse im Dienste der christlichen Archäologie* (Freiburg im Breisgau: 1930) 39–40.

10. Flavius Victor (Diehl 3754B); Soteris (Diehl 3754D); Constantius (Diehl 3761); Auri solidum un[um] et semes[em] (De Rossi 1:653).

11. In the *Edict of Diocletian on Maximum Prices* (A.D. 301) a worker in wall mosaics, for example, was to receive 60 denarii a day, while a painter of figures was to receive 150. See *Edict* 7.6, 9 (ed. E. Graser in T. Frank, *An Economic Survey of Ancient Rome* 5 [Baltimore: 1940] 338). In a letter of Aug. 2, A.D. 337, addressed to the prefect of the praetorium, Constantine freed the artisans from civic duties so that they might have time to perfect themselves and train their sons in their various skills. See *Cod. Theodos.* 13.4.2: *Artifices artium brevi subdito comprehensarum per singulas civitates morantes ab universis muneribus vacare praecipimus, eis quidem ediscendis artibus otium adcommodandum, quo magis cupiant et ipsi peritiores fieri et suos filios erudire.*

Chapter XII

1. Styger, *Grabeskunst*, p. 7.

2. T. Kempf, *Christus der Hirt. Ursprung und Deutung einer altchristlichen Symbolgestalt* (Rome: 1942).

3. For a description and sketch of the lamp, see H. Leclercq, "Astres," DACL 1 (1907) 3010–11, fig. 1040. For the dwelling of the demons in the upper atmosphere and their delight in the savor of incense and burnt sacrifices, see Origen *Exhort. ad martyr.* 45; Euseb. *Praepar. evangel.* 5.2. These crude concepts about the evil spirits and the arduous journey confronting the soul after death are part of the pagan cultural inheritance from which the early Christians did not entirely escape. See A. Rush, *Death and Burial in Christian Antiquity* (Washington: 1941) 30–39.

4. Marucchi, *Catacombe*, p. 3.

5. This caricature, which was found on the wall of an imperial palace dating back to the time of Septimius Severus, represents a man with the head of an ass upon a cross. Near it stands another man, and beneath it is scrawled in Greek: "Alexamenos adores his God." See Marucchi, *Manual*, p. 44.

6. For the concept of the Church as "Mother" in early Christianity, see J. Plumpe, *Mater Ecclesia* (Washington: 1943).

7. *Attice, spiritus tus in bonu, ora pro parentibus tuis* (Diehl 2338)!

8. Styger, *Grabeskunst*, p. 7.

9. H. Leclercq, "Mages," DACL 10.1 (1931) 1033–34, fig. 7482.

10. For the epitaph of Abercius see G. Rauschen, *Monumenta minora saeculi secundi* (Bonn: 1914²) 3–9, 37–41; H. Strathmann and T. Klauser, "Aberkios," *Reallexicon für Antike und Christentum* 1 (1950) 12–17.

11. *Irene, de calda! Agape, misce mi! Agape, misce nobis! Irene, porge calda* (Diehl 1569)!

12. Wilpert, *Sarcofagi* 1:90: *Quos paribus meritis iunxit matrimonio dulci omnipotens Dominus.*

13. J. Wilpert, *La fede della Chiesa nascente secondo i monumenti dell'arte funeraria antica* (Rome: 1938) 146.

14. Styger, *Grabeskunst*, p. 7.

15. Wilpert, *Sarcofagi* 1:173.

INDEX

Abercius, 238 f
Acilius Glabrio, 38 ff, 122
Acolytes, 163
Acta martyrum, 135
Acts of the martyrs, 142
Ad Catacumbas, Coemeterium,
21, 85; *see also* Sebastian, St.
Ad Clivum Cucumeris, Cata-
comb, 13, 20, 21
Ad Duas Lauros, Catacomb, 21,
75
Ad Ursum Pileatum, Catacomb,
21, 63; *see also* Pontianus, Pope
Africa, cult of martyrs in, 77
Agape and Irene, meaning of, 241
Agnes, St., Catacomb of, 2, 20
Alexander, St., Catacomb of, 20
Altar, in Christian antiquity, 239;
facing people, 66; papal, in, St.
Peter's, 88 f
Altars, simple, 165 f
Ambrose, St., 76; baptism of, 172
Anthony, hermit, desire for mar-
tyrdom, 149
Antoninus Pius, rescript of, on
Christians, 126
Apocrypha, and Christian art,
238, 242 f
Apollonius, St., acts of, 142
Apostasy, 124, 130 f, 148;
attitude toward, 161, 162; by
surrendering books, 136
Archaeologists, 10
Archaeology, problems of, 206 ff
Archives, episcopal, of Rome
seized, 135 f
Arcosolium, description, 24
Art, of Catacombs, origin of,
196 ff; Christian, origin of early,
198; *see also* Christian art;
Apocrypha and Christian art;
Pagan symbols in Christian art;
etc.

Audiens, meaning, 172
Augustine, St., and baptism, 171

Bakers, burial chamber of, 185 f
Balaam, 235
Baptism, of adults, 168; in catacombs, 175; ceremonies of,
172 ff; of children, 168; and
Eucharist, 158; examination of
candidates, 170; of infants, 169;
persons excluded from, 170;
postponement of, 171; prepara-
tion for, 169 f; represented in
catacombs, 236 f; of St. Per-
petua, 148
Baronius, Caesar, and Church, 4;
and catacombs, 5
Basilica, on site of martyrdom,
114
Basilica of the Apostles, excava-
tion beneath, 107 f
Basilica of St. Sebastian, excava-
tions beneath, 107 f
Basilica of Sts. Alexander,
Eventius, and Theodolus, 65
Bassilla, Catacomb of, *see*
Hermes, St.
Bene merenti, 191
Blandina, tortured for faith, 148
Blessed Sacrament, carried by
boy, 161
Bosio, Antonio, 5, 16
Brandea, 65
Bribery, of officials, 131; of prison
guards, 147
Burial, forbidden within walls of
city, 19; types of, in ancient
Rome, 21 f

Caecilia, St., crypt of, 50, 51
Caius, Church historian, on St.

267